GINGER NUTS

the unauthorised biography of

CHRIS EVANS

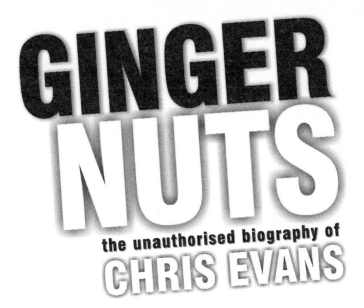

the unauthorised biography of

HOWARD JOHNSON

André Deutsch

First published in 2003 by
André Deutsch
An imprint of the
Carlton Publishing Group
20 Mortimer Street
London W1T 3JW

ISBN 0 233 05117 1

Typeset by E-Type, Liverpool
Printed and bound in Great Britain by Mackays

Dedication

Writing a book takes patience and dedication. But *being around* someone who's writing one takes infinitely more of the stuff. So absolute thanks and total love to Louise, Elliott and Gabriel.

Picture Credits

The publisher would like to thank the following sources for their kind permission to reproduce the pictures in this book:

Lee Burgess Page 1
Paul Carrington Page 6 (top left/right)
Getty Page 5 (top)
Matrix Press Agency Page 10 (bottom)
Mirrorpix Pages 6 (bottom), 7, 8, 9, 14, 15, 16
PA Photos Pages 12, 13
Rex Features Pages 5 (middle and bottom), 10 (top), 11
Sports Photography Edward Garvey Pages 2, 3, 4

Contents

Acknowledgements

Thanks and respect to the many people who have freely given their time and knowledge to help create this book. Above all, to everyone who agreed to be interviewed and helped to create a clear picture of Chris Evans; John Aizlewood, James Ashton, Jamie Broadbent, Lee Burgess, Paul Carrington, Professor Cary Cooper, Simon Garfield, Tim Grundy, Sarah Harker, Chris Howe, Gareth Johnson, Stuart Maconie, Tich McCooey, Simon Morris, Phil Mount and Trevor Palin.

Thanks, too, to my editor Lorna Russell and copy editors Ian Gittins and Louise Johnson, who have all contributed hugely. And let's not forget Paul Elliott, Robert and Nicola Swift and The Angleseys.

The following books proved invaluable when writing this book:

Freak Or Unique? The Chris Evans Story by David Jones (Harper Collins, 1997)
The Nation's Favourite by Simon Garfield (Faber and Faber, 1998)
Just For The Record by Geri Halliwell (Ebury Press, 2002)

Prologue

The suit is sharp but sober, black with a red pinstripe that would look at home on any City slicker, topped off neatly with a salmon pink tie and a crisp white shirt. The ginger hair isn't entirely ginger any more, but flecked with a grey that hints at new-found maturity, maybe even sobriety. And it's not misleading. Christopher Evans isn't drinking anything stronger than water on this particular night. After all, he has a script to get cracking on bright and early tomorrow morning. On his arm is his bride of almost two years, Billie Piper, matching her husband's well-groomed appearance in a refined trouser suit, her hair freshly highlighted. With matching smiles as wide as the Thames, Mr and Mrs Evans are attending a charity fundraiser at London's Old Vic theatre on February 5, 2003, and the celebrity couple look every inch the picture of contentment.

Mind you, why wouldn't Chris be smiling? If you had a fortune estimated at £50m, a pop star wife sixteen years your junior, luxury homes in Portugal, the United States and England, and no need ever to work again, you might just be cracking a grin yourself.

But where Chris Evans is concerned, things are never that simple. This, after all, is the man who said, 'I've been to the top, and it ain't all there.' The man who dragged himself up by his bootlaces to escape a life of drudgery in an insignificant suburb of Warrington, and who took the early death of his dad from cancer as a signal never to let the grass grow under his feet and to achieve, achieve, achieve. But achieve what exactly? And at what price?

Despite becoming the biggest British media star of the last decade, despite transcending his position as the sharpest, funniest broadcaster out there to first own his own media empire, then flog it for a vast fortune, and despite a string of beautiful girlfriends, there's been plenty of self-doubt, heartbreak and tragedy along the way. Chris has never really done contentment. There has been the debris of a failed marriage and other failed relationships, including one that yielded a daughter that he never sees. The seemingly never-ending outlandish behaviour, the marathon drinking sessions, bust-ups and fall-outs (often with his fellow celebrities), high-profile court cases, rantings and ravings and ... well, the ongoing desire to expose himself to the world in more ways than one.

Of course, there have been plenty of grand times along the way, too. The vast amounts of money and the mansions and motors it has bought, the hanging with pop stars, the pranks and the schemes. And let's not forget the million laughs we've all shared as Chris Evans has entertained the nation every step of the way with such cultural milestones as the *Big Breakfast* and *TFI Friday*. If anyone has managed to live a life less ordinary, then this is the fella.

So, as Chris Evans heads into middle age, who exactly is he? Are those crazy days and crazy, crazy nights behind him now he's found true love and happiness in the arms of his young bride Billie? Can he re-invent himself as the power behind the throne of his new production company UMTV? Or will Chris's ego simply demand a return to the spotlight once again to reclaim his crown as the Man Of The Moment?

From Manchester to Vegas, from London to Hollywood and taking in most of the world's glamour spots in between, Chris Evans's life has been nothing if not one long, strange trip. But to follow it properly, first we need to pay a visit to a little-known place called Orford ...

1 Something Got Me Started

Capesthorne Road cuts right through the middle of Orford, from Blackbrook at the one end out towards Longford at the other. It would like to think it acts as the main artery, pumping life right through the heart of this Warrington suburb. Some might say it's just the quickest way in and (more importantly) out of the place. For while the word 'suburb' may conjure up romantic notions of leafy lanes and twee homes sitting in quiet repose throughout the day, shorn of their workers, but calmly awaiting their return from the town's throbbing commercial centre in the evening, Orford really isn't that kind of suburb at all.

Originally a small manor attached to Warrington, there'd been a community recorded at Orford since the Doomsday Survey of 1086. It grew as a village built around the imposing Orford Hall, but as recently as 1961 Johnson Ball, a former Orford resident who went on to become Principal of Queen's College, Stourbridge, was reminiscing that Long Lane, now one of Orford's main thoroughfares, had been 'a quiet country lane with tall hedges on both sides' at the turn of the twentieth century.

Nobody living in Orford today could relate to such a countryside feel. Functional, characterless and uniformly grey, Orford looks and feels like the quintessential 1970s council estate, only one step forward from the high rise monstrosities town planners had sworn by in the 1960s, two steps back from the redbrick terraces which had housed the British working classes for decades before. Orford today is not the jewel in Warrington's crown. It has a tired air about it. It's not that its residents don't care; the many neatly maintained gardens and brightly painted doors show there are plenty of them that do. It's just that the raw materials these people have been given to work with are so uninspiring.

The expansion of a new motorway complex across the Northwest in the 1960s helped Warrington to become designated a 'New Town' in 1968, opening up possibilities not only for its own commercial development, but also as a feeder of workers to the infinitely more powerful commercial centres of Liverpool and Manchester. Commuting was suddenly easy, and Warrington began to gobble up the fields to the north of the town centre as prime land for both new residential areas and commercial sites. And, as was so often the case with these new houses, it proved very hard to immediately turn them into homes, with all the attached sense of community, roots and tradition. As families were displaced from the centre of town to make room for commercial redevelopment, there were some noble attempts to keep people who knew each other together in their new environments. This plan met with only limited success, though, and as new areas grew up together with new faces, community spirit suddenly wasn't so easy to find.

It was to Orford that Christopher Evans was brought just before he turned four. Born, some might say appropriately, on April 1, 1966, little Chris had spent those first formative years with his mum Minnie, dad Martin, brother David and sister Diane in the corner shop that the family ran at the junction of Bostock Street and Selby Street in the Bank Quay area of Warrington. Martin was a charming man who was both devoted to Minnie and fully prepared to put in the hours to support his family. Sharp as a tack, he'd made a living as a local bookie's clerk after the Second World War, working out the odds in his head and paying lucky punters as quickly and efficiently as he could. Of course, it wasn't until 1961 that off-course betting was legalised in England, but bookmakers were well-known in Warrington, as in most other cities, and had been tolerated by the police as a relatively harmless diversion. While he and Minnie ran the shop, Martin still took bets out of a wooden garage in Selby Street and even ran a black Morris Minor as a taxi, anything to support Minnie and the children. When Chris was born his dad was 45 years old, his mum was almost 40, and it was hard work bringing up three children. But both parents were full of love for their offspring, so nothing was too much trouble. They had roots in the area, too. Minnie's parents had lived in Bostock Street and Martin's family was also from Warrington, which meant there was always a willing pair of hands ready to muck in.

On March 16, 1970, though, the Evans family were suddenly taken away from the familiarity and friendliness of Bank Quay. Bostock Street had been earmarked for demolition and redevelopment, and they were moved the short distance out of town to 113 Capesthorne Road in Orford. Even to a small boy like Chris, this must have felt like a real culture shock. There was no doubt that the house the family were moving to would be seen as a step-up. After all, it was new, it was semi-detached, and it was even blessed with such fancy new trappings as gas central heating and a garden. But Orford was already developing a reputation as a place where you had to be careful, a place where juvenile gangs roamed the streets and petty crime was becoming commonplace. It's a reputation that remains to this day. *Warrington Guardian* journalist Sarah Harker covered events in Orford for eighteen months between 2000 and 2002, and has seen more than most of the day-to-day trials and traumas of living there.

'I have to be careful here,' she muses, when asked about what kind of a place Orford is. 'You'd have to say it's a deprived area. There's a lot of unemployment, single parent families and whatnot. If you asked anybody what Orford was like, they'd tell you it was pretty rough. The council has tended to concentrate its regeneration efforts on the town centre and that's been a big bone of contention for a lot of the suburban residents of Warrington, Orford very definitely included. There's a huge water feature that's been built in town that cost millions … and it's lovely. But people who live in Orford, Dallam and Westy are asking why none of the money is going to improve things for the town's suburban residents. They're asking why the council aren't looking on their own doorstep.' And, given some of the things that Sarah Harker has seen in Orford, the residents are right to be asking such questions. 'I'd say there are definitely certain parts of Orford that are no-go after dark,' she claims.

So was that the case back at the dawn of the 1970s? Not according to Trevor Palin, an Orford resident at the time and Chris's best friend when they were both growing up on the estate. 'Chris and I lived about half a mile apart,' he says. 'The estate then wasn't like it is today. The flats and houses were relatively new, with a lot of young families. There were good times and bad. Kids played and fought together, the usual.'

Certainly, Trevor has no recollection of anywhere being a no-go area back then. Neither Capesthorne Road, nor Greenwood Crescent, where the Evans family ended up three years after their arrival in Orford. Minnie and Martin swapped houses with Kathleen and James Smith to move just round the corner to 319 Greenwood Crescent opposite those three bastions of British working class estates, the chippy, the newsagent and the pub. Lee Burgess, who also lived close to the Evans family at Mill Farm Close, doesn't remember the estate as particularly violent either. 'I have no memory of that at all,' he says. 'My mum being the person she is, she would never have let me walk through it if it was dangerous. I would walk home in the dark across fields with no problems. It was nothing by today's standards.'

Trevor Palin remembers having a very close relationship with six-year-old Chris. 'We'd be together a lot,' he says. 'I would stay over at his and vice versa. I remember he made brilliant paper aeroplanes ... at one time, he even made great models out of balsa wood and paper, the sort you would soak and then stretch over the frame. I was totally impressed.' Despite the fact that Chris was extremely bright and possibly too quick with his tongue, Trevor says that it was he who copped most of the flak for the typical naughtiness that young lads get up to. 'If we ever got into trouble, I would always be the one who got blamed for it,' he says. 'I was a cheeky little sod at the time.'

The pair were soon palling up at the local St. Margaret's Church of England Infants' School. With his shock of red hair, impish grin and sharp wit, Chris was already showing all the characteristics that were to make his name less than 20 years later. Here was a boy who already stood out from the crowd. Of course, it's always tempting to look at a person's childhood for clues as to what shapes the character of the adult. Many have done so with Chris, reaching the conclusion that his fierce determination to succeed, perceived lack of sensitivity to others and tendency towards bullying fellow workers all stem back to the fact that he himself was bullied at school.

Well, it's an easy conclusion to jump to. He was new to the area, had shocking ginger hair that made him stand out, and was always there with a sharp or sarcastic response. *Obviously* he would have been picked on. And Chris himself claimed in a 1994 newspaper article: 'Being a ginger kid was hell on earth. I got into a lot of fights, but didn't win a single one. I wasn't the cheeky chappie you might think.' Some former class mates of Evans remember differently.

'I can't remember any special attention that was doled out to Chris,' says Trevor Palin. 'We had these chaps at the school, but as I can recall it was never really that heavy. I do remember that Chris could certainly stick up for himself verbally.' Lee Burgess, who was also one of Chris's classmates at St. Margaret's, is even more unequivocal. There was no bullying.

'I've read stuff about him being bullied, but that's absolutely not my recollection,' says Lee. 'No way was he bullied in the year I was at the school. I don't know whether at that age children are that aware of people's looks or characteristics, anyway. Chris was popular and bright and funny, the sort of person that people would rather be friends with. He had a big mop of ginger hair and freckles, and topped it off with a cheeky grin. He was very confident and popular. Anyone who was a huge achiever at St. Margaret's was popular.'

Both Trevor and Lee agree that St. Margaret's took a very traditional approach to the education of their little ones. 'It was a good school with a decent standard of discipline,' says Trevor. Lee, who was a sensitive child, paints a much bleaker picture of the place, though. 'It was very disciplined and compared to a lot of the other schools I went to – my step-dad was in the army and we moved around a lot – St. Margaret's was quite antiquated. I remember that there were 36 pupils in our class sitting at six round tables with six kids on each. Every Friday there was a literacy and numeracy test that determined where you would sit the next week: the brightest on the top table, and the least bright on the bottom one. Chris was always on the top table and I was always on the bottom one. I remember being really happy if someone from my class was off school, because it meant that I wouldn't have to sit in the last place on the last table.'

In fact, Lee hated the place so much that he ran away from home three times in the year he was at St. Margaret's. Popular Chris, though, had no such problems.

'He was extremely bright and very confident. He was a part of the in-crowd with two or three other lads and was quite a joker even then,' Lee explains. 'Chris was always the class comic, telling jokes and making everybody laugh. He was the one who'd be very quick to answer the questions in class. I remember that he was so confident he'd debate with the teachers, even at that age. There were two or three boys who seemed very much ahead of the rest of us, and Chris was certainly one of them.'

And even at primary school Chris was already showing off his individuality. 'He was very eccentric,' says Lee. 'You were free to wear your own clothes at St. Margaret's; there was no uniform. In the class photo that year Chris was wearing a nylon T-shirt, one half of which was orange and the other half purple. I was wearing a sensible blue jumper and grey trousers.'

This extraordinary confidence was a direct result of the stable and loving family unit that Minnie and Martin had constructed at home. 'Chris doted on his mum,' says Trevor Palin. 'She was everything to him, even though she was quite strict.' Indeed, Chris would talk about his mum with great affection later in life, though he would find it difficult to devote a lot of his time to her, especially since Minnie chose to remain at Greenwood Crescent despite her son's phenomenal success. Even when Chris had become an extremely rich young man, Minnie still felt a kinship with Orford and didn't want to move somewhere *swanky*, away from everything she knew. Chris meanwhile, had no such fond feelings for the place. Asked whether he missed Warrington, he would respond with 'Yes, I try to miss it every time I go past on the motorway.' A convenient gag? Not according to one of his future colleagues, Jamie Broadbent, who would talk of being sent to deliver Minnie's Christmas present of two tickets to Australia to her in 1996, because Chris didn't want to go back to Orford.

But that was a long way in the future, and if you were to look for signs of Chris's unease with the place while he was actually living there, it would be hard to spot any. In fact, the only thing that appeared remotely strange about Chris's upbringing was that he seemed remarkably different to both Diane and David, respectively three and 13 years older than him. Neither of his elder siblings seemed to have Chris's bulletproof confidence or his outgoing nature, and as such there didn't seem to be much closeness between the three children. Trevor remembers them being peripheral figures in Chris's life. 'I vaguely recall his sister Diane,' he says. 'But that's about it.'

Around the age of nine, Chris was also beginning to show signs of one of the traits that to this day many still find baffling. Despite his freckly ginger look, which was hardly the stuff of your average pin-up, he was definitely attractive to girls. Jane Pucill was the first to fall for Chris's schoolboy charms and according to Trevor Palin even at that young age she was quite a catch. 'Jane was a lovely girl, way beyond her years and very mature for a young lady,' he says. Chris wasn't going to be put off by such perceived unattainability, though, and devised his own peculiar method of impressing Jane. On a school coach trip, he sat on the back seat of the coach and serenaded her with a word-perfect rendition of Tommy Steel's ancient pop hit 'Little White Bull'. It did the trick.

Life was fun for the young Evans. He was enjoying his school and was popular there, while his home life was settled and loving, even despite the lack of real closeness with his brother and sister. Chris's dad had taken a job as a wages administrator at the local Winwick Hospital when he'd moved to Orford, but there was still plenty of time for bonding between father and son, who loved to discuss sport and play mini-snooker in Chris's bedroom. There were walks over the local fields with the family Alsatian, Max, and laughter was in plentiful supply. And when Chris passed the exam for the Thomas Boteler Grammar School, where his brother David had been a pupil 12 years earlier, it seemed as if his life was going perfectly to plan.

He started at the school, which was a three-mile bus journey away in Latchford, in September 1979 together with Mark Rutter, another St. Margaret's boy. Academically, the place held no fears for him. Chris was exceptionally bright and one early end-of-term report proclaimed 'enthusiasm and ability in a broad range of subjects ... excellent.' Chris even played for the cricket team and appeared in the school production of *Androcles And The Lion* in his second year. Boteler certainly did have some boys who liked to throw their weight around, just like any place where young men are sparring for position. But Chris's sharp mind and ready wit was enough to keep them at bay, and he was confident enough not to keep his head down.

One former schoolmate, Barry Melton, remembers Chris wandering around the school corridors bashing away at a guitar that he'd borrowed from the music teacher. It's hardly the sign of someone lacking in self-esteem. His imagination was now being constantly fired by entertainment; songs, television, radio. *Multi-Coloured Swap Shop* and *Tiswas* on Saturday morning telly, Piccadilly Radio 261 or Radio 1 on the radio. Listening to the breakfast show before heading out to school was, as Chris later said, ' ... the ultimate. It was the golden years of Radio 1.' Chris Evans's own life, too, had a golden glow, but then out of the blue a family tragedy unfolded which would instantly take the shine off everything.

Before Chris had started at Boteler his father, Martin, had been bothered by pains in his abdomen and bowel trouble, and was referred to a specialist by his local doctor. The news couldn't have been worse. Martin was diagnosed with an advanced state of bowel cancer and told that the condition was terminal. He lost weight rapidly and was forced to walk with a stick. It was obvious to everyone on the estate that Martin Evans was in a bad way. And through the winter of 1978, Minnie, David, Diane and Chris were all seen pushing Martin around in a wheelchair.

The outlook was bleak, everybody knew it, and there wasn't a thing that could be done about it.

Martin Evans died in Warrington General Hospital on Wednesday April 25, 1979, when Chris was just 13. On his death certificate, the cause of death was listed as carcinomatosis. The cancer had spread throughout his body. The obituary, which was published in the *Warrington Guardian* on Friday 11 May, was touchingly simple; 'Lived in the Bank Quay area for many years, and worked for ten years as a clerical officer at a local hospital. In his earlier days was a keen billiards and snooker player. Before moving to Orford was a proprietor of a shop in the Bank Quay area. He leaves two sons and a daughter.'

The family was absolutely devastated by Martin's death. As the eldest son, David took care of the arrangements, despite having already left the family home by this time. Minnie was heart-broken, saying on many occasions in the future that she felt cheated by the early loss of her partner. At the impressionable age of 13, Chris was extremely vulnerable, and dealt with the loss by attempting to blot it out of his mind completely. He admits now that his mother shielded the real seriousness of his father's illness from him, and after he died Chris couldn't bring himself to attend the funeral, which took place at the Walton Lea Crematorium.

Whether it was nothing more than simple coincidence, or whether the death of his father really did trigger a rebellious streak in Chris, the third year of his education at St. Thomas Boteler proved to be his last. There are various explanations as to why Chris left the academically superior Boteler in 1980, aged 14, for Padgate High School, just a short walk from his house in Greenwood Crescent, but sorting the truth from the fiction is no easy task. Chris himself is supposed to have a told a friend in later years that he crowned a science teacher with a wooden stool, leading to expulsion. He also told Alison Ward, his future girlfriend, that he'd been given his marching orders for tying a science teacher to a tree.

All this seems highly doubtful. There was nothing on Chris's school record to suggest that he was booted out of Boteler, and the most likely explanation is that he simply wanted to be closer to his mum. The fact that Chris settled so well at Padgate would also seem to suggest that he hadn't been expelled from Boteler. He played football, table tennis and golf, became a prefect, and was a valued member of the school.

The fact that Padgate High was co-educational was also a bonus for Chris. He loved girls and, despite his oddball appearance, they certainly loved him. There was a short relationship with a Tamara Bradshaw, then a more serious thing with Tina Yardley for about a year. Indeed, years later, Chris would still remark on how special Tina was. Outside all the new relationships and school activities, Chris also found time to start delivering papers for a local newsagent, as well as broadcasting on the local Warrington General hospital radio. With typical decisiveness, he resolved there and then that his future either lay in broadcasting or as a newsagent.

The death of his dad hadn't sent Chris off the rails, as his own stories about St. Thomas Boteler might have suggested. In fact, what it most likely did was provide the drive, energy, focus and determination that would fuel Chris Evans's single-minded pursuit of fame and recognition. If death could take his father so unexpectedly, he figured, then there wasn't a single second to be wasted. Professor Cary Cooper, a psychologist from the University of Manchester Institute of Science and Technology is convinced that Martin's death was absolutely crucial in shaping Evans's character.

'I've done research on a number of successful people,' he explains. 'And there is one characteristic which emerges: that a disproportionate number of them have lost a parent early in life, either by death or by estrangement. It's not unusual at all, and it would appear that these people are trying to gain control of the world later in life in a way that they couldn't when they were young. It's not necessarily power or control over others that they seek, but control over events, things that might happen to them. This is often illusionary, because of course they can't always control events. But even so, there's no doubt that you *can* exert more control over things if you're at the top of the tree rather than the bottom. So that's where they always feel they need to be.'

As Chris himself famously said, Martin's death was, 'the shotgun that started the race – that's when my life started. I grabbed every moment of every day.'

2 New Kid In Town

Hanging about waiting for things to happen wasn't Chris's style, so sticking around at school just wasn't on his agenda. Impatient to start his new life, the 16-year-old Chris had had enough of Padgate High. He left in 1982 with eight O-Levels and two CSEs to his name, despite careers advisor Bob Lowe's attempts to get him to stay on into the sixth form. 'He always wanted to be a newsagent,' he explained. 'And we couldn't persuade him to stay on at school, even though he was capable of doing well.'

Chris later claimed that all he ever wanted to be was a fireman, but that he was told he wouldn't make it because his eyesight wasn't good enough. Being a newsagent seemed a rather more realistic proposition, especially when Brian McLoughlin, who ran a chain of three Newsheet shops with his brother Tom, took Chris on at the shop on Battersby Lane, about a mile from Greenwood Crescent, for a wage of £50 per week.

Chris was delighted. It may not have been much, but it was regular money and it was a start, although he was equally determined to make a break into radio. Even as a 15-year-old with no experience, he'd demonstrated a natural aptitude while broadcasting on hospital radio, showing a maturity and ease with the microphone that was way beyond his years. Chris was confident he could do something in broadcasting, and started out on his quest by writing to Piccadilly Radio in Manchester, asking to replace one of the dogsbodies who worked on Timmy Mallett's show.

Chapter 2

Mallett had quite a local reputation thanks to his evening show *Timmy On The Tranny*, a typically wacky extravaganza where music was almost incidental to the on-air japes and jests. It was comedy of a sort, and Chris knew that his own brand of rapidly developing eccentric humour could add something to the mix. Station controller Tony Ingham was so impressed by the boy from Orford's front that he took him on to become part of Mallett's team, where Chris quickly gained an on-air character, a supposedly useless no-mark called Nobby No-Level.

Two-jobs Evans now had to start work at Newsheet at 5.15 in the morning, then race home after work to grab a bite to eat and be out of the house for Manchester, where Timmy Mallett's show started at eight in the evening. It was a punishing schedule which only allowed Chris three or four hours sleep a night, but despite making mistakes through tiredness which were covered up by loyal workmates, he still managed to impress the McLoughlins enough to be moved to the Woolston branch to assist Tom.

Trevor Palin remembers picking up his friendship with Chris again at this time. 'Chris and I had bumped into each other again purely by accident. I was riding my bike not far from where he lived. I was having guitar lessons at the time and was struggling on the bike with an oversized case. Anyway, next thing we're both back at his place strumming away. That was the start of our teenage years together. After leaving school I had a job as an apprentice French polisher and Chris was working at the local paper shop. I remember going round there one day and he had Radio 1 playing at absolutely full volume. The guy who owned the shop was moaning, but it took a while to get the volume down. I remember Chris laughing. He really didn't care!' Indeed, Chris's love of cranking up the radio eventually led to the beleaguered newsagent giving him his marching orders, effectively forcing him to devote his energies wholeheartedly to broadcasting. Inadvertently, Mr McLoughlin had just given Chris Evans the biggest break of his life.

Having passed his driving test soon after turning 17, Chris could now drive a battered old Mini down to Manchester, where he persuaded Piccadilly's Tony Ingham to take him on as a freelancer at a massive £2.50 an hour. As well as continuing as Nobby No-Level, Chris now had to do a bit of everything, learning the ropes of radio from the bottom up. Whether it was getting records from the library, sorting out interviews or editing newscasts, Chris had to be on hand to provide some manpower when it was needed. It may have been the bottom rung, but at least he was definitely on the broadcasting ladder now. And while it may not have been his on-air skills that did it, Chris made an immediate impression.

'He became a favourite around the station very quickly, considering that he was just hanging around in the evenings,' says Tim Grundy, who was himself starting out on a broadcasting career that would see him become both a respected DJ and TV broadcaster. 'He suddenly turned up helping out on Timmy Mallett's show, this gawky, tall, odd-looking lad, who would always be hanging about in what we used to call the lines room, where all the telephone lines came in. He'd just be answering the calls.'

'Chris and I started out working for Timmy at about the same time,' says Paul Carrington, one of the people who knew Evans best during his time at Piccadilly, and now a DJ at station Magic 828 in Leeds. 'Timmy was very hard on everyone. I remember him yelling through the studio talkback. 'I want a caller! NOW!!' and there's no doubt that he was horrible to some people. I wouldn't dream of slagging Timmy off, because I owe my break in radio to him. But I would equate him with a spoilt little brat who would throw his toys out of the pram if he didn't get his own way.'

Trevor Palin, who had been drafted in by Chris to give the team a hand on the strength of his guitar playing and composing abilities, is even less charitable. 'Chris needed some sort of angle at Piccadilly, and he knew I was quite good on guitar. More importantly, I had the ability to pen a tune in no time. So we went to Piccadilly and I was introduced to Timmy Mallett, who was a total arse. There we all were, messing about, writing jingles and doing OBs with this lunatic little Hitler in the background whinging at everybody. It was a very strange time.'

'I had my first show at Piccadilly, which went on air after Timmy, running from 10pm till two in the morning,' recalls Tim Grundy. 'So I watched them all at work while I was preparing my show. Timmy worked the kids hellishly hard; he was absolutely brutal.'

'Chris was totally unfazed by everything, though,' says Paul Carrington. 'Timmy's shouting, being on air himself, whatever. You could spot the talent straight away. There was nothing forced or manufactured about Chris. Everything he said was funny and I don't know if Timmy resented that. He certainly saw the value in Chris, though.' And Chris definitely saw the value in Timmy. The anarchic feel to Mallett's shows, the constant stream of ideas, and the fast pace and outlandish jingles; there's no doubt that Evans took a lot of his ideas from his first boss. And he may well have inherited some of his less pleasant characteristics from Mallett, too.

'In a way Timmy's way of dealing with us was good, because it certainly taught us discipline,' says Paul Carrington. 'But I don't suppose he set a terribly good example of how professional people should perform.' Indeed some of Chris's legendarily volcanic outbursts later in his career would appear to be a direct imitation of his former mentor, though Paul believes a fiery temper was always part of Chris's own make-up. 'He could fly off the handle even back then, very much so. He could really lose his temper over trivial stuff and he hated it if people didn't have the same attention to detail that he had.'

Yet there was no denying the quality of material that Chris produced. He was palpably an absolute natural. 'Chris was incredibly enthusiastic, clearly talented, and he made Timmy laugh a lot,' says Tim Grundy. 'He made all of us laugh. But there were always arguments. Chris and Timmy would fall out, and Chris would be a bit sulky for a while. But it never lasted long, because Chris desperately wanted to learn. He became very popular around the station because he was so maverick, so awkward and different and unpredictable that he had an instant charm about him.'

Chris's popularity wasn't confined to his on-air persona,

either. Whenever the Piccadilly crew went out of their HQ at Piccadilly Gardens for an outside broadcast, Chris immediately shone. 'We used to do this show called *Timmy's Funday Sunday,* which was an outside broadcast with an open top double-decker bus that would go to different locations throughout the summer,' says Paul. 'Parks, basically. And before Timmy went on to do the live broadcast, Chris would go out to warm the crowd up. The trouble was that he would do a better job of warming the crowd up than Timmy did on air, and I think that put Timmy's nose out of joint.' But if Mallett was miffed by the fact that Nobby No-Level had stolen some of his thunder, it seemed as if the rest of Piccadilly Radio had no problem at all with Chris.

'He was a lovely guy,' says Paul Carrington, who still has a genuine affection in his voice. 'He had that enviable gift of being in a group of people and always being the one who could make people laugh. But he was also likeable in a Frank Spencer kind of way. There was this element of calamity that seemed to surround him permanently. He seemed to be able to attract disaster, then walk away unscathed.'

The stories of Chris Evans's early mishaps have become the stuff of legend. There was the time he was supposed to drive a group of competition winners down to London for a Prince's Trust concert, only to stall in the radio station car park when he jammed the mini-bus against the low ceiling. He only managed to free the vehicle by letting the tyres down. Then there was the time when he attempted to drive the Piccadilly Radio car with a broken leg. 'He was having a go at driving it with one fully-plastered leg hanging out of the driver's window,' laughs Paul Carrington incredulously. 'Of course he crashed the car!'

'I'm not entirely sure he even had a driving licence when he took the radio car out,' recalls Tim Grundy. 'The Piccadilly Hotel, where the radio station was based, had a corkscrew ramp. Once Chris came out of the end of it like a rat out of a pipe, careered straight into the road and smashed into the wall on the other side!' Predictably, word of the young idiot's mishap spread through the station like wildfire. 'Everybody bloody well knew about it,' says Paul. 'Anyone else would have been fired on the spot, but Chris simply used his charm to get away with it.' Grundy agrees: 'Every week there was a "You won't believe what he's done this week" story going around the station. But Chris just laughed his way through it.' Even when, on one occasion, he lost Piccadilly thousands of pounds through sheer bone-headed stupidity.

'At one stage, I was doing a mid-morning show,' explains Tim Grundy. 'Mark Radcliffe, who would end up as a presenter on Radio 1 with his mate Lard, was my producer. Mark and I often flew off to do interviews with pop stars that would then be networked out to other stations to make some extra money for Piccadilly. Now the two of us got a chance to fly out to Gibraltar where there was this big TV show being filmed called *Rock Around Gibraltar* where loads of acts were appearing on board the Ark Royal aircraft carrier. Bob Geldof had decided that this was where he would make his first appearance after Live Aid, so when Mark and I grabbed him in the hotel and he gave us this long and fascinating exclusive interview, it was a real coup. When we got back I went straight to the radio station and put it in my locker for safekeeping, with "Bob Geldof Master" written across it in huge letters. When I came into the station after the weekend there were people avoiding my glance. I asked what they matter was and it was "Nothing, nothing, nothing". Eventually, I got to hear that Chris had found this hilarious comedy sketch about boxing and was looking for a piece of tape to dub it off on. He'd opened my locker, found the Geldof tape and recorded the whole of the boxing skit over the Geldof interview, even though he *must* have known what it was because it was so clearly marked.'

It was classic Chris, and Grundy was understandably furious. His big coup had been blown by a piece of vintage Evans stupidity and thoughtlessness. 'Mark told me the whole thing was ruined and we couldn't use the interview. Had Chris been in the building on that day, I would have punched his lights out,' he admits. 'But he wasn't and eventually Mark and I both calmed down. We weren't so much angry in the end. It was more a question of "When is Chris Evans ever going to grow up?" Then the next thing we heard was that the station boss, Mike Briscoe, had heard about the incident and was going to sack Chris. Mark went into Briscoe's office and said, "Don't sack him. He's a talent, and you'll lose a great presenter if you do. He just needs to understand his responsibilities." Then I went in after Mark and said exactly the same thing.'

Thanks to the intervention of Evans's more senior colleagues, Briscoe relented. 'I think he might have sent Chris a nasty memo,' says Grundy. 'But he didn't even give him a formal warning.' And did Chris get to hear about this charitable act? 'I don't know,' says Grundy. 'Probably. I don't think Mark or I went up and told him what we'd done, but the chances are that word would have got around. It wasn't ever mentioned by him, though, as far as I remember.'

Remarkably, Chris was never sacked for any of his many mishaps at Piccadilly Radio. Technically he probably couldn't have been given the boot anyway, because he was only being paid a freelance pittance for the experience he was gaining. But a few quid here and there while he tried to break into broadcasting was hardly enough to survive on, and he was always looking for other ways to supplement his meagre income. Part-time glass collecting at a rockers' pub in Warrington called The Lion wasn't going to swell the coffers, yet there had to be a better way which didn't entail taking the regular jobs that his mother kept hoping he'd accept to get his life on an even keel. Inevitably Chris came up with a scheme, and this time it was one that needed the help of his old school mate Trevor Palin.

'Away from the station, we decided that we needed more to do,' says Trevor. 'So we set up a Tarzan-a-gram business. I borrowed a pair of leopardskin-style trunks from dad and gave them to Chris. I would wear a pair of boxer shorts. We put an ad in the paper and bookings started to follow. It was new at the time, so clients weren't aware of what they were really going to get. Instead of two hunks they got a couple of wimps. We'd get hold of some info about the unfortunate client and pen some lyrics together to sing when we ambushed them. They were very rude sometimes, but the fact that it was all a bit of fun meant they normally went down well.'

Chapter 2

For the first time, Evans had shown he had the knack of making money out of his own inventive and unique entertainment ideas. He was totally unafraid of making a fool of himself, using his wit to charm and disarm anyone, and he'd also realised that he could utilise the talents of other people – in this case, Trevor – to make his 'act' even more appealing. The Tarzan-a-grams were fun and also lucrative. The bookings rolled in. Yet given their mainstay's unerring ability to attract trouble like some kind of wonky lightning conductor, there was plenty of madness along the way.

'One time we were doing a gig,' recalls Trevor. 'We had just finished and were upstairs changing. A lady came up, and was laughing about our performance. Chris came straight out and asked her if she would like some whipped cream on her. Next thing I know, Chris has put this stuff all over her and then proceeded to lick it off. I was sure that her husband was downstairs, so I started to get panicky. But as usual, Chris really didn't care!'

After eventually ditching the Tarzan-a-gram business, Chris and Trevor decided it would be fun to spend the summer of 1984 hanging out in the Welsh seaside town of Rhyl, living from hand to mouth, blagging a bed, doing a bit of busking for cash and having some fun. 'We'd just finished watching one of the *Lemon Popsicle* films, so it seemed a good time to go,' explains Trevor Palin. 'And Rhyl was the nearest seaside resort that had any sort of youth culture. We initially drove down in a mini that Chris had bought. He'd been having problems with Timmy, so we decided that we'd run all the outside broadcasts from a phone box in Rhyl! We would busk in the day and then do the stuff for Mallett's show from a telephone box in the early evening.'

This innovation was typical Evans. Why *shouldn't* he and Trevor do radio from a phone box? And, of course, with a boss like Timmy Mallett, the pair weren't going to get any resistance from upstairs. There were unforeseen problems, though. 'After sleeping in the mini for several nights, it became apparent that we needed to sort out a hygiene agenda,' says Trevor. 'For a while we'd nip into one of the guest-houses when the patron was otherwise engaged and use the facilities. But after getting caught a few times we decided on an even better plan. Chris and I made a pact; we'd try to stay in as many guest-houses along the front as we could. Not as paying guests, of course. As our faces started to get recognised around the coast it became easier to mix and mingle with people. We would suss out which girls were staying where and then befriend them in the hope that we could get a sleepover. I remember many a time when Chris and I would be escaping down the fire escapes in the early hours. The ploy of wooing them with romantic guitar and song always worked!'

Back in Warrington after their summer expedition, Chris decided that he wanted to keep his hand in at DJing and pestered local pub owners – including The Lion, where he was still collecting glasses – to give him a shot. The results were mixed. Some remember him being timid and characterless, others recall him being eclectic and charming. But there was a six-month slot at The Mersey pub, and even a gig at The Tropical Fun Pub in exotic St. Helens. There were odd jobs at the local Top Man shop, and even in a car showroom for about five minutes. But Chris's heart was never in it. He simply *had* to entertain people, and that was what he was going to do.

While he was scrabbling around trying to find his way career-wise, in May 1985 Chris's personal life took a dramatic turn when he started seeing Alison Ward. A pretty local girl with a dash of Goth style about her, the pair became friendly when Chris started playing squash with the boyfriend of one of Alison's sisters. Though she claims she didn't fancy Chris at first, the pair started dating, Alison tagging along when he had a DJing job, with the young couple often ending up back at her parents' house in Gough Avenue. Chris, she says, was a gentleman at first and it was months before they slept together.

Once again, some people were surprised that the blonde and attractive Alison was seeing the awkward, gawky-looking Chris. But, not for the last time, people had underestimated his appeal to women. 'Girls loved him,' confirms Paul Carrington. 'I think it's that he was very unthreatening, and that's quite an attractive quality for a woman. He was always very easy in women's company and very attentive, though he wasn't any kind of slimy flatterer. I don't know whether it was contrived, but I believe it was just him. He was just a nice guy and girls couldn't help but like him.'

Tim Grundy, too, experienced first hand Chris's rather remarkable way with the ladies. 'We were becoming very close friends at that time,' he says. 'We spent a lot of time at my house out in Cheshire, went out together and did some fairly crazy things together, usually involving far too much alcohol. And Chris was the one who always copped off. He always seemed to attract mature, classy, well-heeled, intelligent, extremely pretty women.'

Or maybe that wasn't so surprising, after all? On the surface, Chris Evans was perfect; funny, attentive and unthreatening. But Alison Ward has made explicit claims that their sex life was far from satisfactory.

The work at Piccadilly was still very casual. Chris wasn't tied down with any kind of contract and while he was determined to make it as an entertainer, he was prepared to explore any and all avenues to achieve his goal. Trevor Palin remembers heading down to London to see if the streets really were paved with gold. 'I remember standing outside Stringfellow's and Chris getting all excited because he had spotted Bruno Brookes,' recalls Trevor. 'It was about this time that a more determined side of Chris started to come out. He really wanted to make a name for himself and he was going to make it happen. He even went into a bar in the West End and got a gig as DJ for a couple of nights just on the strength of his mouth. He'd really started to get balls.

'We were only about 19 at the time, and I recall him saying that by the time he was 21 he wanted to be a millionaire. The strange thing is, I didn't even doubt he would do it.' But, despite such high falutin' talk there was never any money of course, and just like in Rhyl, sleeping arrangements in London had to be improvised. 'We fell asleep on the steps of the Bank of England, and stayed in Centre Point for while,' says Trevor. 'But they ended up kicking us out. We even went into the offices of the YMCA on Tottenham Court Road and went to sleep under a banqueting table.'

Back in Warrington again, having failed to persuade anyone

that they really *were* the Second Coming, Chris and Trevor then decided that in their search for stardom it would be a good idea ... to go to college. 'We were always influenced by films and saw one about college life that made us think it would be a laugh,' says Trevor. 'Chris lasted about an afternoon, but it was the changing point in my life. I met a wonderful girl who was later to become my wife, so I stuck at it.

'During one college session I peered up to see a long-haired stranger banging on the window. At first I didn't have a clue who it was, but this person was beckoning me to come outside. When I got out the door I burst out laughing. Chris had got this wig from somewhere and had come to get me out of college! At this time he had an old Spitfire motor. Sometimes I would borrow it so that I could take my future wife for a spin. But after nearly going underneath a lorry I decided it was better to give it back for good.'

The decision not to borrow the car any longer turned out to be symbolic. Chris and Trevor's lives were heading in different directions, and besides, Trevor was getting tired; 'Chris was always up all night. The guy never slept.' Trevor had found his own niche, a love of photography that would later develop into a highly successful career with his own creative design agency, Yap Yap. He had also found a girl he would stick with. Chris, for his part, was still searching ... but he wasn't sure exactly what for.

3 Baby Love

So Chris Evans was bobbing around on a sea of energy and half-baked ideas. He had talent, certainly. He could make people laugh, he could talk the hind legs off a donkey and he could invent madness in his head almost without thinking. But he needed to find some structure, some way of drawing all these strings of lunacy together to make one cohesive, understandable whole. Was it going to be nightclub DJing that would do this? Posing about in a pair of Tarzan pants? Or working on the radio?

It soon became clear that the only thing that was likely to give Chris's life the shape it needed was Piccadilly. He had never completely severed ties with the station, and the longer he hung around, the more he started to find that his skills were becoming valued. He was now even getting the chance to present his own late night shows when other DJs went on holiday, although Chris was still required to do plenty of menial tasks. After broadcasting late at night Chris would often still be at the station when Tim Grundy, now elevated to presenting the breakfast show, arrived for work. 'I remember saying to the Programme Controller, Mike Briscoe, that if Chris was hanging around at the station at that time then I'd like him to be involved in my morning show,' says Grundy. Thus was born 'White And Two Sugars'.

'That's how I took my coffee, and Chris was my coffee boy, so that was how he got the nickname. He was only ever referred to as White and Two Sugars, but he was soon quite heavily involved in the show, popping on air and saying "Hiya maaaate" in that way of his. Most of the time I had no idea what he was going to do when I opened the mic to him. Once he came in and just put his hand straight on the record while it was playing and stopped it. I opened the mic and said, "What the hell are you doing?" but he just laughed and said "Hiya maaaate". Incredible.'

Sometimes, Chris's unpredictable behaviour would rile Grundy, especially when Evans would take huge pleasure in ruining a gag or set-up that the jock had spent hours, even days, teeing up. One time, Grundy actually snapped. 'Chris had ruined something on air again and I'd just about had enough. I pinned him up against the studio wall by the throat to let him know I wasn't best pleased. Chris stormed out and sat on his own for a bit, then put his coat on and went home. I don't think he came in the next day, but on the following day he came back and sat sheepishly in the lines room for ninety per cent of the show. Eventually, he came in and said "I've been thinking about this, mate. You spend a long time dead." Then he put his arms around me and gave me a hug. That was typical Chris: unpredictable, but loveable. He loved the role and he wanted so much to be what I was, this breakfast show presenter with a good salary with all the perks.' Like a company car ...

'He came on the show one day and started off,' recalls Grundy. 'He said, "You've got a fantastic company car. It's like a spaceship." I said "Yeah, it's a nice car, isn't it?" "It's amazing, mate," he went on. "It goes at nine million miles per hour and it's got all these gadgets." Then out of the blue he said "Well, I want a company car." I fell about and said, "Oh yeah, so what kind of company car do you want?" He said "I want a Skoda. I'm going to write: 'I'm Tim Grundy's coffee boy' down the side." Twenty minutes later, a Skoda dealer was on the phone saying "You've got it"' And two days later there was a Skoda outside the office for him, with "I'm Tim Grundy's coffee boy" down the side. He wanted to put a giant cup and saucer on the roof, but never got around to doing it, but he was ever so proud of it and drove it all around town. I think he blew it up on the M6 by dropping a spanner in the engine in the end, which was no surprise to anyone.'

With the talent he was obviously showing, albeit a tad unpredictable, Chris wasn't going to stay as coffee boy for long, and it was Timmy Mallett's move into TV that propelled him to the next level. Mallett left Piccadilly Radio in 1985 when he was poached by fledgling station TV-am, where his *Wacaday* show would become one of the biggest children's hits of the era. Back in Manchester, the gap for the evening slot was there to be filled and, according to Paul Carrington, 'Chris was hotly tipped to get the show, and it was quite a surprise when he didn't.' Instead, the job went to a rival DJ named Steve Penk, who would cross paths with Chris Evans again much later in life.

Chris did end up with his own slot, though, a Saturday show called *Saturday Express*. It was no surprise to Paul Carrington that he positively revelled in being able to do his own thing. 'That was where his talent really shone through, as a naturally gifted communicator,' says Paul. 'Chris was someone who could take any situation and make it entertaining. I remember covering for him once when he was away and I was absolutely hopeless. I had to have everything scripted and written down. But Chris did it all off the top of his head and had a whale of a time. You could see it a mile off, that if he had the luck he'd go on to better things.'

The luck duly came. Steve Penk had quickly proved his worth in Mallett's old slot and was moved to a more prestigious, prime-time daytime show. Ironically, given what the future held, Penk had done Chris a huge favour, because Evans was then seconded onto the evening show, broadcasting from seven till ten throughout the week. Now that he was captain of the ship, Chris could set the agenda, both creatively and operationally. But there was no doubt that he was influenced by what he'd learned from Timmy Mallett, both then and now.

'A lot of the stuff Chris has done on the radio, Timmy did years before,' says Paul Carrington. 'It's just that Chris did it better. He had a better connection with people and his success on air was due to the fact that he could relate to a wide audience.

Timmy could relate to four and five-year-olds, but Chris was multi-faceted.'

Evans had never doubted his own ability to succeed as a DJ, and now he was proving it. His private life was less successful. It had looked as if Chris was at least going to try when he and Alison moved in together, lodging with one of her sisters and her husband in Warrington. By autumn 1986, Alison was pregnant, though she's admitted it was by mistake, and Chris's reaction to the pregnancy was mixed, to say the least. While he certainly didn't encourage Alison to have an abortion, Chris decided they should move out of her sister's house – not such an unreasonable notion.

There was a cottage in the village of Ainsworth near Bolton that was being converted by the parents of Mike Gates, one of Chris's colleagues at Piccadilly. It wasn't quite ready, but Chris reasoned that it would be perfect for the young couple when it was finished. So far, so sensible. But Chris then decided what would really be best would be if *he* moved away from Alison and in with Mike Gates in Ainsworth immediately, leaving her in Warrington. The eccentric arrangement lasted until Alison was eight months pregnant, when she was finally summoned to Ainsworth, only to find that Chris actually wanted her there to take part in a PR stunt, where he would claim he was living with Alison in a tent in his friend's back garden. The local paper duly ran a story about the 'wacky' DJ, but Alison maintains that she never spent a single night in the great outdoors. She must have been wondering what kind of a man was going to be the father of her child too, given that he'd been living away from her for the majority of the pregnancy and appeared only to have brought her to Ainsworth for a photo opportunity. But if this was both strange and selfish behaviour, it was as nothing compared to the sensational events which were to unfold when the baby finally arrived.

'In May of 1987, I'd got a couple of weeks' holiday,' explains Paul Carrington. 'I fancied some sunshine, but I didn't want to go by myself. So Chris said "I've got a couple of weeks, too, we can go together. I'll go and book it." So off he went to AA Travel in St Anne's Square in Manchester, and came back saying "I've got a brilliant deal – £138 for two weeks in Gran Canaria. Should I book it?" I was like, "Yeah, fantastic". So there we were – your typical couple of lads going on holiday. In fact, Chris was doubly excited because he'd never actually been out of the country before, and had never even flown in an aeroplane.'

'Now, a few things stand out from that holiday for me. Firstly, I took Trivial Pursuit in my suitcase and we were sitting outside on our balcony one night drinking wine and beer and playing the game. We were talking about life in general, as you do, and suddenly Chris just came out with it. He said "I'm going to be a huge star one day" in this very matter-of-fact way, like it was the most natural thing in the world. I just said "Oh right, very good". He said, "You don't believe me, do you?" to which I replied "You obviously think you will be, so good luck."

'I wondered years later whether he had some sort of prophetic gift. He didn't seem to get over-excited about this revelation, but that wasn't unusual. If he was down he wouldn't be able to get excited about anything. If anything, I'd say Chris bordered on being a manic-depressive. He wasn't suicidal or anything like that, but his mood very much went in peaks and troughs – and not always reacting to things in the way you'd expect. Big things made little impression. Little things would sometimes really bother him.'

Carrington has a point. It wouldn't be unreasonable to look at Chris's behaviour patterns – frenetic energy, a constant need to move on, low boredom threshold, a capacity towards selfishness – and see signs of depression there. Because when he was in those moods, nothing would be able to motivate him to show interest. Not even, apparently, the prospect of losing a leg.

'As you know Chris is ginger, with very pale skin,' elucidates Carrington. 'He didn't understand the nature of sun cream and sunbathing in that you have to use sun block and high protection if you've got that type of complexion. Well, on the last day of the holiday Chris was determined to get some sort of tan to go back with. But instead of using sun cream, he smeared baby oil all over himself, and he got so badly burnt that his leg came up the size of a balloon. Honestly, it was huge, the size of a crown green bowling ball. The reps took him out to see a doctor and he came back and told me that the doctor had said "Prepare yourself to lose your leg. You're going to get gangrene in this, and it wouldn't surprise me if you have to have your leg amputated." But Chris wasn't at all fazed by the news, and we just packed up and headed for home. Getting on the plane he was walking with a massive limp like he'd broken his leg, but Chris is the luckiest person I've ever met, and within two or three days and with a bit of cream it had all gone down.'

Yet the most amazing episode of this holiday had already happened a few nights previously. 'Again, we were sitting on the balcony,' says Paul. 'All of a sudden, Chris said to me, "I'm just going to call Alison and see if she's had the baby." Now I was astonished. I didn't know *anything* about it. "What baby?" I asked. "Didn't I tell you?" he replied. "She's pregnant." I thought for a couple of seconds, then said, "Riiighhhttt. So who's the father?" "Well, me!" "And you've come away on holiday with me when your girlfriend's just about to drop a sprog?" And Chris said, "Well, yes." And he didn't see anything wrong with that at all. It was as if it hadn't even occurred to him that there was anything weird about this.

'So then he went away and made the call. And when he came back I remember thinking about this whole affair, and being shocked by the fact that he seemed totally unbothered, unexcited and unenthusiastic that he might be a father.'

There are unsubstantiated stories that Chris Evans had made mention of the fact that he was going to be a father on air at Piccadilly Radio. Tim Grundy, for his part, gives no credence to them. 'He didn't really talk about Alison or his daughter,' he says. 'I certainly don't remember us having any conversations about it, so I doubt very much that he would have talked about it on air. And the idea of being a dad certainly didn't fit with the image that Chris was portraying of being the young lad about town.'

Jade Lois Ward was born at 11.45pm on Thursday June 4, 1987 at Warrington General Hospital. Chris's name wasn't on the birth certificate, with Alison later explaining that they thought social benefits would be increased that way. When Chris got to see Jade, his daughter had been taken to intensive care after having some difficulties breathing. He started crying; the first and only time Alison Ward ever saw her partner break down.

'I think he was scared as much as anything,' she says. Indeed, Evans seemed scared of responsibility, and scared that his chance of fame might be messed up by the arrival of a daughter who needed to be looked after and put first. After all, he'd hardly taken Alison's needs into account to date. She hadn't liked being cooped up miles away from friends and family while Chris spent much of his time at Piccadilly, so she moved out of the house in Ainsworth and headed back to her mother's in Warrington. Dutifully – for a change – Chris followed, and even said they should look to buy a house in the area. Towards the end of the year he bought a two-bedroom terraced house at 285 Lovely Lane, right round the corner from the hospital where Jade was born.

The family hardly got a chance to live there, though, because by the time October came around, and with Jade just a matter of months old, Chris and Alison had split up. Rightly concerned that Chris was far more interested in his work than in his family, Alison moved back to her mum's again and the relationship broke down.

It didn't appear that this 21-year-old DJ was suited to domestic bliss, but that didn't mean Chris Evans's interest in the opposite sex had diminished. No sooner had he and Alison knocked things on the head than he was hopping into bed with a newsreader at Piccadilly named Sara Green. Tim Grundy still can't quite believe how he found out about the affair.

'Sara was this absolutely gorgeous blonde, a really attractive girl,' he says. 'Now, Chris was telling me one day how he'd just bought a futon, and casually said that he and Sara had had the best night's sleep together ever. He definitely wasn't bigging it up about how he was sleeping with Sara – Chris was never very open about his relationships, and was generally very discreet. It seemed like he'd mentioned her very much by mistake. So I said, "Hold on. You're *with* Sara?" And it was like, "Well, yes." Things like that would happen on a regular basis.'

Chris Evans may well have just come out of a serious relationship with Alison Ward – in which there was now a child involved – but it wasn't long before he was spending much of his time at Sara Green's house in Cheadle Heath. Only a complete cynic would suggest that this might be because it was a lot closer to his work at Piccadilly than Warrington was …

4 London Calling

Chris Evans has a habit of walking out on jobs. Later in life, he would famously quit his two biggest gigs – as breakfast show presenter on both Radio 1 and Virgin Radio – over what he perceived to be terrible personal injustices. Attempts to curb his creative instincts when he'd supposedly sailed too close to the wind and, worst of all, people actually trying to tell him what to do, were anathema to him. Further down the line, Chris – a man whom numerous people say doesn't relish confrontation – would have an entourage of people to deal with those difficult conversations when he wanted shot of a gig. But the first time that Chris Evans told his boss to stick his job where the sun doesn't shine, at least he had the balls to do it himself.

The legend of the incident that led to Evans leaving Piccadilly Radio at the end of 1987 has been blurred by time. What is certain, though, is that Chris was sitting in for another DJ, hosting the afternoon show, when a casual comment about cats caused absolute meltdown. One story goes that he read out a story on air about a wealthy woman who had left a considerable fortune to a cat. His then boss Mike Briscoe insists, however, that the item had been a serious piece of news about a rather nasty case of cruelty against a cat. But what is certain is that Evans followed the item with the comment: 'I like cats, lightly grilled on both sides.'

It's the kind of nonsense anyone might say in a pub conversation, but unfortunately for Chris, he wasn't talking to his mates in the boozer. He was broadcasting to the whole of Greater Manchester including, it transpired, many of the area's cat-loving population. The phones lit up with listeners complaining about the off-colour remark. Immediately after the show, Evans was summoned to Mike Briscoe's office for a dressing-down, with Briscoe clearly expecting the 21-year-old presenter to apologise profusely and assure him it wouldn't happen again.

Chris Evans, however, had other ideas, as Paul Carrington clearly remembers. 'It wasn't necessarily what Chris said on air that got him fired,' he explains. 'It was his outburst in Mike Briscoe's office. It was about five past six and most people had gone home for the night, but I was having a little listen. It was a muffled conversation, but from the tone it was obvious they were having a blazing row. Chris definitely told Mike Briscoe to fuck off. In fact, the only words I did hear clearly as he came out were "Well, *fuck off!*" as he slammed the door, which resounded throughout the building. The door sort of wobbled, like a cheap BBC sitcom set.'

Seething with anger, Chris stormed out of the radio station vowing never to return. It was exactly the kind of response you would have expected from the headstrong Evans. No matter that he had just thrown away one of the most prized broadcasting gigs in the Northwest over an absolute nothing incident; someone was trying to exert editorial control over him and he absolutely, wasn't going to stand for that. According to Tim Grundy, though, he did return to the station the following morning.

'I was on air doing the breakfast show when Chris came into the studio and announced he was leaving. I asked him what was the matter and he simply said, "Oh, I'm leaving. I'm going to London." That was his very first thought; that he was off to London. He spouted on about Mike Briscoe for a bit and then said to me, "Open the mics". I was worried he was going to say something obscene on air about Briscoe, but he was like, "No, I just want to say goodbye to everyone." So I opened the mics and Chris said "Maaaate, I've had this fantastic idea. I'm going to sell Scotch air to the Americans. I'm going to go to Scotland and get cans of air and sell them to the Americans. I'm going to make *millions*. Hey, thanks for being there. See ya. Bye." And that was it. He was off.'

Bemused and confused, Grundy quickly found out about the previous night's bust-up with Mike Briscoe. 'I found out later that Chris had told Briscoe: "I'm the best effing disc jockey on this station. If you sack me, you're losing the best effing DJ here." And Briscoe had said "Well, watch me." But Chris had said "Too late, 'cos I quit." He told Briscoe to stick it up his arse and went.' This would all fit in with Chris's belief in his own ability and his devil-may-care attitude, of course. But despite his bluff manner, which was designed to tell the world that he couldn't care less about Mike Briscoe and his poxy job, Paul Carrington claims the reality wasn't really like that at all.

'I remember going round to see Chris in Cheadle Heath where he was living with Sara Green, a couple of days after he'd walked out,' he says. 'And Sara told me that he'd actually been very down about the whole affair. I think it probably hit him more than he thought, even though he was determined to brush it aside and bounce back. But that was another insight from her into how depressed he really could get about life.'

None of Evans's high-profile strops would ever again carry such a risk. Whenever he would waltz off into the sunset in the future, at least Chris knew he already had hits under his belt and cash in his bank account. This time he had nothing to take with him except a burning sense of injustice and, very quickly, the feeling that he might have blown things big time. Speaking to Loyd Grossman in the *Sunday Times Magazine* in January 1994, Evans reflected on that fateful flounce.

'I walked out thinking the world was my oyster, and that I was really good,' he said. 'I got paid every third week, left on a Wednesday and was due to get paid on a Thursday. But because I'd broken my contract, they didn't pay me at all. And then the garage rang up and asked for my car back. So literally, within 24 hours of walking out on one of the biggest radio stations in Britain, I had no money and no car. I was a 21-year-old, totally unemployable arrogant little shit. I'd blown it in a big way.'

As it turned out, Chris Evans hadn't blown it at all. Rather, he had unwittingly sown the seeds for a stellar career path that would turn him into the biggest media noise in Britain. Not that Chris looked much like the biggest media noise in Britain when he sat down opposite Rob Jones, Managing Director of Radio Radio, in Rathbone Place, just off London's Oxford Street, early in 1988. He'd managed to wheedle himself an interview at the new station on the back of a recommendation from his acquaintance and one-time Piccadilly Radio producer Andy Bird, who'd recently taken a job 'down the smoke'.

Radio Radio had been formed, with the backing of Richard Branson, as an attempt to offer a broadcasting solution to a tricky commercial problem. Radio Radio would produce programmes hosted by some of the biggest names in broadcasting, including Ruby Wax, Johnnie Walker and Jonathan Ross, that could be syndicated to commercial stations for use in their graveyard shifts. The appeal for the potential buyers was clear. They would get top quality broadcasters for a fraction of the cost of putting their own people on air at a time when listener numbers were minuscule. So the names might pull in extra numbers *and* help save money.

Jones took a shine to Evans, calling him 'a very polite young man,' a reaction that might cause a double take in some quarters. Maybe the Piccadilly experience had caused a bit of a reality check. Jones didn't have a presenting job for Chris, but he did offer him the chance to help produce Jonathan Ross's show. This could have felt like a step down for the man who'd already been presenting himself, but if it did, Chris certainly wasn't about to show it. He needed the break. And besides, the fact that his starting salary of £18,000 was as near as dammit double what he was on in Manchester certainly helped soften the blow. Plus Jonathan Ross was the media darling of the moment – a man who Chris had identified as the figure who could kick-start his career in London the fastest.

'Chris set out on an incredible mission of getting to know Jonathan Ross and it was the single most driven thing I've ever witnessed in my life,' says Evans's former Piccadilly Radio mate Tim Grundy. 'Within moments of Chris going down to London, he invited me down to stay with him in Belsize Park in a house he was sharing with a TV producer. It was a really nice place in a mews terrace, and Chris had a couple of the upstairs rooms. We went to his health club, which was the same club where Jonathan Ross was a member. We went to the same restaurants where Jonathan ate, the same pubs where he drank. Chris had absolutely set his sights on getting to know him.'

And once he'd wormed his way in with Ross, Chris didn't waste his opportunity. Rob Jones's hunch that Evans was 'obviously bright and sparky' proved to be right. Despite the fact that Ross was a big star already on the back of his Channel 4 chat show *The Last Resort*, Chris was far from intimidated, weighing in with plenty of ideas to improve the presenter's syndicated show. And within a matter of weeks it came as no surprise to Jones that Evans was badgering him about getting his own show, claiming he was already more accomplished than Ross.

Jones wasn't at all convinced. 'He was very Manchester at the time,' he said. 'And as we were a national service, putting on a blatantly regional guy would have brought complaints.' Jones was convinced that Chris Evans wouldn't make it as a national radio presenter, but recognised a masterful producer, even going so far as to call him a genius. It wouldn't be the last time the word was used in connection with Evans's all-round broadcasting skills.

While Chris talked down Jonathan Ross's talents to try to secure his own radio slot, his behaviour suggested that was a tactic rather than a genuinely held belief. He had quickly recognised that schmoozing would be a vital component of the armoury he'd use to drive his way to the top, and spent much of this first period in London shamelessly buddying up to Ross. But there was another member of the team who was going to end up as an even more important part of Chris Evans's life, even if he hadn't quite realised it himself yet.

Carol Deirdre McGiffen rejoiced in the title of traffic manager at Radio Radio, but neither that nor a rather prissy way of dressing did her personality much justice. The 28-year-old from Kent was an absolute livewire – especially when the drinks were flowing in the station's local pub, the Bricklayer's Arms – and had been known to flash her impressive boobs once in a while when the mood took her. The story goes that she once got down to her knickers, jumped on a table and persuaded Richard Branson to dance with her at a Christmas party when she was working for the part Virgin-owned Music Box TV channel. If there was ever a woman who'd be able to hold her own in the face of Chris Evans's quick-fire wit and repartee, not to mention general outrageousness, then this was her.

It was obvious to everyone working at Radio Radio that there was an immediate attraction and chemistry between the two of them, despite Chris being six years younger than Carol. But Chris was still dating Sara Green, seriously enough, in fact, for Sara to have moved to London from Manchester to be with him. She'd scooped a job at the new BBC station GLR, and the pair of cub presenters were by now settled in a rented one-bedroom flat just off the Camden Road.

With his exciting new life in London, it would have been easy for Chris Evans to have forgotten all about his other existence in Orford; his mum, his mates, and his baby Jade. It would have been so easy, in fact, that that was exactly what he did. After he had failed to make Jade's christening at The Church Of The Transfiguration in Birchwood it was obvious to Alison Ward that the relationship with her daughter's dad, which had been hanging by a thread anyway, was almost over. Alison had decided that if Chris was only going to be a dad when it was convenient, then it would be better if he didn't see his daughter at all. 'He used to phone now and then,' said Alison Ward. 'And he always asked how Jade was. But it was all done out of duty.'

At this stage in his life Chris Evans was either a man who'd recognised he had great talent and was rightly making sure he made the most of it, or a charmless careerist who was prepared to neglect his duties to suit himself. Or maybe both. 'He was totally upbeat at this point,' says Tim Grundy. 'A wide-eyed kid in the big city. Chris took me round London like he'd lived there all his life. He was really excited at being surrounded by celebrities. He'd point out Tony Hadley from Spandau Ballet's house, and stuff like that.'

In later years, Evans blamed the death of his father for this single-mindedness. 'I just don't have any fear,' he told Mariella Frostrup in *Vogue* in July 1997. 'A friend says my emotions are fireproof, and when you lose your dad, they just *are*. When someone you love dies you think,"Fuckin' hell, don't want any of that; better get on with it; didn't realise it could happen." And so you run and run and run, looking backwards to make sure you're getting further away, and then, if you're not careful, you've run so fast that you realise you're running not only away from his death, but towards your own.'

Meanwhile, Evans's relentless desire for upward mobility in the world of media saw him hot-footing it out of Radio Radio less than a year after arriving at the station. The BBC were launching London network GLR, for which they'd already recruited Sara Green, and the station's young, ambitious and bullish bosses Matthew Bannister and Trevor Dann were on the lookout for fresh talent. Bannister and Dann had been mates since their days working together at Radio Nottingham, and after floating around the London radio scene at Capital and Radio 1, Bannister had seen an ad in the paper for the job of managing director of Radio London, which became GLR. He applied, got the job, brought Dann in to 'pick the records' and by October 1988, they were up and running.

Bannister and Dann were interviewing for producers, including a guy called John Revell, who had set up Virgin Megastores' in-store radio station. They also interviewed Chris Evans, who by now had made friends with Revell. When Evans came in to put his case for employment to his prospective new bosses, something about his appearance seemed oddly familiar to Trevor Dann. Then the penny dropped. Evans was wearing the same tie that Revell had worn a couple of interviews earlier.

When Dann picked him up on this, Evans was unconcerned: 'This? It's Revell's tie. I borrowed it. I didn't realise you had to wear a tie for the BBC.' Dann couldn't help but laugh inwardly at this. And then things got better still. In a section on the application form which asked candidates to add any other information which they might consider relevant, Evans had written a couple of slightly cocky points about his contacts in the industry. His third point in this 'extra information' section read: 'Pressure is my middle name. See over.' Dann flipped the sheet over, and saw that Evans had filled his name out on the form as Christopher Pressure Evans. This wit and disregard for formality won him the job.

While Bannister and Dann were congratulating themselves on poaching a hot new talent, Radio Radio boss Rob Jones was seething when he found out that Evans was leaving. Just a few hours earlier, knowing that GLR were sniffing around his talent, he had offered Evans more money to stay and been told by his protégé that he absolutely, definitely wasn't about to walk out on the station. Later the same day, he'd found out that Chris *was* leaving. Not that Evans had told him personally. He'd left that dirty job to his producer mate, Andy Bird.

Chris Evans's first job at GLR was once again acting as a producer, this time to Emma Freud, the daughter of hangdog MP Clement Freud and sister of a man who would eventually become very influential in his life, one Matthew Freud. Trevor Dann recalls that at this stage, the idea of Chris presenting wasn't an issue. 'I'm not ready yet,' the new boy had claimed, rather surprisingly.

Despite this, Evans's new bosses were highly impressed by his production work with Freud on her weekday show, which ran from 10am till midday. She was a decent broadcaster, but not a girl with an instinctively common touch. Evans, though, could tap into her intelligence and rework it to give it an almost game show appeal. He instigated a slot called 'Name That Pope', wherein Freud read out details of a historical pope from a reference book and asked viewers to, well, Name That Pope. Evans had great instincts and was prepared to fight for what he believed was right for the show. And fight hard, if necessary.

'You hear stories about how he would drive Emma to tears on a regular basis,' says Radio 2 broadcaster and journalist Stuart Maconie. 'And on meeting Chris, I could kind of see how he could have done that. He's very full on and blunt, although I certainly wouldn't say in a malicious way. When I interviewed him once I actually asked him about whether he had made

Emma cry, which was a rumour going round the industry, and his answer was, "Well, if I *did* do that, then it was only for her own good, to get better programmes out of her".'

Evans moved on to produce Danny Baker's weekend breakfast show, and a lasting friendship and working relationship was formed. It wasn't hard to see why the two men would hit it off. Baker, a former music journalist, had found his true vocation in radio. The environment suited his nature. The microphone fuelled his fierce intellect, lop-sided view of life and, let's be honest, rampant ego. His shows were fast, freaky and above all, very funny. Here was someone that Chris admired and was maybe just a touch in awe of from the get-go.

By the summer of 1990, Chris had finally decided that the time was right to go on air himself. Dann and Bannister were happy to accede to his requests, and put him onto the Saturday afternoon slot. Within three or four months, however, DJ Dave Pearce had upped sticks for Kiss FM, leaving weekday evenings free. Chris was moved into the slot with a show called *The Greenhouse*. If the title sounded pompous, the idea was even more so. An environmentally friendly radio show? Presented by Chris Evans? It sounded horrific.

Evans, however, threw himself into the spirit of things by surrounding himself with a load of plants in the studio. He then proceeded to ridicule the ecological subjects he was duty-bound to bring up. His natural aptitude as a broadcaster simply shone through. It was as if he'd never been off the air, and the ideas poured out of him. He was an extremely potent force at GLR in that he was unknown, and therefore highly capable of pulling pranks on the famous, the stupid and the unsuspecting. He would ring up people like Michael Parkinson and cheekily wind them up, which made him very endearing. Eventually Chris ended up in the station's Saturday morning slot, where he devised a show that to many still remains the absolute peak of his broadcasting creativity.

Round At Chris's was the perfect vehicle for Evans to show his skills. Loose and unstructured, the show relied almost entirely on his speed of thought. This was truly broadcasting for the fearless, and once again Evans demonstrated that he is far more comfortable in front of a microphone than he is in real situations. For a 23-year-old, his confidence was astonishing.

Evans based much of the show on inviting listeners down to the studio to act as a kind of unpaid 'crew'. This was an idea that he had discovered on American radio and which he would use time and again throughout his career, from the breakfast posse at Radio 1 to the zoo TV of *TFI Friday*. But the *Round At Chris's* volunteers weren't broadcasters; they were regular punters, doing it for fun and not as a career move. Controlling them on live radio would be a daunting prospect even for an experienced presenter, but Chris took it all in his stride. So what that there were anything between 25 and 50 people slopping about in the GLR studio at Marylebone Road? Evans believed he could handle it, and he mostly did. Brilliantly.

Yet away from the radio job, other things weren't running as smoothly. Chris's relationship with Sara Green was on the wane, and by the time of his twenty-third birthday in 1989 it was just about done. Evans had by now bought himself a ground floor studio flat in Parkhill Road, Belsize Park and while Sara still worked at GLR, she no longer held any fascination for him. As so often in his life, he'd simply moved on – this time, inevitably, to Carol McGiffen.

The split certainly wasn't a clean break. 'Sara is the only person with a worse story to tell than mine,' admitted McGiffen, when she and Chris were no longer friendly. This was because their affair had started while Chris and Sara were officially still an item. Carol insists that the pair didn't actually sleep together while Chris was with Sara, but she does admit to 'this mad snog for hours' on a company jolly to Dunkirk. Bizarrely, though, the catalyst for their first act of sexual congress turned out to be none other than the footballer Gary Lineker.

In the summer of 1990, Britain was gripped by football fever. The World Cup was being held in Italy and England, under manager Bobby Robson, had progressed to the quarter-finals to meet Cameroon. Seven minutes from the end of normal time, it looked as if the unthinkable was about to happen as Cameroon led 2-1. Up stepped Lineker to convert a penalty and take the tie into extra time. Chris was watching the events unfold up in Belsize Park with a bunch of mates, and when Lineker scored with an another penalty in injury time to send England through to the semi-finals, the party began in earnest.

Had Lineker not sealed an England victory, the chances are that the party would have fallen flat and petered out. As it was, Chris acted as house DJ and vast quantities of booze were supped. Carol McGiffen was there, and by the end of the night she had bedded Evans, an experience that she later decided was 'really, really funny.'

However, it may not have been quite so amusing for one Holly Samos, a young woman who'd helped out on *The Greenhouse* and shared a flat with Claire Houghton, a researcher on the programme. Evans – ever one for a complicated love life – was also dating Samos. McGiffen kept a diary on her computer at the time, and merely entered, 'Wonder what Claire thought of me sleeping with Chris. Isn't she good friends with Holly?' But this comment was an afterthought for Carol, having already noted the England score.

Clearly the young Holly was no match for the independent, worldly, confident and sexy Carol McGiffen. And nobody knew that better than Carol, who was quite happy to see the object of her affections carry on with this young girl, to 'get it out of his system' as she put it. She was proved absolutely right when Chris soon ended his relationship with Holly.

Really, it was no surprise. Carol was besotted with Chris, while Chris had found a woman who was both feminine and laddish at one and the same time, someone who was sexy but who could always hold her own in the pub. The couple discovered the Haverstock Arms in Belsize Park and soon became friendly with the landlord, Andrew Carey, a man who would later play a part in *TFI Friday* as Andrew The Barman. They would spend leisurely hours drinking, laughing and being daft, and it was fun. In fact, it was so much fun that Chris eventually decided that the relationship could entertain London.

Round At Chris's was elongated to *Round At Chris's And His*

Missus, and the show became even more popular. Carol and Chris were a potent brew. Both were fiercely intelligent and quick-witted, yet happy to see the value of a bit of base humour. Ideas such as 'Pregnant Pause', a phone-in competition that was only for women who were, you guessed it, pregnant, weren't beneath them. And their instincts were good.

Out of a rather weak pun, the pair manufactured one of the most successful phone-ins ever staged by GLR. Laugh In The Bath – only for people who were naked and soaking – and Tickle Your Trout (for people in bed together) were variations on a theme, but the variations always seemed to work in their very capable hands. A year after Chris and Carol's Lineker-induced coupling, they were being hailed by London's media industry as the best thing on radio. 'I just count myself really fortunate to have been around Chris Evans at that point,' says Trevor Dann. 'He was just brilliant. He was George Best.'

5 Video Killed The Radio Star

Brilliance is in short supply. One glance at the TV schedules for any day you choose will tell you that. So Chris Evans was never going to remain a secret for very long. In fact, the British public were about to experience Chris the TV presenter for the very first time.

British Satellite Broadcasting, or BSB, had launched into the burgeoning satellite television market with their gimmicky 'squarial' – the hook on which they hung their marketing drive. Unfortunately, they found themselves up against Rupert Murdoch and his muscular Sky network, in a war that they were destined to lose within a year. BSB, however, was the place where Chris Evans made his TV debut when the network first opened for business on April 29, 1990. As the front man of the music video show *Power Up* on BSB's music channel The Power Station, Evans initially seemed an odd choice for telly. Nobody doubted his broadcasting abilities, but many were in agreement with the old adage – he truly had a great face for radio.

'Evans came in and he was really ugly, a ginger-headed bastard with these great goofy glasses.' It's fair to say that Evans didn't make much of a first impression on Don Atyeo, Managing Director of The Power Station. Yet within the course of that one interview, the 'ginger-headed bastard' convinced Atyeo that he should be awarded a job in a medium where he had precisely nil experience. When The Power Station launched out of a dingy old studio in West London's Parsons Green area, it was Evans who was live on screen.

If the fledgling station's bosses were nervous about taking such a risk, they very quickly realised that they'd struck TV pay dirt. Evans was an immediate sensation, at ease in front of the camera, a natural entertainer with an unerring instinct for what would work. What was more, he was capable of doing it without a director prompting him through an earpiece. Evans could remember links, where he was supposed to be in the show, what he had to do next and how long he had to do it in … *everything*. 'I was really quite in awe of him,' admitted Atyeo.

Evans's gags and sketches seemed never-ending. From inventing stuff like Man In The Cagoule (who had a cagoule buttoned up right over his head) to doing the show naked behind a desk in the car park, the atoms whizzing around his brain were in constant motion. He also had his old mate, Tim Grundy, involved as The Man With The Fish. 'I'd walk on with a 10lb salmon under my arm and Chris would say, "What do you want, Man With The Fish?" I'd say something daft, and he would always respond with "That is *astonishing*!" We did dozens of sketches and they were dead funny.'

Yet if it appeared that Chris Evans simply plucked ideas from the air as easily as kids nick apples from a neighbour's tree, appearances were deceptive. 'Loads of the features that Timmy and I had used at Piccadilly, he then did on *The Power Station*,' says Grundy. 'But why not? Chris did them in his own particular way.' Yes, he had a natural gift for creativity, but he also knew that he had to work at it. The *Evening Standard's* music critic John Aizlewood stumbled into a scene by complete accident a few years later, in the middle of 1997, where he got to witness Evans's creative processes at first hand.

'I happened to meet Chris in a pub in Notting Hill through mutual friends,' says Aizlewood. 'And what was incredible was that everyone seemed to have this need to share stuff with him. Complete strangers were coming up to him in the pub and saying, "I've got this idea for your show". Now, I'm sure a lot of people would have just said "Yeah, yeah, whatever". But Chris listened really attentively to everything that these people said, and then he would write a kind of shorthand version of these ideas on his hand in ballpoint pen. By the end of the night he was literally covered in pen all the way up to his elbow. I had a conversation with him about this, and we agreed that the pub was an amazing place, because it was where you always had the best conversations and the best ideas. He was quite open about the fact that he got loads of his ideas from conversations in pubs.'

Indeed he was. Chris Howe, a respected director who worked with Chris on *Tee Time*, a golfing show that was produced by his production company Ginger in 1998, also confirms Evans's shameless magpie tendencies. 'Chris loved nothing more than having a few beers around the table, and being one of the boys. You'd tell him a joke, and it would be on the radio the next day. And if you had a go at him, saying, "You're nicking my jokes", he'd just laugh and say, "That's what I do, you fuckin' idiot. I get my jokes from you and tell 'em to the nation!".'

It was this attention to the minute details of everyday life and everyday conversation that Evans wove into his frequently inspired TV shows. But as impressive as his skills were, and as accomplished as he undoubtedly was, it was also clear that where someone so exuberant and yet so young was operating there was always going to be friction. 'He was very single-minded about what he wanted to do,' reflected Don Atyeo on the subject, but that was probably being a little kind to Chris.

In fact, when he thought about it a little more, Atyeo went much further in describing Chris's *modus operandi*, calling the star 'a demanding fucker and an egotistical son of a bitch' when he spoke to David Jones for *Freak Or Unique: The Chris Evans Story*. Most of the time Evans's headstrong attitude would be tolerated because his hit rate on ideas was so consistently high. But clearly some people thought that Chris Evans was getting too big for his boots.

Up in Manchester, Tim Grundy received a call asking for his help. 'I was told "Chris is behaving like a cunt. Can you come and sort him out?" He was doing the big "I am" and it was thought that it would be good for him to have some Northern levelling. I liked him, and I didn't want him to cock things up by being arrogant. Word like that gets round the industry very quickly, though judging by the success Chris has had, you'd have to say he got away with it. But he's still known as a bastard by an awful lot of the people that worked with him.' Still, Tim Grundy headed down to London to try to straighten his mate out.

'I stayed for about a week, and we went out most nights and enjoyed ourselves. I remember his future wife Carol joining us for an Italian meal near to where he was living. There were about six of us, and I'd offered to pay. Then at the end of the meal I got my credit card out and the waiter said they didn't accept them, which left me looking very foolish. I didn't even have a cheque book, but fortunately Carol happened to have a float with her because she was working on a kids TV programme. She paid. Chris was angry about how we'd been treated, and so on the way out he stole the sign on the door as an "up yours" to them.'

The thieving of the restaurant sign was a minor incident, but inevitably Chris's up-for-it nature soon landed him in serious, this time trouser-related, trouble. According to Jules Fuller, who worked on the Power Station programme, Chris was in the habit of forever getting his dick out in the studio. 'I would walk into the studio and his dick would be sticking out of a hole in the curtains surrounding the studio walls,' Fuller said. But when the TV watchdog organisation, the Independent Broadcasting Authority, filed a complaint that Chris Evans had exposed himself on live television, that was another matter entirely. Surely Chris hadn't? Surely Chris wouldn't ... Would he?

A crisis meeting was convened with The Power Station's chiefs to run a video tape and see the outrageous and lewd behaviour of their presenter for themselves. The trouble was, nobody noticed anything at all. Not even when the tape was run in slow motion. Finally, it was only when freeze-frame was used that anyone could see what the fuss was all about. Chris had been leaping around his studio doing kung-fu kicks wearing a pair of shorts, and his penis had appeared down the side of them.

Given the fact that the public wouldn't have been able to see the dick in question unless they had an *awful* lot of time on their hands, it seemed like a real storm in a teacup, but reactions from executives differed wildly. Some of them thought nothing of it, saying that Evans should simply wear a tighter pair of shorts in future to avoid accidental flopping. Others, though, believed it had been a deliberate attempt to sabotage the station. Jules Fuller thought it would have been entirely in character for Evans to expose himself like this. And he claimed – like some sort of bizarre penis detective – to have uncovered two other instances of times when the Evans todger had been on screen. Don Atyeo, too, thought Evans had been stirring things up deliberately.

'Every show had to be watched before it went on air after that,' said Fuller. 'I think it went to his head. He was going slightly out of control,' he reasoned, blaming the pressure of working for both GLR and BSB as the primary factor behind Chris's wild ways. Tim Grundy is more forgiving. 'I'm convinced it was a genuine mistake,' he says. 'I was actually there when the gaffer of The Power Station came down to have it out with Chris, and people shook when this bloke walked into the room. He frogmarched Chris across the yard to have a look at the offending piece of footage and it was put it up in slow-mo on 14 screens in an edit suite. There were 14 different versions of his knob right there. Chris was mortified that it had been broadcast, especially because it was half term and all the kids were watching. He apologised profusely to the management and in the end they gave him the benefit of the doubt. His attitude saved his bacon.' Grundy recognised that Chris was fraying around the edges, though, and decided it was time for the heart-to-heart he'd been asked to come to London to deliver.

'I did it subtly, not the sledgehammer way. I never said, "You're behaving like a cunt, get a grip", as has been reported. Chris was already beginning to live the high life. He was getting £900 cash to buy clothes for his TV appearances; he didn't, he just pocketed it. And he was on good money at The Power Station to start with. There was a lot of money in satellite stations at the time, a huge pot of money for young people to spend, and they were spending it very enthusiastically. Plus a few kids used to hang around the studio wanting to see Chris, so he was getting a bit of a following.

'I told him, "There are some really important things to

remember in telly," and then advised him that you shouldn't be a bully just because you're the star in front of the camera. Well, it must have worked because some time later I got a phone call saying, "He's a completely different bloke", and Chris even gave an interview to some magazine saying he'd been behaving like a cunt and some of his friends had told him so, but now he'd come back down to earth and that he was going to be Mr. Nice for ever more.'

If it was the pressure of work that was turning Chris into a monster, he clearly needed to get off that particular merry-go-round. As it happened, he did so by pure chance. November 1990 saw Sky merge with BSB, and in April 1991 the squarials disappeared. So too did The Power Station. Chris, and his penis, were off the air. But by this stage, the DJ wasn't worried. He knew he had talent. Another opportunity was bound to be just around the corner ...

6 Breakfast Time

It's fair to say that a great deal of Chris Evans's behaviour to this point had been governed by unpredictable and impulsive decisions. Nothing, however, was a impulsive as his sudden decision to get married.

Anybody who knew Chris Evans and Carol McGiffen found their decision to tie the knot a little hasty ... and close to downright madness. Yes, the couple had a good time. They were both possessed of sharp and lively minds. They both liked a drink or two. Yet they also had plenty of darker moments. There were arguments, over pretty much anything and everything. They were loud and physical arguments, too. 'Chris never attacked me,' says McGiffen. 'But he had a temper like you wouldn't imagine. He would throw stuff at me and I would chuck it back.'

Nevertheless, Chris had an undeniable hold on Carol that she simply couldn't shake. It even extended to the point of agreeing to become his bride. 'I went to his place one Sunday morning to tell him, "I never want to see you again," she once told the *Mirror*. 'We ended up having a bit of a row and stuff, and then he said "Let's get married". I suppose he thought everything would be alright if we got married, and I believed it. I really couldn't imagine living without him.' Ten days later that was exactly what they did.

Chris Evans and Carol McGiffen were married on September 17, 1991. 'We told no-one because we thought it would be funny to surprise our friends, who had no idea why they were meeting us at Camden Town Hall with a video camera,' explained Carol. As it happened there were only five pals present anyway when, at 3.30pm, Deputy Superintendent Registrar Mrs Susan Bloom married the pair in a ceremony that could hardly have been more low-key. No family attended, the reception consisted of drinking champagne in a bar where the couple promptly lost the wedding certificate, and the wedding night was spent in the distinctly downmarket Holiday Inn in Swiss Cottage. As a start to married life, it was rubbish. But it proved to set the tone for the couple's time together as Mr and Mrs Chris Evans ...

TV mayhem. Chris had caused it at BSB right enough. Now it was time to create it. When The Power Station closed its doors Evans wasted no time in plotting his next move in television. Getting together with his old Piccadilly and Radio Radio mate Andy Bird, he began to devise a kids' Saturday morning show for TV-AM and pitched the idea for *TV-Mayhem* (TV-AM. TV-Mayhem. Get it?) to the station's boss, Bruce Gyngell. To Evans's delight, Gyngell went for the idea and commissioned 17 shows that would fill his autumn scheduling, with the traditional option for more if the show was a success. Here, though, was where the clever stuff happened.

Chris and Andy's lawyer knew full well that the station was about to go into a franchise battle that it might very well lose. On that basis, he insisted on a clause in the contract guaranteeing Big And Good, the company formed by Evans and Bird, the full financial terms of the deal if *TV-Mayhem* were scrapped mid-series for whatever reason. So when TV-AM lost the franchise battle and announced on October 19, 1991 that the station would be replaced by GMTV when its licence expired, it was no surprise when Bruce Gyngell called Evans and Bird into his office. *TV-Mayhem* had been doing reasonably well up against Philip Schofield's *Going Live* on BBC1, but Gyngell explained that he had to get his costs down to return as much value as he could to shareholders now that the licence had been lost. The show would have to be scrapped immediately. Evans and Bird sat in the office doing their level best to look depressed at the news.

Then as soon as he was out of the meeting, Chris phoned Tim

Grundy in Manchester. 'He was highly excited and said, "I'm retiring, mate," ' remembers Grundy. ' "Gyngell's just given me my retirement. He doesn't know there's a clause in the contract that says even if he drops the show he still has to pay us for them. It's brilliant. I'm going to collect cars and play golf." ' The next day, the pair's lawyer walked into TV-AM with the contract and the two unemployed kids/TV gurus were handed a great big cheque.

'Chris said it was £750,000,' says Tim Grundy. 'But Andy Bird later said it wasn't as much as that. But it *was* a lot of money, certainly enough for Chris to tell me he was retiring. And he did indeed buy a Ferrari and go off to play golf for a bit. He was seriously wedged.' Yet even with all that dough in his pocket, the idea that Evans was going to knock it all on the head at the age of 23, with the amount of energy he had, was palpably absurd. He needed a fresh adventure. It soon came.

Radio 1 controller Johnny Beerling didn't see Chris Evans as 'early retirement' material either, which was why he got in contact with him early in 1992 with an offer to present the Sunday afternoon slot just vacated by his kids' TV rival Philip Schofield. On the surface, the two presenters couldn't have been more different. Schofield was the squeaky-clean, blandly handsome, super-safe reliable sort. Evans was more your off-the-wall, 'interesting-looking', dangerous penis-flasher. But Chris was absolutely delighted to accept the offer, having worshipped Radio 1 from far-off Orford when he was a kid.

Warrington wasn't trendy enough for anyone to entertain the notion that Radio 1 was less than cool – and certainly not our little ginger-headed hero. His new vehicle *Too Much Gravy* hit the airwaves in March 1992. Evans had named the show on the basis that his listeners would have stuffed themselves with a Sunday roast before tuning in from 2.30 to 4pm, but within a few weeks his excitement at going to his favourite radio station had turned to despair.

Chris didn't like his relatively inexperienced producer, Lucy Armitage, and felt that his ideas were being constricted. This wasn't *Round At Chris's* for the nation: this was torture. Chris confided in the veteran DJ Johnnie Walker, who recounts that the young tyro told him: 'All I ever wanted was to work at Radio 1, it was the realisation of my lifetime's ambition. And now I'm here, it's completely crap.'

The rows with Lucy Armitage didn't help matters. Armitage was trying to get Chris to play by the BBC rules, turning up in good time, making sure he played all the right trails and the right records. It was never going to work. And, to her credit, Armitage praised Chris after the event for showing her there was another way. 'Chris let me know there's more to life than following everybody's rules,' she reflected. Indeed he did. Whatever people's feelings about Chris Evans, he can't be accused of lacking the courage of his convictions.

Within six months of going on air with *Too Much Gravy* Chris was out of the station he'd grown up loving. It can never be said that he sticks around anywhere where he feels under-valued. His instincts, though, were about to be proved spot-on yet again. There were no regrets: not when he was already hard at work on his next project, the one that would both transform his career and completely change his life.

In May 1992, Chris began shooting pilots in Lewisham for a new morning TV show. Channel 4 had experimented in the breakfast slot with a serious-minded news magazine show called the *Channel 4 Daily,* and it had bombed in the ratings. There was a gap for an innovative breakfast show, and a £10m franchise was up for grabs.

A new production company, Planet 24, fronted by the nation's favourite scruffy bloke Bob Geldof, decided that they wanted the slot and so began the *Big Breakfast.* Using a real house and Lewisham neighbours to create a unique atmosphere, Planet 24 were hugely innovative. Breaking with the established tradition of getting a face to front a programme and give it an immediate ratings shot in the arm, the company decided from the off that they wanted two presenters, a male and a female, who wouldn't be well-known, but who would bring freshness, enthusiasm, vitality and youth to the screen.

A dark-haired looker named Danielle Lux was being tested as one half of the team, while Chris was the only name seriously being considered for the male presenter's role. 'Jonathan Ross had bumped into Bob Geldof, who was pitching for the new breakfast show,' explains Tim Grundy. 'Geldof had said, "We're looking for someone really wacky to present this show, someone no-one's ever seen before." Ross looked him in the eye and said, "I've got just the bloke." From Chris telling me he'd retired, the next thing I knew there he was presenting the *Big Breakfast*.'

During the four days of shooting pilots, it quickly became clear that Evans was a natural for the job. His experience at The Power Station meant he was relaxed in front of the cameras, quick to respond to any item, and utterly confident that he could be entertaining. Lux, however, was less convincing, and was overshadowed from the off by Evans. Nevertheless, Planet 24 seemed happy enough with their new talent, as did Channel 4 who awarded them the commission. Things couldn't have been going any better – at least, not as far as Chris's career was concerned.

As usual, however, Evans's domestic life had soon broken down into a state of chaos. Within eight months of tying the knot, Carol Evans had walked out on her husband and moved in with friends. The only outward indication that there was anything wrong was the fact that, all of a sudden, *Round At Chris's And His Missus* failed to feature the missus at all. Another member of the GLR team, a girl called Cecile, replaced Carol on air.

In an unusually self-aware moment, Chris Evans began to analyse his life. Yes, his career was going well and looked as if it was about to enter a new, even more successful phase with the *Big Breakfast*. But his personal life was a shambles, and instead of simply running away from the bad things as quickly as possible, for once he decided he was going to do something about it. Astonishingly, and bravely, Chris opted to face up to his demons, and called psychotherapist Claire Chappell. According to Evans himself, the 10 weeks of sessions were hugely beneficial.

'I started to realise how scared I was of dying,' he's admitted in interviews. For the first time, he felt that he was beginning to understand his hypochondria, which meant that the minute he had the slightest sniffle he would be convinced he was about to expire. And, of course, it doesn't take a psychotherapist to work out that most of the demons inside Chris were a direct result of the death of his dad at a crucial age in his development.

'Looking back, my immediate reaction to his death was, "Right, you've got to get on with things now,"' he's reflected. 'My mum was devoted to him, and although I didn't think about it much then, I think I blamed myself. I started running to get on with my life with such a sense of urgency I was too scared to stop. My mum was fantastic at the time. But it was then that I developed a huge fear of death, because ever since I've done nothing but work.'

The therapy had a degree of success in enabling Chris to step outside of himself and face up to his demons. 'I'm coming to terms with slowing down,' he said. He also had a brand new philosophy: 'Take part in the race, but as you pass each spectator have a good look. Remember what they're like and, for heaven's sake, don't miss out on what's around you.'

Brandishing this newly discovered wisdom, Chris was determined not only to enjoy the moment for the first time in his life, but also to try and patch up things with Carol. He quickly brokered a reconciliation with his wife, and the summer of 1992 proved to be one of the happiest times in his life. Evans heeded his own advice and really did take the time to appreciate what was going on around him. He even took Carol on a Caribbean cruise to show that he could be caring and considerate, and for once the pair seemed happy and contented. Chris even put weight on, though Carol didn't care.

'When we were on our own, away from everyone, and there were no pressures we got along fantastically,' she explained. 'We didn't argue at all.' There was even talk of starting a family, though even when engulfed by such apparent domestic bliss Carol wasn't entirely convinced that Chris actually meant it. The most enthusiastically pro-children statement he managed to make to her was, 'If you want to have kids, you can have kids.'

Not the most maternal of women, Carol sensibly dismissed this rather half-hearted suggestion. Her only regret, she was to claim later sardonically, was that if the couple had had children, 'I would have got more money after we split up.' However, such animosity seemed a long way off in 1992, especially when Chris let out his own pokey flat and the couple moved to a rented home in London's Parliament Hill area, where Evans began to prepare in earnest for the launch of the *Big Breakfast* and what he also saw as his big break.

Chris had achieved major local success with GLR. He had been part of the new wave of satellite broadcasting at BSB, and he had entertained the nation at his favourite station, Radio 1. But the *Big Breakfast* was different. This was national, terrestrial TV, and a show that Channel 4 hoped was going to be broadcast into the homes of just about every family in the country. Chris immediately understood the opportunity that offered him and he was determined he'd make the most of it. Perhaps mindful of what Tim Grundy had said, Chris was really making an effort on the show.

'I remember Paula Yates saying in an interview that the amazing thing about him was that he was this fantastically talented guy, but that he was the most down-to-earth person she'd ever met,' says Grundy. 'That he loved everybody, and everybody loved him. At this stage, he was still Mr Likeable.' Simon Morris, one of Chris's oldest friends, a man who has known him from his earliest days in London and who eventually worked with Chris at a very senior level at Ginger, confirms this view. Morris has a unique view of Evans, being both his friend and a former business partner. And he's in no doubt as to the basis of their friendship.

'I met Chris through work, originally when he was first on the radio at GLR,' he says. 'I was working as Marketing Director at Sega and he did some PR thing for me, and we just got along. A lot of planets came into alignment at the same time. He and Carol used to come out with my wife Helen and me, and we became good friends quite quickly. I remember I was very wary of being seen as someone who was latching on to him, because by the time he got the *Big Breakfast* gig he was being touted as the Next Big Thing. So we had a drunken conversation about "mates first". I specifically remember saying to him, "I don't want anything out of you." And that was the way he liked it.'

'Chris nearly kills himself trying not to upset people,' said

Paula Yates, his co-presenter and wife of Planet 24 figurehead Bob Geldof at the time. Then she added, 'All my girlfriends think he's gorgeous.' So too did Gaby Roslin, a 28-year-old who had been drafted in to co-present the show just four days before the *Big Breakfast* was due to launch. It had been decided that Danielle Lux just didn't have the on-screen presence needed to make the show really sing.

Big Breakfast launched on Channel 4 on September 28, 1992 and from the very first minute it went on air it was obvious nobody had ever seen anything like it. Not in this context, anyway. Taking its cues from youth-focused entertainment shows and kids' series such as *Tiswas* and (no surprises here) Timmy Mallett's *Wacaday* rather than the typical news shows and 'on the couch' breakfast presentations, the *Big Breakfast* was a riot.

Broadcasting from three lock-side cottages which had been knocked through in East London's Bow area, the location was inspired, immediately producing a sense of controlled chaos that was perfectly suited to Chris's quickfire wit. The walls were decorated with large and hyper-real breakfast items – fried eggs, sausages and the like – and the walls were painted in day-glo colours. And in the middle of all the madness was Evans, laughing and joking and firing off one-liners with the precision of a TV veteran. Next to him sat Gaby Roslin, who was almost sisterly in her indulgence of the hyperactive lunatic next to her and the perfect foil to his entertaining nonsense.

There was no attempt to pretend that this particular breakfast show was aiming for anything highbrow. The news was read almost as an afterthought, a necessary evil that was getting in the way of the stupidity. It was unashamedly populist (Paula Yates lying on a bed flirting with pop stars was about as deep as it got), but it was far from dumb. The presenters needed quick minds and an unerring ability to deliver with precision timing, and it was demanding work.

'It was terrific, revolutionary, and never surpassed,' says Tim Grundy. 'Chris was a very wealthy man even before he became properly famous, so why would he do a job that was so punishing? Because he was driven by fame. He had always said he wanted to be famous. Anyone in this line of business who claims they don't is a liar. We all go into this business because we want to be loved.'

But to earn that love and fame, Chris had to be out of the door at 4am each day to drive down to Bow and prepare for the show. OK, so he was driving a Porsche by this stage, but it was hard going nonetheless. There was an editorial meeting at 5am, where they toyed with ideas and scoured the tabloids for topical titbits. This meeting severely tested Evans's new-found resolve to become a nicer guy, and he couldn't always hack it. Tired and sometimes irritable, if someone else's idea wasn't to his liking he would then go through it in a surly fashion. 'He would make you look like a complete fuckwit,' explained Courtney Gibson, who was a producer on the show.

An hour later, when the meeting had broken up, Chris would go off for a bath to get himself psyched for the show, then it was into a dressing gown and off to make-up. It's no surprise to learn that Chris was blithely unconcerned as to whether the robe was properly done up or not. 'He didn't care who copped an eyeful of his dick,' recalled Gibson, helpfully. By the time the ritual was complete and the show was on the air, though, Chris had got himself focused and he performed with a zest and freshness that was immediately apparent.

It may have taken a couple of months before people got used to such a radically different format, but by the turn of the year people were starting to get the *Big Breakfast*. Writing in the *Independent* magazine on January 23, 1993, James Saynor explained Evans's appeal: 'He talks a mile a minute in tones packed with incredulity, his on-screen routine a carefully patterned mix of gags, wind-ups, up-your-jumper whoopery and occasionally sullenness (reminiscent of Eric Morecambe or Basil Brush). He has a profound understanding of the meaningless chaffing of young people, but also incarnates the more ancient values of good old British "cheek", tickling people's fancies across the generations. To moppets, Evans is a teasing older brother; to young adults he's the office wag; to those with wrinkles he's a chirpy, hormonal nephew.'

All those days of sitting at home in Orford, soaking up all forms of popular entertainment without the filter that being 'cool' naturally imposes, had clearly done Chris Evans a power of good. He was able to orchestrate the madness brilliantly, the ability which, arguably, remains his single most valuable and remarkable asset. He keeps his head when it would be so easy to lose it.

In these halcyon early *Big Breakfast* days, was Evans being falsely modest when he told James Saynor, 'I don't find it easy. There are things I overlook. I make ten or 15 mistakes every day'? Or was it his demand for high standards, from himself as much as from the people around him, that forced him to be this self-critical, even when he was turning in phenomenal performances? It seems that, a lot of the time, Chris Evans simply couldn't believe what was happening to him.

'We'd speak regularly, mainly on the phone,' says Tim Grundy. 'We'd meet up in London occasionally, but we were both working flat out, seven days per week. Chris was in awe of everything that was happening to him, he was totally gobsmacked. He'd say, "I can't believe it's all happening. I just keep pinching myself." People that he'd always idolised were coming up and saying *they* idolised *him*. He was blown away by all of that. And as far I could see, he was still very humble about the whole thing. He was the kiddie in the chocolate factory.'

Yet for all of Evans's brilliance in front of the camera, and his stated desire to be a more reasonable person off it, the demands and pressures of fronting the *Big Breakfast* began to take their toll. In many ways, it was understandable. The stress of working on a daily show was immense. Researchers and producers would work on one episode per week, and would often enter the building at nine in the morning the day before going on air and not leave at all until more than 24 hours later, when it was all finished. It was brutal stuff and Chris naturally suffered, too.

Soon there were plenty of days when Evans was turning up for work like a bear with a sore head, 'wearing his grumpy trousers' as Paula Yates so graphically put it. Courtney Gibson was in no doubt that Evans could be tyrannical, shouting and screaming his instructions and demands. But such was the value he brought to the show that, once again, nobody dared to pull him up when he was ignorant or rude.

This is by no means an unfamiliar situation in the media, though, where 'The Talent' is indulged and treated with kid gloves for fear that the magic ingredient which is delivering the ratings should suddenly up sticks and leave. Yet this invariable proves to be a self-fulfilling prophecy. You allow people to get away with bad behaviour and they will almost inevitably see how much further they can push the envelope. And Evans did, even going so far as to use the old 'dick out' routine on series editor Fiona Cotter Craig when he was aggravated with her for one reason or another. 'It was very unpleasant. It was at eye-level, inches away from my face,' she explained.

Tim Grundy, who had given Chris the benefit of the doubt over The Power Station incident, doesn't doubt Cotter Craig's story one iota. 'He is a bit of a flasher, is Chris,' he notes. 'I don't mean that in a particularly perverted way. I think he just finds it funny. When men get drunk, a lot of them have to take their trousers off. If you said, "Let's see who's the first person to drop his pants and run across the room", well, that would be Chris. He had no shame about his penis. He was very upfront like that. Maybe it's a good thing to be that OK about your body, but he did have a reputation.'

Paul Carrington, who shared an apartment with Evans on holiday in Gran Canaria in their days together at Piccadilly, also remembers the dick in question. 'Chris would always walk around the apartment completely naked without bothering one iota,' he recalls. 'And it wasn't as though there was anything humongous nestling between his ginger nuts!'

'Chris loved, loved, loved taking his clothes off,' says one former *Big Breakfast* employee. 'He would do it all the time, and would often try to force other people to do the same.' Some folk didn't take kindly to these antics, though. There's always a risk attached when you maltreat the people working under you. They may not be able to challenge your authority openly and directly, but they'll certainly find other, devious little ways in which to even the score.

Courtney Gibson claims that one disgruntled member of the *Big Breakfast* team would spit in Chris's coffee; another would do the same into his pre-show bath. Gibson, meanwhile, found a more public way to humiliate Evans. When she ended up producing *The Girlie Show* for Channel 4, she made sure Chris got his comeuppance by giving him the dubious honour of winning their famous award: 'Wanker Of The Week'.

7 Mr Loverman

There certainly were people working on the *Big Breakfast* who couldn't stand Chris Evans. However, it would be painting an overly negative picture of the show to suggest it was a programme wracked with internal strife and squabbles. Firstly, it would have been nigh on impossible to conceal such massive negativity on a chaotic live show. Secondly, there were people who clearly did like and respect Chris. One of those individuals was a softly-spoken Oxford graduate and Old Etonian named Will Macdonald, who had just landed his first major TV job as a researcher for the *Big Breakfast*.

On the surface, it was hard to imagine two more different characters. Evans was the brash, go-getting working class bloke made good: Macdonald the studious, well-educated background boy. However, they quickly established a mutual respect based on intelligence. Chris's vitality was appealing, as was his refusal to play by the rules. Fuck it; if things were getting too boring in the office, why not just go to the pub? Will was also naturally wily enough to know that it would do him no favours to undermine the star, although he claims not to have been a 'cap-doffing syco-phant'. In no time at all, the pair became inseparable.

The stress and pressure of presenting at the required energy level, and at such a ridiculous time of the morning, definitely took its toll on Evans. He suffered from an illness called phlebitis, which made his legs go a strange shade of blue and swell up in a disturbing fashion. In addition he was plagued by hay fever, which drove him to distraction. A hypochondriac at the best of times, Chris fixated on his illnesses more than ever, even declaring on occasions that he was convinced he wouldn't live too long.

What to the outside world was seen as Chris's ultimate moment of triumph, the time when he finally arrived as a major national celebrity, was proving to be a hollow victory. As successful, confident and happy as he appeared to be to casual observers, Evans was actually a bundle of neuroses. Consequently, he went back into therapy. Despite the fact that he had been a media figure for some time already, moving up into the A-team had changed his life beyond all recognition. And the first thing that happened was that the tabloid newspapers – as they always do – began to delve into his past.

In February 1993, less than six months after Chris had first appeared on national TV, the tabs uncovered the news that Evans had a secret love child with Alison Ward. The *Daily Star* phoned Alison to let her know they had the information. She maintains that she refused to co-operate, but the paper said they'd print the story anyway. So what could she do except phone the *Sun* and offer to work with them, in return for cash? Unluckily for Evans, the story ran on February 13. In it, Alison explained that he hadn't seen Jade in more than two years, and said she felt Chris had done the dirty on her by failing to face up to his responsibilities. 'He'll be on a few thousand a week, a lot more than the £72 benefits I get,' she moaned. Then she admitted: 'He's sent £150 per month for Jade since we split.'

It certainly didn't help Chris's cause in the eyes of the public that the previous week he'd been offered a three-year deal by Channel 4, worth around £1.1m, and had apparently negotiated his fee upwards to £1.5m. It was a complete no-win situation. Chris had taken on a publicist Matthew Freud, the brother of Emma, whose show he had produced back at GLR. Freud tried to diffuse things by saying Chris had never tried to hide the fact that he had a child. Evan's old mate Simon Morris agrees, and is scathing of the media's treatment of Chris in this instance: 'The dark side of someone sells, and the media is very callous. In my time I've spoken directly to very senior editors about deal making. It's all, "If you give us *this*, then we won't print *that* about you," so don't imagine that the papers do these things out of a sense of moral responsibility. That stuff about Chris and his first child drove me mad. It's just not right, because the papers fuck with people's lives. All I can say is that Chris is a good person and he never tried to hide that part of his past from anyone.'

In response, Evans claimed that he was on 'amicable terms' with Alison. She thought this was stretching things a bit, but was even more amazed when Chris phoned her up to ask if she would bring Jade down to London to take part in an article for the *Daily Mail*, which would portray all three of them as perfectly happy with the arrangement. Scornful of the scheme, she refused.

Yet the revelations about his private life only served to increase Chris's celebrity profile. It was all grist to the mill for the tabloids, and TV executives got to see the first signs of what many would later recognise as The Evans Effect. Chris's personality meant he had broad, almost universal appeal. There was always an angle on Chris that newspapers and magazines with vastly differing demographics could twist to appeal to their particular readers. Rarely, if ever, had there been a star that could reach so many different types of people. Terry Wogan had come closest in his BBC chat show heyday. However, young people never found Wogan remotely cool. Evans was a different story.

And, of course, as people began to realise the value that Evans could add to a media property, his fees began to skyrocket. In April 1993, he was lured away from GLR to Richard Branson's Virgin Radio to present one weekly programme, *The Big Red Mug Show*, for £60,000 a year. Despite this, he was unhappy at the prospect of leaving the station he'd grown emotionally attached to. In a heartfelt speech at his leaving do, and failing to hold back a few tears, Chris assured everyone that GLR had been the best job he'd ever had – and nobody doubted his sincerity. By the same token, nobody blamed him for leaving. He would have been barking mad not to take such a lucrative offer.

For the first time Chris Evans was beginning to understand the real value of his biggest commodity – himself. He was also thinking hard about a new project that was to take his media profile even higher. Even as the *Big Breakfast* continued to be a ratings winner, he contacted Michael Grade at Channel 4 with a pitch for a new game show: *Don't Forget Your Toothbrush.*

The concept behind ... *Toothbrush,* like all the best TV ideas, was simple. A studio audience would interact with guest stars, with the possibility of a member of the audience winning a luxury holiday at the end of it. So far, so normal. But the unique selling point that Evans believed would give ... *Toothbrush* its edge was the fact that each and every member of the audience would have to turn up with their passport (and, naturally, a toothbrush) and be prepared to leave the studio and head off directly to the airport to claim their prize. Potential winners had to be able to take the next seven days off work, or be unemployed, or not care if they got the sack! This would add the extra frisson of excitement needed to lift the programme out of the ordinary and establish it as a unique proposition. Grade was impressed and commissioned ... *Toothbrush.* Now Evans had to make it.

Under the guidance of his agent, Michael Foster, Chris formed his own company, Ginger Television Productions Ltd, on May 17, 1993. It was hardly a big deal to start with, consisting merely of Evans and Will Macdonald together with a secretary jotting down ideas, but soon two other Planet employees, Lisa Clark and Stephen Stewart, were brought on board to develop ... *Toothbrush.* The business and legal side of the new company went through Planet 24. Increasingly – and not for the first time – Chris was prepared to let his home life suffer for the sake of his ever-increasing workload.

'When Chris was spending all his time at work,' Carol recalled, 'I told him that if I couldn't get involved, we really didn't have a life together. There was a definite sense of walking on eggshells.' However, Carol wasn't the only one who was sensing a change in Chris. Tim Grundy, his closest associate from Manchester and the man who'd helped to save his hide over the Bob Geldof tape at Piccadilly and had done his level best to keep Chris's feet on the ground in London, suddenly found that Evans no longer seemed to care about retaining his friendship.

'I phoned Chris up the day after he'd been a big part of Red Nose Day 1993,' says Grundy. By now Evans and Carol had bought a three-bedroom house, and had moved to a quiet private road called Fitzroy Park in Highgate. 'A couple of months earlier nobody even knew who he was, and now he said, "Mate, can you get your head round what's happened in the past 24 hours?" I said no, because I just kept seeing him everywhere. Then he announced that he'd just bought a helicopter. I was like, "*What?*" I thought he meant a real one. But he said, "No no, it's a model one. You've got to come down and fly it with me. When can you come?" I was free the next weekend, and he told me to sort it out with Carol, then he put her on, saying, "Here she is. I know you don't like her."

'I was gobsmacked. I said, "Carol, I don't know why he's just said that." But she was quite cold towards me, and obviously believed Chris. I mean, she'd bailed me out in that restaurant when they wouldn't take my card. Why would I hate her? Anyway, I can't remember whether I cancelled or they did, but for whatever reason I didn't go down that weekend, and there followed a long period of not talking. It wasn't a falling-out, it just happened. Then, after a while, I'd set up a charity, and thought there was no harm in getting in touch by letter to see if Chris would do something for me. I never even got a reply. I then left a couple of messages at his house, and never got a reply to them either. That's when I got a bit disheartened, and quite a few people started saying the same thing. Chris's behaviour pissed me off. I'm a Northern lad, and you don't forget your mates. It's not what you do. And that was pretty much the end of my contact with him.'

White And Two Sugars. 'I'm Tim Grundy's coffee boy'. The Man With The Fish. Pulling women in Cheshire. Suddenly, it was as if none of it had ever happened. Because Chris Evans was moving on up. Chris Evans was now a superstar.

'Successful people have very few continuous friendships,' explains Professor Cary Cooper, 'because they are always fully immersed in whatever project they're working on at that time. Relationships simply disappear when they're no longer working with that person. If someone is highly achievement-oriented, then it's not easy for them to either invest in a relationship or sustain it.'

Evans was clearly determined to enjoy his new-found status, and his mate Simon Morris was there to open doors for him. 'Chris started to get a reputation as a bon viveur and a laugh, and he always had a posse around him. Carol was always out; there were always attractive women, free drinks, free food, free passes and lots of laughs. When you're becoming successful you can do anything you want, people indulge you. Who wouldn't have some of that?

'I remember getting involved with sponsoring the Williams Formula One team around this time,' Morris continues. 'Chris and I would spend all our time in the pits. We were only supposed to have a passing interest, but no, we were messing around in there doing everything bar getting our hands on the engine. Chris loved being on the monitors with the headphones on, taking the piss out of Alain Prost. It was a lot of fun. We'd always catch each other's eye when were at a Grand Prix, standing next to Damon Hill or whatever. We didn't have to say anything, but it was like, "Why us? How did *we* get here?" We couldn't believe it. And all the pit crew loved us, because we were a bit rock'n' roll.'

In truth, there's nothing a presenter likes more than being loved. But for everyone who loves a celebrity, there's always someone who hates them too. And the bigger the star, the more they will be hated. Simon Morris remembers one particular incident from that heady period that crystallised the issue. 'A bunch of us went down to Bournemouth for the launch of Segaworld, or something like that. I paid for Chris and Carol, Will Macdonald and his missus and a producer friend Dan McGrath and his girlfriend Lisa to stay at the Brighton Grand. Anyway, before the launch party we went for a sit-down Chinese. There were about 10 of us there, all having a nice time. We weren't being remotely lairy. Someone else who was in the restaurant came over and asked Chris for an autograph for a little girl who was with them.

'Now, I've seen Chris knock people back when they've asked for autographs. He could be very blunt, especially if he was working. But nine times out of ten he was great, especially with kids. On that occasion he was absolutely fine, and even personalised the autograph for the girl. Anyway, a bit later someone else from the table came back over, obviously for a dare, with the piece of paper on a silver platter and said that whatever the girl's name was said thanks, but she didn't want his autograph. He then proceeded to rip it up in front of us. Chris was really upset by that, but he did nothing about it. Looking back, maybe that was the point where the public started to crystallise into two camps. They either really liked Chris Evans or they thought he was a mouthy git.'

Yet it didn't seem possible to ignore Chris Evans, even though the public had a pretty good go at ignoring his *Big Red Mug* show on Virgin Radio. Having a headline sponsor, in this case the coffee manufacturer Nescafe, was never likely to sit easily with Evans, a man whose instinct was not to worry too much about upsetting anyone while he was on air. However, in the bigger scheme of his career, the show wasn't terribly important. It was more significant that it once again gave him the chance to hook up with John Revell, the man whose tie he'd borrowed for his GLR interview, Virgin Radio's joint programme director, and a man who would eventually play a big part in Evans's move from highly-paid A-list entertainer to something else altogether. Evans made a mental note of Revell as he worked towards developing *Don't Forget Your Toothbrush*. While that notion was gestating, however, there were some other major changes taking place in his life.

On June 30, 1993, Chris Evans sensationally quit Virgin Radio, less than three months after arriving at the station. The decision to stand down so suddenly and so soon was attributed to the fact that Chris hadn't realised quite how punishing his *Big Breakfast* schedule was, and how much it would take out of him. There may even be an element of truth in that, although the stress hadn't seemed to have unduly bothered him while he was still presenting for GLR. And Virgin, after all, was only a weekly show.

No, a more likely explanation for the decision was that Evans had realised the potential of being the *owner* of creative content rather than simply the provider of it. Just like with ... *Toothbrush*, through Ginger it would be possible to devise ideas for shows and sell them to TV stations, with the hook being that Evans himself would present the programme in the UK to what was pretty much a guaranteed audience. Once the show had proved successful, the format could be flogged off around the world, thereby guaranteeing income from each individual deal that was done. Chris would earn twice on the UK version – Ginger would produce the show, he would present it – and any number of times on the format as it was rolled out across the world. No wonder he figured that his time away from his day job at the *Big Breakfast* would be better spent developing Ginger rather than presenting a show for Virgin. The potential financial gain would make Virgin's £60,000 a year look like peanuts.

Yet Chris's excitement about the potential of ... *Toothbrush* and Ginger, and what it might do to take him to another level as a media *player* rather than a media *presenter*, may have been tempered in the summer of 1993 by the fact that his marriage to Carol McGiffen was on the rocks, less than two years after their shambolic Camden Town registry office wedding had set the tone for the liaison. 'It was me who made the suggestion that we should break up,' claimed Carol. 'It just went horribly wrong, and I don't know the real reason.'

Maybe the split had something to do with the fact that Carol was no longer working. Somehow, her career had been sidelined by Chris's meteoric rise. 'Chris was doing really well,' she claimed. 'And I don't begrudge him any of that. But I think I may have felt a bit of a spare part.' Carol was neither the first nor the last person to feel that way around Chris, but she had to accept that things were over between the two of them. Evans moved out of the Highgate house and crashed with friends for a short time, then headed for a flat in Narrow Street in Docklands that was owned by Planet 24. It was primarily used by two Irish guys, Mick and Kieron, who were the voices behind Zig and Zag, the two outlandish puppets who regularly sparred with Chris on the *Big Breakfast*. The pair would fly over every couple of weeks to film. Now they had a new lodger.

A marriage that lasted for less than two years might have filled some men with a sense of failure, but if Chris Evans was feeling bruised by his experience, he certainly wasn't about to show it. He threw himself into developing ideas for *Don't Forget Your Toothbrush,* and decided that he and Will Macdonald should head over to Los Angeles, stay in the ultra-fashionable Sunset Marquis, and do some writing. They had a fine time driving around in a white Ford Mustang convertible and enjoying a city which neither had visited before.

By the time the pair had returned a week later, the *Sunday People* had managed to get hold of shots of the two of them hanging out in LA together, supposedly sharing 'intimate' moments. There was even a shot of two pairs of their shorts hanging out to dry on the balcony of the room they were sharing. Under the headline 'Big Breakfast Buddies' the intimation was clear. Chris and Will had split up with their partners so they could have a gay relationship. Perhaps it was a good job the hacks hadn't seen the practical joke Chris had played on Will when they were up in the Lake District together writing for ... *Toothbrush*: 'Will told me that he had woken up one morning and reached for his spectacles, only to see them balanced across the bridge of Chris's penis a couple of inches from his face,' says an insider. Nice.

However, the tabloids may have held fire on their insinuations had they known that Evans was about to start dating Kim Wilde. The 1980s pop star had been called in to the *Big Breakfast* to stand in for Gaby Roslin, and Chris wasted no time in making it clear that he fancied her something rotten. Wilde was nervous about presenting a live TV show, but Chris was charm itself as he put his arm round her, told her things were going to be OK, and mollycoddled her through her first performance. His charms worked, and much to his own amusement, they were soon an item.

'Do you know when I was lying on my bed back in Warrington all those years ago, I used to wank myself to sleep over her?' he confided to a colleague. 'Now I'm going out with her!' Naturally, the notion of the geeky ginger bloke romancing a pop star made the tabloid editors rub their hands in glee. Was the relationship borne partly out of hype for the show? Well it was certainly possible, especially when Chris's spokespeople sent out the not-very-cryptic message to the *Sun* that he was 'a Wilde and crazy guy'. When Evans did talk about Kim, he was the same gushing self that he nearly always tends to be in the first throes of a relationship. 'I fell for her and we are having a completely wild, wonderful romance,' he bubbled. 'Kim is just the most amazing, beautiful, sexy, intelligent girl. This is the real thing. I am head-over-heels in love. We literally can't take our hands off each other.'

No-one can say for certain whether Chris Evans actually wrote these words down on a piece of cardboard, ready to pull out and regurgitate at the outset of any new affair. However, he would be prone to using very similar protestations of undying love many times in the future. Still, at this point Chris was so infatuated with Kim that he actually appeared on Jools Holland's annual Hootenany show at the end of the year and boldly claimed that he'd be married to Kim Wilde in 1994. Carol Evans might have found this a little far-fetched, considering that she and her husband were yet to divorce, and indeed hadn't even discussed the question.

Yet suddenly, less than a week after the 'marriage' declaration, all bets were off. Chris and Kim had knocked it on the head. So why did things fizzle out just as quickly as they had sparked into life? Chris would only say that the whole affair was absolutely crazy: 'It started madly, it ended madly and what happened in between was equally crazy.' Kim eventually offered a bit more insight into the dynamics of the relationship, saying: 'I've never been comfortable with the public side of my life, and being with Chris made it worse.' Perhaps more pertinently, she also talked about her own career needs. 'I was working a lot,' she explained. 'I'm very independent and don't like having my wings clipped. Anyone would have to take all that on if he stayed with me.'

No matter. Our boy was young, free and single again … . but not for long. Evans had met a young girl, Rachel Tatton-Brown, with her sister Claire when the pair had been studio guests at his GLR show. Rachel had first appeared in the papers in 1988, modelling in the *Daily Mail*'s fashion pages. A year later, at the age of 20, she was named British Supermodel of the Year, yet somehow ended up working on the *Big Breakfast* and 'stepping out' with its carrot-topped presenter. When the news broke, the tabloids dusted down the inevitable 'Beauty and the Beast' headlines and paraded gorgeous Rachel and geeky Chris as London's craziest celeb couple. It can't have pleased Carol to find that her picture was also gracing the articles as she was compared in a none-too-favourable light to her husband's new, young and very attractive girlfriend ... but it was unlikely to bother Evans too much.

8 Big Time Operator

Don't Forget Your Toothbrush simply had to work. The stakes were high. It was the first show Chris Evans had devised, it was Ginger's first commission, and it had been bought by that doyen of British television, Michael Grade. This was the big league, Saturday night prime time telly, and Chris was the sole presenter. He just couldn't afford for it to fail, and would make the show a success if it killed him – or anybody else, for that matter.

However, as … *Toothbrush* was piloted for the first time towards the end of 1993, everyone could see that it was a mess. Even Evans himself admitted that it was 'all over the place' and Michael Grade dismissed it as 'amateur hour'. The hours that went into creating three more pilot programmes were painful and full of bad blood, terrible atmospheres and Chris ranting and raving as he handed down his instructions. The days of Paula Yates thinking that Chris was the most down-to-earth guy in the world were long since past. He knew he was being unreasonable too, admitting: 'I used to shout a lot and I know that I'm doing it now. But that's because I care.'

It certainly wasn't unusual for Chris's explosive outbursts to reduce people to tears. 'He can make you feel very small,' explained one insider from that time. 'But some of the people he worked with in the early days, particularly on the *Big Breakfast*, weren't very good at their jobs and that was why it was going on.

Most of the ranting would come out of the fact that Chris had a reasonable point. But he would make it in an unreasonable way. He would scream, "This is fucking terrible and this is fucking useless". I think it was all about control, and I didn't let it bother me. I got used to it, and in the end I hardly even heard him when he was screaming.

'When you work with him – or, at least, if you worked with him at that time – there was a culture of fear, because you didn't know what mood he'd be in. Every Friday morning, before rehearsals, every single person there would be incredibly apprehensive about how Chris would be when he turned up. If he was in a foul mood it would be, "This is shit, this is shit, this is shit. Sort it out." But it's better to be in that situation, rather than going out with him when he might come home and throw plates at the wall.' Luckily, chain-smoking Rachel Tatton-Brown, who also acted as Chris's on-screen sidekick on the first series of … *Toothbrush*, had the patience of a saint.

In a bold move to try to ensure … *Toothbrush*'s success, Evans chose none other than veteran *Fifteen To One* presenter William G. Stewart to produce the show. Nevertheless, it still took four pilots before the team were happy with what they were about to present to their primetime audience. No matter. The blood, sweat and tears delivered the goods.

The first *Don't Forget Your Toothbrush* aired on February 12, 1994 and was hailed as great television entertainment. Writing in London's *Evening Standard*, TV critic Matthew Norman drew comparisons between Chris and some of television's greatest presenting figures: 'If Evans's looks, gestures and frequent "whey-heys" are reminiscent of Morecambe, then his warmth and ease with people suggest Michael Barrymore, while his mastery of a tricky format conjures Brucie to mind.' This was high praise indeed, and Chris would have been absolutely delighted to be compared with some of his personal favourites. Yet what was even more incredible was that Chris had never before hosted his own show – or worked with a live TV audience. And he was just 27 years old. Norman concluded that, 'Chris Evans may well be something of a genius himself.'

With *Don't Forget Your Toothbrush* Chris had not only rubber-stamped the notion that was being whispered about the place, that he really *was* a genius at presenting shows, even at devising shows, but his financial savvy was also revealed. When foreign TV networks were jumping up and down to buy the ... *Toothbrush* format, it was revealed that Ginger had a 50% share in all the foreign rights. So Chris was not only a genius. He was also a fantastically wealthy genius.

... *Toothbrush* was a major success, then. It no time at all, it was commissioned for a second series. Even so, Chris Evans still wasn't happy. Working as hard as he was on the *Big Breakfast* and *Don't Forget Your Toothbrush*, he suddenly decided he didn't like Rachel working as a researcher and appearing on the show. Was this down to a new insecurity about whether people – and girls especially – only liked him for his money? Carol McGiffen had her own opinion: 'Women who wouldn't have given him a second glance before he appeared on the telly approach him now because he's got fame and money. It's a big problem for Chris, and I hope he realises it.'

Characteristically, the manner in which Evans chose to resolve the issue was extreme. 'Chris didn't want Rachel to work,' explains an insider. 'He said that there was so much pressure on him that when he got home from doing the *Big Breakfast* he wanted Rachel to be there waiting for him. It became a really big thing, and in the end she gave in and went from being this bright and outgoing career girl to someone who stayed at home all the time decorating cake tins.'

The newspapers, for one, never saw this as a problem. During June 1994, tabloid headlines appeared proclaiming that the pair were about to marry. Such headlines had screamed out from the front pages before, of course, and they proved no more reliable this time around. Evans and Tatton-Brown began the usual round of splits and reconciliations, but by the end of the year the relationship was over for good. Carol McGiffen even offered some sisterly support to Rachel via the *Sunday Mirror*. 'I'm not surprised they split up,' she snarled. 'She's a numbskull.'

So what now for Chris Evans and the *Big Breakfast*? In a way, the show had served its purpose for him. It had brought Chris to the attention of the nation, and established him as the pre-eminent media figure in the country. And, more importantly, it had given him the chance to build his own production company, develop his own ideas and become very, very rich.

Money had always been important to Chris. He'd walked out on Radio Radio for a better gig despite promising he wouldn't, and had pocketed his clothes allowance back at The Power Station. It now became obvious to him that Ginger should be the focus of his energies. He managed to cut a deal with Planet 24 that would reduce his early morning starts to three days per week to give him more time to devote to developing new series and new opportunities for Ginger.

By now, Chris had moved out of Narrow Street and into a bigger flat in the shadow of Tower Bridge at Cinnamon Wharf, and it was easy for him to jump on a bicycle to pedal like fury down to the office at Planet 24. The Ferrari, Cherokee Jeep and MGA that he now owned weren't much use in London's car-clogged streets, so he left them in the garage. Yet what with ... *Toothbrush* and the truncated *Big Breakfast* appearances, he was still working at a pretty frantic pace, filling his life up with so much work stuff that it effectively became his social life as well. Evans was very aware of this, and explained as much to the *Times Magazine*.

'Apart from the people I work with, I haven't got any friends,' he said. 'Well, maybe a couple, but I haven't got a network of friends. Most people set up a network of friends, and then they get a job that sustains their life. What I've done is, I've got a job that sustains my life, but I haven't really got a life out of work. So I'm having it the wrong way round, and it's quite difficult.'

Professor Cary Cooper says this isn't uncommon amongst high flyers like Evans. 'People like Chris tend to be so busy achieving that they simply don't have the time to develop friendships,' he explains. 'You have to spend time developing a friendship, growing it, and that's not a pastime which is achievement-oriented. These people tend to wish they had more friends, but only when something goes wrong – something like a heart attack or the collapse of a business – do they truly understand their significance. And then it's often too late, because at that stage they're usually in their mid-fifties. In Chris's case it wouldn't be too late to rectify that problem if he wanted to, to re-orient his life.'

According to a former work colleague who doesn't want to be named, it is only half the story: 'The problem with Chris is that he's socially inadequate in normal domestic and friendship situations. He was always the first to suggest that the gang at work should all go to the pub. In fact, he would get a bit irritated by anyone who said they didn't want to, because they had to get home to their girlfriend or whatever. It would always be, "Give me one good reason why you have to go. Just one." But as soon as you took him out of that rather superficial "matey" environment, it was as if he didn't know how to handle it. There was one time when he was invited round to the house of someone he worked with for a little dinner party. It was nothing to do with work, just a social occasion for couples – and he couldn't handle it. He drove round to the house where the party was happening with his girlfriend, then they both sat outside for hours while Chris agonised over whether he could face going in or not. Eventually, he just drove off. In those kind of social situations he was hugely dysfunctional.'

The idea of Chris Evans, inveterate socialiser and life and soul of all parties, sitting outside someone's house afraid to knock at the door may seem far-fetched ... but it didn't to Evans. 'On Friday night I'd get home,' he explained in the *Times Magazine*. 'And literally – and I'm not joking – the phone wouldn't ring until Monday morning. What I did, for a while, was just go out for a drive in my car on my own.'

The single life living in a trendy part of town with no responsibilities and buckets of cash to slop around may have seemed appealing when Evans was holed up with Carol in Highgate, but now it just seemed empty. He had a crew of people up at Ginger, sure. But Chris was now the guv'nor, *their* guv'nor. The dynamic of his relationship with workmates had changed dramatically and it had changed forever. Now there would be numerous awkward little scenarios to deal with. When he was in the pub should he be the one to stand all the rounds? He was absolutely loaded now, after all. Or should he just carry on as before and work hard at maintaining his position as one of the boys? These were the kind of personal dilemmas that he wrestled with and they just didn't make him happy.

Despite the phenomenal success of his career to date, Chris Evans felt unfulfilled. And as he said to Matthew Norman in the *Evening Standard*, even … *Toothbrush* was starting to lose its appeal. 'I'd achieved my life's ambition at 27,' he explained. 'So what do I do next? It's not as if I can bask in it, because there's no emotion at all. There's no sense of achievement, no sense of adulation, no sense of anything. You can compare it to climbing Everest. You climb Everest, and what do you do then? Climb the north face? Okay, but so what? And then? Climb the north face with a grand piano over your shoulder? There has to be more in life.' If Evans was already feeling this way about his latest project, a project that he had devised, presented and also owned, then the *Big Breakfast* must barely have been registering on his creative monitor. There was only one solution …

On September 29, 1994, two years and one day after launching the show, Chris Evans left the *Big Breakfast*. His departure wasn't exactly a formal affair. After he'd been given a fake script so that he wouldn't know what was in store for him, the gags to mark the end of the Evans *BB* era included a can of beans blowing up in his face and Chris being spun around on a huge fairground wheel. For his part, Chris relayed his thoughts about the programme with great sincerity, telling the viewers he would often stick a lighter under the arses of the cameramen when Gaby Roslin was interviewing, so the heat rising up their backsides would make them wobble the camera.

Yet unbelievably, from such schoolboy pranks great television had been made. The *Big Breakfast* had been very good to Chris Evans, as he had been good for The *Big Breakfast*. But now it was time to move on and look for new challenges. Chris had managed to turn himself into a media legend within the space of two short years. All he had to do now was work out what he was going to turn his talented hand to next.

9 Saviour

While Chris Evans was busy building himself into the hippest, most bankable and most savvy broadcasting phenomenon of the time, one of his former employers had been busy getting itself onto broadcasting's critical list. Radio 1 was in crisis.

Matthew Bannister, Chris Evans's boss back at GLR, had been appointed controller of the station in the middle of 1993 on the back of a radical set of proposals. Bannister had argued that Radio 1 was in deep trouble, staffed by an old boys' club of DJs and producers who had grown ancient together and lost touch with the popular culture and music that they were supposed to reflect. He believed passionately that the station should be dedicated to delivering new, exciting and challenging music, just as much as it was about telling people what was top of the pop charts. What he didn't believe it was about was DJs who were twice or three times the age of the station's target listenership using the airwaves as a platform for their monstrous, egos.

Bannister wanted a total change in what Radio 1 was going to represent, and he didn't have time to mess about. His first introduction to all of the staff did not augur well: 'There was no doubt from the staff meeting I attended that these people, by and large, didn't want to work with me. They were going to resist change.' He was right on both counts.

So ensued a period of plotting and scheming on both sides

that would have been worthy of any Shakespearean drama. Bannister decided to rip up the old rulebook. Those DJs that he considered dinosaurs would be going, pronto. The cleverer ones saw what was coming and resigned before they could be sacked, making sure they used the airwaves to justify their own position and stick the knife in. Dave Lee Travis, a.k.a. the Hairy Cornflake, used his show to vilify Bannister and what was going on behind the scenes. Many big names, including Simon Bates and Bruno Brookes, made capital out of the media as they left the building for the last time. It was a nasty business. Bannister took an awful lot of flak from the tabloids as he ripped the heart out of Radio 1.

Matthew Bannister's cause really wasn't helped by the fact that, almost inevitably, the station's listenership plummeted. In June 1993, two months before the Hairy Cornflake flounced out, Radio 1 had 19.23m listeners. In November 1993, just one month after Bannister had introduced his first changes to the station's broadcasting schedule, the figures were down to 16.86m. Two months later, the number was 14.84m. Bannister had lost Radio 1 almost four-and-a-half million listeners in just seven months. Naturally, the 36-year-old exec copped some serious media flak. The *Sun*, in particular, was merciless in its treatment of the station's controller.

Yet amazingly, and impressively, both Bannister and his bosses at Radio 1 held firm. Even when the network was haemorrhaging listeners, and disgruntled DJs were leathering Bannister in the most public manner imaginable, the controller didn't waver. His vision of a Radio 1 that would truly reflect the nation's youth culture and which would differentiate itself from the plethora of commercial stations that had sprung up in the early 1990s stayed true.

To enable him to develop his grand scheme, Bannister decided he needed a new head of production for the station. He knew his old GLR mate Trevor Dann was floating around and had even done work for the station as an independent producer, but Bannister was wary of pushing forward a former colleague and friend for the position, for fear of being seen as a 'jobs for the boys' kind of guy. His solution was to employ a head-hunter to sift out suitable candidates. Dann was one of six people interviewed and, according to Bannister, 'did the best interview'. So Trevor Dann joined Radio 1 in January 1995, and immediately set about putting the building blocks in place to construct his friend and boss's brave new world. His first idea was that the station should stop playing records made before 1990. This was serious, radical stuff.

Bannister and Dann's violent shake-up of the airwaves was soon in full effect at Radio 1. Bannister had taken a flame-thrower to pretty much everything and everyone who was a part of the old ethos, and there was no going back. With Trevor Dann now also on board, the new guard were now in the ascendancy. Steve Wright, for so long a mainstay of the station and still a very capable broadcaster, didn't like what was happening around him and got his retaliation in early. Wright resigned from the station's flagship breakfast show a couple of weeks after Dann had arrived.

There had been no suggestion that Wright was about to be axed and it came as a massive blow, even to a duo so hellbent on massive change as Bannister and Dann. It put enormous pressure on them to bolster confidence within the station and in the tabloids. They needed to pull a pretty big rabbit out of the hat to compensate for the loss of Wright – and they had to do it quick smart.

Out of the clear blue sky one of Dann's former GLR colleagues, John Revell, phoned. Revell had been working at Virgin Radio as launch programme director, but was now on the lookout for new projects to get involved with. By Dann's own admission they'd had a slightly sticky parting of the ways at GLR, so maybe his suspicions should have been roused by this sudden act of camaraderie. Nevertheless Dann and Revell met, and Revell was shown around the Radio 1 building before the pair retired to a pasta bar and got to talking about the old days.

One name that inevitably popped up was that of mutual friend Chris Evans. However, it was only when the conversation had been going for quite some while that the penny dropped with Dann. Revell was sounding things out on Evans's behalf, sniffing around to see if there would be any interest in them taking on the breakfast show now that Steve Wright was on his bike. Dann suspected that Bannister might very well be interested, and said Evans should get in touch. He never got the chance. No sooner had Dann gone back to work after lunch and told his boss of the conversation with Revell than Bannister immediately phoned Chris at home and left a message. When Evans returned the call, he didn't beat about the bush. 'I know what you want to talk to me about,' he said and promptly invited Bannister to visit him at his flat that very afternoon.

Sitting in the penthouse, with Tower Bridge adding some imposing background scenery, Bannister prepared to dazzle Chris with his pitch. He wanted to tell him why it would be a great thing for both parties if Evans took on the breakfast show, how it was still culturally important, and how Evans could be a key part of his Radio 1 revolution. He didn't manage to say anything. 'You don't have to sell this to me,' said Evans. 'I'd really like to do it.' Radio 2 broadcaster Stuart Maconie, working as a freelance journalist at the time and just starting his own career in radio, confirms the story.

'I met Chris a matter of days before he was due to start presenting the breakfast show,' he explains. 'I'd been commissioned to write a cover story on him for *FHM* magazine, and was very keen to meet him. He was the biggest thing in the British media at the time. Anyway, I asked him a pretty blunt question about how many millions he was getting paid to do the breakfast show and he said, "No, no. It's nothing like that." He explained that when he spoke to Matthew Bannister he'd said to him, "Ah, Matthew. I wondered when you'd call."

'Now, that might sound a bit arrogant, but it didn't come across that way to me. It just seemed very perceptive. Why wouldn't Matthew Bannister ring his old mate? He was copping a lot of flak for what he was doing at Radio 1 and needed a big name. Evans then said he'd told Bannister, "Don't make me offers of money, because the most important thing first off is that I *want* to do it." He told me, "I'm a rich man. I'm a very rich man because of ... *Toothbrush*. I won't get up that early in the morning for money. I need another reason to do it. And my reason for doing it is because the Radio 1 breakfast show is part of my heritage." And I don't think he was bullshitting. I absolutely believed him.'

Matthew Bannister claimed Evans had a slightly more prosaic way of illustrating his enthusiasm. Reasoning that he should only do things that excited him so much he immediately wanted to go to the toilet, he confirmed that he was definitely getting a distinct stirring in his bladder as the two men sat there in the swanky flat. Things were looking good ... but, of course, Evans's idiosyncratic brand of water divining didn't mean he was going to throw himself headlong into a commitment just like that. He was way too shrewd an operator. So he announced to Bannister that if he was to take the job – and he wanted to think about it overnight – then he would only do it if he could produce the breakfast show himself with John Revell via Ginger, as an independent company. This didn't perturb Bannister, who left the meeting frothing with excitement.

Evans was true to his word. The following morning he spoke with Bannister again. He'd lost none of his enthusiasm, again confirmed that he wanted the gig, and told Bannister to get in touch with his agent Michael Foster and his publicist Matthew Freud to do the deal and start thinking about how the coup (because it was definitely a coup) could best be exploited in the press.

The idea of stage-managing news for maximum impact is all well and good. The only trouble is that news always seems to have a mind of its own. No matter how hard you try to keep a secret people start to get wind of it, and almost immediately rumours were starting to fly. Freud spoke to Bannister at his cottage in Sussex, concerned that if the story leaked out they wouldn't be able to control it. They decided that Bannister should drive up to London straight away so that a photograph could be concocted of him and Evans supposedly doing the Radio 1 deal. Evans was rehearsing for *Don't Forget Your Toothbrush* down at LWT's studios on the South Bank, and Bannister met a *News Of The World* photographer there. The pair found a balcony outside one of the complex's canteens where the snapper could hide behind some bushes to make it look as if the 'exclusive' snap of Bannister and Evans, holding plastic cups and 'doing the deal', had been taken without the pair of them knowing about it.

The shot never made the *News Of The World*, which cheesed Bannister off no end after he had driven all the way up from Sussex. But he felt a whole lot better about it the following day when the *Sun* started the week with the deliberately blurry photo, used full page, under the evocative headline 'The Million Pound Cup Of Tea'. Bannister is in no doubt as to the significance of the event. 'That was the moment that it stopped being "Radio 1 is shit" and started being "Something exciting's happening at Radio 1",' he says.

Something exciting *was* happening at Radio 1. Chris Evans was coming. And while the news might not have made people want to go to the toilet with joy, there was a real buzz about the appointment. However, amid all the hoo-ha and in-house back-slapping there was one man who definitely wasn't smiling. Head of Production Trevor Dann could see trouble looming large.

When Bannister told him Evans was only prepared to present the breakfast show if it could be produced independently by Ginger with John Revell as producer – and that he'd agreed to the demand – Dann was distraught. You could see why. Dann had just arrived at the station as the bloke in charge of actually getting programmes made and onto the airwaves, so he must have felt that the rug had been pulled from under him. He was already in a difficult spot, trying to keep everybody upbeat when the station was going through radical upheavals. Now he was going to have to convince everyone that he really was in charge of his department when the jewel in the crown, the breakfast show, was no longer under his control.

Dann voiced his concerns to Bannister: 'You're not giving me a chance,' he moaned. Bannister's assertion that there were other shows being independently produced for Radio 1 (he cited hip-hop DJ Tim Westwood's programme as an example) was technically correct, but it was also irrelevant. This was the breakfast show they were talking about, the flagship of the station, not an underground dance programme.

Yet despite Dann's chagrin, the die was already cast. In his desire (or possibly his need) to have Chris Evans at the station Bannister had given the DJ exactly what he wanted. The fee of £1.4m that was paid to Ginger was the biggest sum paid to any independent production company by Radio 1, but Bannister asserted that in terms of output, the deal was hugely cost-effective. For two-and-a-half hours' broadcasting per day, five days per week, the controller thought he was getting a bargain. The total cost per show was around £7,000, which was hardly exorbitant. And with the PR value that Evans would bring, Bannister could argue – with some justification – that he'd done a tidy bit of business. All he had to do now was pray that his Golden Boy would deliver.

Chris Evans's first day as presenter of the Radio 1 breakfast show, on April 24, 1995, was utter madness. Media interest was extraordinarily intense. Inside the studio, cameras – for the papers and even for television – were everywhere as the media gorged itself. If anyone had been in any doubt about The Evans Effect and what he might bring to Radio 1 in addition to the show itself, they should have been at Broadcasting House when the first programme got underway at 6.30am.

Evans himself was remarkable. In truth, the key moment happened the minute he started broadcasting. Amid all this madness, where it must have been impossible to hear yourself think, never mind compose yourself to present what was probably your most important show ever, he showed his broadcasting genius. 'All right, all right,' he hollered above the kerfuffle. 'Everything's all right, everything's going to be OK. I'm here now.' This opening gambit didn't come across as remotely arrogant, but rather as soothing and reassuring. Radio 1's breakfast show was in safe hands. We could all forget about the trouble and the strife, because there was now a man in charge who truly loved and cared about the show and the station. We could all stop fighting, and get on with simply having a good time. Stuart Maconie felt the passion that Evans had for the show.

'There is no doubt about it,' he says. 'This was a kid from Warrington who had grown up on the show and who had loved it in a very pure, non-cynical way. He would have thought that for him, getting to present the breakfast show would have been *the* thing to do, in the same way that bands always wanted to get on *Top Of The Pops*.' But amid all the fanfare and the trumpeting, there was one tiny incident right at the end of the show that made the biggest impression on Maconie.

'After I'd finished interviewing Chris for *FHM* before he started, I told him I was off to Broadcasting House,' he remembers. 'Now, Chris got the wrong end of the stick and thought I was off there to interview someone else at Radio 1 for the piece about him. So I explained to him that I was actually going up there to talk about *Collins And Maconie's Hit Parade*, which was the first show I did for Radio 1 with my colleague Andrew Collins. Anyway, Evans thought about it for a moment, then said, "Oh, I think I've heard of you. It's you and another bloke, isn't it? Oh, I like that show." It turned out we were both starting on the same day, so he wished me luck and that was that.

'On the day of his first show I was listening to it like everyone else in the country, and then right at the end when the champagne corks were literally popping, he said, "Coming up tonight, there's a new series of *Collins And Maconie's Hit Parade* which you should check out. They're two sharp guys." Now I thought that said a lot about the man, that in the middle of his big moment he still thought about us. He hadn't even promised to mention it. I thought that was very decent of him.' Decent. It's not a word that gets associated with Chris Evans terribly often, but it was definitely valid in this instance.

So maybe the maverick in Evans, the argumentative streak that had seen him cross swords with his producer in his last stint at Radio 1, had been tempered. Maybe it was just that Evans really, really did want the gig. But at first it certainly looked as if Chris, John Revell et al were prepared to be team players, regardless of the fact that Ginger were producing the show out of house. Only three pilots had been made before the show went live, but according to Matthew Bannister everything was very tightly

Even at his first school, St Margaret's, Chris was already showing signs of the entertainer he was to become. Here he is, fourth from the right, second row from the back, displaying a cheeky smirk and eccentric dress sense. Lee Burgess, who talks about Chris in *Ginger Nuts*, is seated on the front row, far left.

St Margaret's Church of England Primary School. Chris's first experience of school was a happy one

Padgate High School. Chris was transferred here from St Thomas Boteler when he was 14. He has claimed he was expelled for tying a science teacher to a tree

St Thomas Boteler. Chris passed for the local grammar school after showing consistent signs of intelligence at primary school

113 Capesthorne Road. The Evans family's first
house in the Warrington suburb of Orford. They
moved into the area in 1970, when Chris was
almost four years old

319 Greenwood Crescent. Chris spent all of his
childhood and youth here after moving from
Capesthorne Road and his mother Minnie still lives
in the house

Chris's main London base is this stylish place in Belgravia

Palatial pad. The Surrey mansion, Hascombe Court, which Chris bought for £6 million in 2000. Definitely a home fit for a man worth £50 million

Des res. Another home in LA is always handy. And if it was once owned by singing sensation Lionel Richie, then so much the better. The rumour is that Chris is now looking to sell - at a profit!

Chris parties on with his Piccadilly Radio workmate Paul Carrington in Gran Canaria, 1987. It was during this holiday that Chris dropped the bombshell that his girlfriend Alison was having their baby

Have a cigar. With Michael Grade after the Channel 4 boss commissioned *Don't Forget Your Toothbrush*. Grade would later call the first pilot for the show 'amateur hour'

So why so sad? It was as
presenter of Channel 4's
The Big Breakfast in 1992
that Chris soared to
superstar status

Mr Ego. Some might say Chris
got a bit big-headed with all his
success. This photo seems to
suggest it could have been true

formatted. No matter that certain ideas – the unfunny Northern comedian Charlie Manning, and a feature called *On The Bog* featuring Evans and sidekick/producer Dan McGrath sitting on a loo discussing contemporary issues – didn't appeal to Bannister personally. At least there was discussion and debate. Despite Trevor Dann's reservations, maybe this set-up could work after all.

Nobody got to see the workings of the Radio 1 breakfast show at closer quarters than Jamie Broadbent. A lad from Stockport with a real love for both radio and music, Jamie had been working in London on an internship at satellite music channel MTV, and had written to Radio 1 on spec seeking work experience. The station took him on, initially for two weeks, about two months after Chris had returned as its star turn.

'On the first day I didn't speak to Chris,' remembers Jamie, sitting in a pub in Leeds where he's now a broadcaster on Radio Aire. 'Someone had brought him toast and marmalade, which he didn't want. So I said I'd go to the shop and get him toast with butter, which he did. I legged it to the shop and he happened to look over the balcony and saw me running. So he decided, "He's all right". I'm sure if I'd been walking rather than running, he would have gone, "He's a lazy bastard." But that chance incident got me in and I started helping on the show.

'John Revell used to answer the phones, but that took him out of the studio, so I got the job of answering the phone. Then there was loads of mail to deal with as well, so they created a job for me. Then after that, Chris created a character for me. He decided I looked like a student, so I became "Jamie The Student". I was still only on work experience at this point, but about four months in I was taken on for about a hundred quid a week or something like that.'

Exactly how much Evans would be able to improve Radio 1's fortunes would be hard to assess in the short term. The show's research team tried their best to measure the new boy's effect by putting together a detailed survey of listeners. 551 people aged between 15 and 44 were sampled after about ten weeks of Evans being on air, the results being generally positive. Ninety

Chapter 9

per cent agreed that the breakfast show was funny and enjoyable, while only thirty per cent found it irritating. Seventeen per cent thought that it was too rude. Some of the more individualistic comments about Evans ranged from 'he's dynamic and takes risks' to 'he's a ginger-haired irritating git.' Well, you can't win them all.

Yet what really mattered were the listening figures, and the numbers that Chris Evans produced in his first three months at the station were sensational. He increased the listenership of the breakfast show from 6.1m to 6.81m. It could be argued that the figures had been on the up even before his arrival, probably as a result of Bannister's changes in music policy starting to kick through, but there was still no denying that this was a remarkable performance. It had almost been forgotten that the reason why Evans had created all the hysteria in the first place was that he was a bloody good DJ.

Stuart Maconie is in no doubt about Evans's talents: 'Chris was amazing on the air. People have accused him of nicking a lot of his stuff, the zoo format with the team and all the rest of it, and to an extent he did do that, but he also brought something particularly British to it. There was a fantastic conjunction of factors that were at play with the breakfast show. Britpop was happening, *Loaded* magazine was all the rage, laddishness was suddenly cool and coming from the provinces and being regional had real value all of a sudden. But that wasn't the whole story.

'Chris was fantastically talented at being able to elevate the stuff that we all do and say in the pub, and turn it into mass entertainment. Girls, football, rubbish old telly programmes, all that minutiae ... Chris could take that stuff and use it in a more witty, clever and pacy way to make enthralling radio, the stuff that would set people driving in to work to thinking, "Me and my mates were talking about that the other day!" He brilliantly tapped into the emerging nostalgia boom, because at that point there really wasn't anything that was specifically designed for thirty-somethings in the way that everything seems to be these days, with stuff like School Disco.

'Chris would also take something that wasn't in itself particularly sharp, like "people who are double-jointed", and make something very listenable out of it. Plus he really did love music, and that wasn't always the case with the frontline Radio 1 DJs. You got the impression that Chris definitely wasn't in it for the helicopters and the supermarket openings. You felt that he really did love the Manics or Pulp or whoever.' But above all of these attributes, Maconie identifies something else entirely as perhaps Evans's greatest single broadcasting asset.

'What really endeared Chris to the listeners was the fact that he was a star, but he was still of their world. Remember all those classic 1970s showbiz figures like Bruce Forsyth? He was very talented, but he was always keen to let everybody know that he was the big star, out playing golf at Wentworth, doing his charity work and all that. You might have liked Forsyth, but you knew that he was nothing to do with your world. Chris was one of us, a cheeky Northern chappie. In a funny way he always reminded me of John Peel, with his "couldn't give a toss" Northern vibe.' And it certainly showed how far Radio 1 had come when a 'couldn't give a toss' Northerner was now the pride and joy of the entire station.

Jamie 'The Student' Broadbent was also blown away by Chris Evans's abilities behind the mic: 'It was great, fantastic. There was nobody else on air at the time who really inspired you, but when I saw Chris he was so fast and so enthusiastic. The first time I saw him performing in front of me I was blown away. It was an amazing place to be.'

The breakfast crew of Jamie, Revell, McGrath, Holly 'Hotlips' Samos (the girl Chris dallied with before settling on Carol McGiffen) and tea boy Justin Bradley became an integral part of the show, foils to Evans's quickfire repartee who added both flavour and spice as support to the main attraction. According to Jamie, Chris had a sharp eye for talent-spotting: 'What Chris actually does is surround himself with very good people. You saw it later on when he had Danny Baker and Will Macdonald as his two key players on *TFI Friday*. But on the breakfast show, Dan McGrath, was exceptional. The music and the jingles he did were established benchmarks of the show. And both John and Holly were very good too. It was the combination of people that made the show so great.'

It seemed everybody loved the breakfast show and the attitude that Britain woke up to every morning. This was the gang you'd always wanted to be a part of. They were living the lifestyle you could only dream of – laughs, booze, more laughs, more booze – and getting paid handsomely for it. At least, that was how it seemed when you tuned into Radio 1. But did the truth match the reality? Well, that very much depended on Chris Evans, the zoo's keeper, who knew the impact that he was having on the station and also knew only too well that he was their biggest asset.

'You would have to indulge him, no doubt about it,' says Jamie. 'Chris would come in one day in a fantastic mood, and you'd love being a part of the show. It felt like it was the greatest three or four hours of your life. Then you'd come in the next day and he would be acting like a complete wanker, you were on the back foot, and it was horrible being around him. You'd have to carry on trying to do your job and trying to keep him happy when he was being a complete arsehole and totally unreasonable.

'You never know what mood he was going to be in from day to day, but the minute he walked in the door you'd know straight away which way it was going to go. If he was cheesed off, he'd storm in, bollock someone for no reason at all and make everyone feel uncomfortable. Then you'd all have to pander to him. You'd take it in turns every two months to get a dressing down. But after you'd worked there for a while, you realised Chris just did that to keep everyone in their place. It's a control trip.'

Yet whatever Chris Evans's off-air behaviour might have left to be desired, there was no doubt that when he was on form he was audio dynamite. 'As a communicator, he was superb,' says Jamie. 'He would tell half of a story, adhere to the rules of radio broadcasting and keep you hanging. The best thing we ever did on Radio 1 was the thing about Dan's girlfriend, and whether he should marry her or not. We stretched it out over five days, the whole "Will he, won't he? Should he, shouldn't he?" thing. The whole nation was gripped, especially when Dan went for it and she said yes. It was classic radio.'

10 Thank God It's Friday

As the presenter of Radio 1's breakfast show, Chris Evans was clearly on top of the world. He was the number one DJ at the station he'd held in awe as a kid, and was recognised – both inside and outside of the network – as its major asset. Not only that, but there was even romance on the horizon again.

During spring 1995, not long after his triumphant return to Radio 1, Chris rang a girl called Suzi Aplin out of the blue. Chris and Suzi had worked together on the *Big Breakfast,* where she'd acted as a celebrity booker. The pair had become quite close, with Chris offering tall, blonde, slim Suzi lifts home from work in his Porsche and Suzi returning the favour in her Mini. His charm, passion and energy had bewitched the Surrey girl and, what was more, Chris definitely had a liking for Suzi too. However, he had chosen to date Rachel Tatton-Brown instead, much to Suzi's dismay.

So when Evans called to ask her out to dinner, Suzi was delighted. She too had left the *Big Breakfast,* in her case to work on a new TV show to be presented by Steve Wright, and was forging ahead with her own career. The initial date with Chris went well, and the couple began seeing each other regularly. Indeed, Suzi was soon working with Chris for Ginger, and the relationship would last for five years, on and off.

Whatever people think of Chris Evans, it seems nobody has a bad word to say about Suzi Aplin, who is universally admired both professionally and personally. 'She is incredibly nice and charming, and very good at her job,' says one source. 'So the fact that Chris was seeing her as well as working with her wasn't a problem for anyone. She was very valuable to Ginger. She and Chris would end up holidaying with people like Bono, and Elton John, and they would keep in touch as much to stay friends with Suzi as to keep in contact with Chris.'

Naturally, life with Chris Evans would never be plain sailing. He had been ruthless and selfish to the detriment of all of his previous relationships, and Suzi would have to put up with some of that attitude herself. On her thirtieth birthday, Chris took her to Barcelona and 'surprised' her by booking two of his drinking buddies into the same hotel. Yet they appeared to enjoy each other's company, and to be happy together.

Evans also began to invest some of his fortune in property. In early 1995, he bought himself a two-bedroom flat in his old stomping ground of Belsize Park, then in June laid out another £300,000 to snap up the Old Rectory in Nettlestead, Kent, a five-bedroom house in two acres overlooking the River Medway. It was exciting to have a posh place out of town to use as a bolt-hole, and Chris enjoyed holding court down there. 'It was a sensible investment,' says Simon Morris. 'Chris did some work on it, but didn't finish it before he decided it was time to move on. But during that period he was rigid in adhering to this idea he had that he'd do his work in town and then get straight down to the house in the country.'

The Old Rectory also became the scene of one of Chris's most famous parties. 'It was a bizarre thing,' says Simon. 'All kinds of weird celebrities turned up for a bonfire party that Chris held there. Tony Mortimer from East 17 came with his own bouncers, and everyone took the piss out of him. Nicky Campbell was there for some reason watching *Match Of The Day* on the telly inside, and wouldn't come out of the house. I took charge of explosives with Andrew The Barman, who Chris knew from the Haverstock in Belsize Park. We built an enormous bonfire and poured a stack of petrol over it to get it going.

'So this fire was burning what looked like the equivalent of a small Welsh cottage on the top of the slope, and Dave and I were laying out the fireworks. We followed the firework code, getting tubes for rockets and sticking them in holes in the ground. There was one rocket, I think John Revell bought it, and it was the size of a cannon. I lit it and stood back, but it toppled out of the hole onto its side and started rolling down the hill, firing rockets out of the top like a Gatling gun. Things were firing out and people were starting to get worried. An explosive charge went through my legs, missing my bollocks by a fraction, and then hit a bush behind me and the whole bush went up! People thought it was all part of a display and cheered like mad! It was hilarious, a great time and it sort of summed things up for me. Everything we touched turned to gold in those days.'

Indeed it did. For most people, the professional and personal success that Chris Evans was now enjoying would have been hugely satisfying. But Evans's kinetic energy, his need to keep pushing himself, to keep proving something, *anything*, meant that resting on his DJ laurels and enjoying his blossoming romance with Suzi simply wasn't an option. The success of *Don't Forget Your Toothbrush* meant that Evans's production company Ginger was now seen as a favoured supplier to Channel 4. When the network approached Chris with the idea of developing a live, early evening light entertainment show, he just couldn't help himself, and immediately began formulating ideas for what would eventually become *TFI Friday*.

Irishman Phil Mount, who is now the series producer of *CD:UK*, one of Britain's most successful music shows, explains how things took shape: 'I was working at MTV in 1995 on a live broadcast called *Most Wanted*, hosted by a guy named Ray Cokes. Because it was satellite and comparatively low budget, it meant that you did a bit of everything, from writing scripts to floor-managing the show to booking the bands, which was kind of my speciality.' On *Most Wanted*, Phil met Will Macdonald, who had moved to the station to produce the show after his success producing ... *Toothbrush* for Ginger. Will had been in on Ginger at the start, but the company had been mothballed from March to December of 1995 while Chris looked for another commission.

'Because Will was there, I met Chris down on the set of *Most Wanted* quite a few times,' says Mount. 'He was Will's big buddy and a major fan of Ray Cokes, who had a sort of chaotic, seat-of-your-pants style that appealed to Chris. Chris would often come down and hang out. He was always trying to persuade Will to go out for a beer; "Will, Will, come for a beer. Come on." He just gave off a vibe of someone who loved life, really. Anyway, Will was obviously cooking things up with Chris for what eventually became *TFI*, and in time it became clear that he'd be leaving MTV for this new project.' Impressed both by Mount's willingness to work and his ability to multi-task, Macdonald spoke to him in the pub.

'Will explained what the idea was,' says Mount. 'It was very early days. I mean, the show didn't even have a name at that point. Will said, "I'm going off to do a big new Channel 4 show. It'll be music-based with wacky guests and celebrity interviews, Chris Evans will be presenting it and it's going to be huge, huge, huge. Do you want to come and work on it?"' Shaking his head, Mount then admits that at first he really wasn't convinced as to the show's prospects.

'It sounds incredible now, but at the time I really did hum and haw about it,' he confesses. 'I was saying, "I don't want to leave MTV because I have a full-time contract here." I'd only been in TV for five minutes, and really didn't know any better. But Will was very patient with me. He said, "This is Channel 4. This is terrestrial TV. It's a really big deal and yes, it's only a three-month contract for one series, but I guarantee you that other things will come out of this." It's incredible to think that a cable TV show was making me hesitate, but Will kept telling me "Don't underestimate this. It's going to be a big, big show."' Finally convinced, Mount threw his hat in the ring with Chris and Will.

The fact that Evans was producing his Radio 1 breakfast show as an external client for the BBC now came in very handy. Evans had held all the cards when Matthew Bannister had come knocking on his door and he'd used them well, renting office space at the BBC's Egton House building for his production team. And now that Ginger was expanding and looked like it would be a going concern after the success of ... *Toothbrush,* he also managed to move his TV arm into the same building.

'I was petrified when I started with Ginger,' recalls Phil Mount. 'It was stepping into the unknown. They had this small office within Radio 1, and for the first two weeks that I was there, all the TV section had was one small room with about three phones in it. Eventually, we moved down to the basement and got ourselves a bit more space.' There again, the team didn't exactly need too much room to stretch out at the time. With a tight-knit hierarchy which included John Revell as executive producer, Will and Dave Granger as producers, Suzi Aplin acting as entertainment producer and Clare Barton as production manager, there were no more than twenty people in the team when Phil Mount started as a junior researcher with a special responsibility to book the bands.

'I'll never forget my first day working there,' he explains. 'I'd virtually produced shows at MTV, so I suppose I thought I'd already achieved something. But that first day I was told about an idea that they needed working up for the pilot. The notion was that they would get some really old mums and dads who would be prepared to French kiss in front of the show's audience. Then we'd get their kids in the crowd and Chris would say something along the lines of, "You thought your mum and dad were safely at home. But no, they're not ..." The old couples would then start French kissing in front of everybody and their kids would obviously be squirming in horror in the audience and on telly.

'So my very first task, on my very first day, was to go up and down Oxford Street with another researcher trying to find old couples who'd be prepared to do this. Now can you imagine how I felt having to go up to couples on the street – *old couples* – and ask them if they'd be prepared to snog on live TV? I remember sitting down on a step somewhere saying to myself, "What the *fuck* have I done?" But that's how shows like *TFI* work.'

Chris Evans was to dust down his French kissing pensioners idea nearly a decade later for his Channel 4 show *Boys And Girls* – but that is another story ...

The energy that these madcap schemes generated meant that,

embarrassing searches on London's busiest shopping street notwithstanding, Ginger TV quickly became a very exciting place to work, full of creative powerhouses generating a mass of ideas. To lead the charge, Chris had brought in respected broadcaster and writer Danny Baker, whom he'd known from GLR days, to help him write scripts for the new show. The relationship between the two men was very interesting, not least because Chris treated Danny in a way that was highly unusual for him.

'Danny is one of the only people I think he's in awe of,' says an insider. 'In fact, I'd go so far as to say that Chris was scared of Danny, because he thought he was the one person who was more of a broadcasting genius than he was. I think he actually aspires to be as good as Danny and looks on him as a big brother. Plus he admired the way that Danny didn't take any shit.' There was one occasion when a Channel 4 exec tried to prevent Baker reading a limerick he had written about Gandhi wearing a nappy on *TFI Friday*. Baker told him where he could stick his opinions, and flounced off the show. 'I can't think of anyone other than Danny that Chris would hate to lose as a friend,' says the source.

'There was a great vibe at *TFI*,' recalls Phil Mount. 'Will and Dave would be giving the orders, Chris was popping in and out all the time throwing ideas at us that he'd developed with Danny Baker, though he was obviously also very busy with his radio show. Then those ideas would filter down to us and we'd have to make them happen. Everyone quickly got a feel for the style that *TFI* was developing – the more madcap, off-the-wall and bizarre, the better. Even after the first pilot, I knew it was going to be huge.'

The debut *TFI* show, which finally went to air on Friday February 9, 1996, had significant differences from the original concept. The location was the Riverside Studios in Hammersmith, and the original notion had been for Chris to anchor the show from the platform in the main studio where the guests walked down to make their entrance. However, it soon became clear that to produce the kind of informal area where guests would immediately be put at their ease, and therefore be more likely to relax into giving a revealing interview, the bar was infinitely more suitable. The show's true point of difference was that it was being created to be something much more intimate than your regular TV show.

'*TFI* felt like a party, where the audience really was a part of the show, whether they were jumping up and down to the live bands or bantering with Chris in the bar,' says Mount. 'You'd see people getting involved. And the fact that the bar really did serve booze – and it was all free – helped to loosen up the atmosphere.'

'It was sort of the hub of the show,' explains 23-year-old Gareth Johnson, who worked behind the bar. 'Nobody had ever had the idea of having guests and audience so close to each other, and with the booze flowing freely it oiled people up and created an instant atmosphere. The free booze really did set the tone, it was very important. They tried the show without alcohol being served for about three weeks at one point, something that Channel 4 instigated if I remember rightly, and it was a disaster. The atmosphere just died. Of course, as soon as they brought the booze back everything was fine again.'

The 'hallowed sanctuary', as Johnson terms the bar area where the bulk of the show was shot, became *the* place to be in London on a Friday. 'Everyone wanted to be in there, and working behind the bar was a privileged position,' he recalls. 'It was shag central. I would have girls chatting me up all the time and you could guarantee they would always ask you the same two questions. The first was, "Can I get tickets for next week?" and the second was, "Is Chris Evans a cunt?" In the end I would start a conversation by saying: "Before we start, the answers are 'no' and 'no'."'

'Because the show was done live in the early evening on a Friday, people would come down to Hammersmith and make a night of it,' says Phil Mount. 'You could start your night off there, have a few pints and a few laughs, see some bands, and when it was all over the night would still be young. So the punters were having a great time, as were the people working on the show and even the guests. We all loved *TFI* and very quickly realised it was having a massive influence on youth culture, because people were really interested in what we were doing. I used to feel very proud when I told people what I was working on. *TFI* had that effect on you.'

11 Under Pressure

It was no surprise that people were talking about *TFI Friday*. The show was sensational. Evans was in his element at the helm, using his unerring ability to put guests at their ease and then coax the most incredible soundbites out of them. And as far as the stunts were concerned, nothing was too wild and crazy if it made for compulsive viewing. From people hitting golf balls full whack in the studio, to floating enormous models down the Thames alongside the studios, to unleashing three tons of chicken soup into the bar, the more outlandish the scheme, the more the viewers loved it.

As word began to spread that this was easily the most irreverent and funny show on television, celebrities started to demand an appearance. Again, the fact that Chris Evans was every bit as famous as the celebs themselves seemed to work in *TFI*'s favour. Chris never deliberately eclipsed his guests, but having someone who was at the same level of fame seemed to allow the celebrities to relax. Suddenly you'd have George Best going up and down on a riser outside the back window, waving various flags. People would do the most outrageous things because it was for Evans. Stars like Jon Bon Jovi, a notoriously difficult artist to deal with, would absolutely insist on appearing on *TFI* whenever he was in London.

'Chris was like Parkinson, in his own way,' says Gareth Johnson. 'He was good at putting people at their ease, and of course that always made for great interviews.' Only once was there a major problem, when Janet Jackson simply froze in the jostling informality of the bar, like a rabbit trapped in the head-lights. Chris calmed the terrified pop star down and was charm itself. The England footballer Paul Gascoigne, a drinking pal of Evans, had no such problems making himself at home at Riverside Studios, though.

'He was often down there, just hanging around,' says Johnson. 'We used to start the recording around three or four in the after-noon, but I remember this one time when Gazza pitched up ridiculously early and I was only just starting to get the bar ready. He sidled up to me and asked if I was serving yet. For Gazza? Of course I was. He asked for a white wine so I started to pour him a glass. He looked at me as if I was mad and said, "What are you doing, man? In a pint glass!" Then he asked me if we had a football in the place, which we did, so the two of us ended up out on the patio playing footy. He'd had two pints of white wine by this time, but I still couldn't get the ball off him. He was absolutely brilliant!'

An appearance on *TFI* had huge social cachet. It was almost as if it was a slight to your celebrity status if you didn't get an invite. Even Paul McCartney wanted to come on so that he could meet Chris Evans. 'Paul always enjoyed talking with Chris,' explains Phil Mount. 'And he was really jealous of the fact that Chris was still in a position where he could come and play foot-ball with all the Ginger team in Regent's Park on a Tuesday night. I heard him saying to Chris: "It must be really great going over with all the boys. I wish I could do that!"'

Musicians, in particular, felt at home on *TFI*, largely because of Evans's obvious love for music. 'He was so into the idea of having all of his heroes performing on the show,' says Johnson. 'He loved his music. Once they had Aerosmith, the Red Hot Chili Peppers and Garbage on one show, which was a fantastic line-up. Both Aerosmith and the Chilis played for an hour or two during the soundcheck, just having fun, and Chris was so into it he just stood there mesmerised, watching the whole thing. One of the production people was saying to him, "Come on Chris, we've got a show to do." Chris was just like, "Don't worry about that. I'm watching *Aerosmith*!"'

'Bands would virtually never just perform their songs and go,' explains Phil Mount. 'You would always see them hanging around in the bar afterwards, and they really entered into the spirit of things. There were no rock star tantrums as far as I can remember. I think they thought the whole thing was surreal, especially because the dressing rooms for the acts were actually across the road. People had to walk across the main road to get to the studio and there were quite a few times when people got lost. One time Lenny Kravitz was walking down the street, dressed in his full rock star regalia, knocking on people's doors saying, "Excuse me, is this my dressing room?" And there was Björk, dreamily wandering out into the main road and getting drivers honking at her, shouting "Get out of the fucking way!" It was incredible!'

Naturally, with some temperamental celebrities involved in a show that was going out entirely live, with no signal delay in case anything went awry, there was always the possibility that things could get out of hand. And, naturally, they did. In a big way, when former Happy Mondays singer and acknowledged toilet mouth Shaun Ryder appeared as a guest. Evans thought that he'd made a pre-emptive strike to stop Ryder from swearing, but things didn't quite work out as planned ...

Evans: 'We talked before on the radio and you know that you swear a lot, don't you? But the thing is, you don't mean to, do you? It's just your lingo, that's just the way it is. Well look, let me tell you this. If you don't swear tonight I'll *give* you my shoes ...'

Ryder: 'Patrick Cox, man. Patrick's a fucking good ...'

Evans: 'You see!' Cue wild applause.

Ryder: 'Patrick makes good shoes, man.'

Evans: 'Now you see that was completely natural, that was completely natural.'

Ryder. 'Patrick makes good shoes man ... and he's cheaper than Fila.'

The incident earned Evans a rap across the knuckles from the Independent Television Commission, who sent him a letter saying that they would take a very dim view of any such transgressions in the future. Two weeks later, actor Ewan McGregor dropped him right in it again, by pronouncing: 'Let's have a go at the Conservative government for just fucking everything ...' 'Do you *realise* how much trouble I'm in now?' retorted Evans, apologising profusely. *TFI* continued to go out live, though, until Phil Mount booked Ryder's band Black Grape to perform the Sex Pistols' 'Pretty Vacant' in a spoof version of the singing impersonation show *Stars In Their Eyes* on March 22, 1996.

'Looking back, it might not have been the brightest thing to do,' admits Phil. 'But Shaun was warned constantly that he mustn't swear and he was fine about it. Anyway, he does the "Tonight Chris, I'm going to be Johnny Rotten" bit and disappears through the smoke. Then he reappears on stage with his hair dyed and looking the part and suddenly he's acting as though he really believes he *is* Johnny Rotten, because he starts decking people and swearing like mad. Thirteen fucks later we cut back to Chris and he was just mortified, going "Sorry, sorry, sorry, sorry!"' Two months later, the ITC issued Channel 4 with a formal warning over the swearing incidents, but Ginger had already grasped the nettle and gone to the network offering to record the show with a delay, to avoid any future embarrassment.

Thanks to Chris's view that the show should continue to be well-rehearsed chaos, the slightly pre-recorded *TFI* still retained its dangerous edge, which made it essential viewing to its hip young audience. And if it came across on the small screen as the best party the viewers could ever be invited to, then that's probably because it *was*. The reason that it worked, according to Gareth Johnson, was because Evans genuinely cared about what was being produced.

'Chris would always make a point of telling us: "We're doing this for the audience. People come from Manchester, Newcastle, Edinburgh, all over to see this show and putting something shit on is not good enough. We're not doing it for the artists we have on. They're there to sell something, and we know that. It's for the audience."'

And yet the enthusiasm he displayed for *TFI* at its peak proved that Chris Evans was doing all this for himself as much as for the audience. Despite the hassle from the ITC, he loved being the ringmaster of this mad, mad circus. 'Oh yeah, he got off on hanging out and being a part of it,' says Phil. 'If it was your production company making the show and you were the executive producer and the presenter, wouldn't you? And the best thing about it all was that you'd finished work by 7pm, a bit earlier once the ten-minute delay had been introduced. You were done and dusted and off to the pub, around the corner for a curry and into the bars, almost always with Chris leading the way.'

'Could Chris hold his drink?' ponders Mount. 'Fuck, yes. Some of the Christmas parties we had at Ginger were absolutely brilliant. You just had to write the next two days off. And then Chris would be there on the radio at 6am the next day and I'd be nursing a ferocious hangover and thinking, "How the hell did he do that?" Incredible.'

'Chris was a great crack on the piss,' confirms Gareth Johnson. 'But he had this uncanny ability never to appear too slaughtered. You'd think he'd just walked into the bar. I'd be all over the place, and he'd be as calm as you like up at the bar going, "Let's have another one".'

According to some of Evans's closest associates, however, there was a manipulative reason for this. 'I've never seen Chris when he's not been in control of himself,' says one source. 'He can hold his drink, and he drinks a lot. But he would always leave before he lost it. It's not an attraction to him to go to another place mentally to escape where he is. He likes where he is just fine, and he's in control there. I've seen Chris pretend to go to the loo and then nip out of the back door when he's had enough, rather than say "That's me finished, I'm off." But he loves having other people around who either don't have any responsibilities or who he can get to forget them. He enjoys creating situations where people get into trouble. Chris loves nothing more than being in the pub with someone with their head in their hands, saying, "Oh God. I should have been home four hours ago. She's going to kill me." He would laugh his head off. Chris loved it if he could, say, persuade someone who shouldn't to go off with a lap-dancer. He's the king of *Schadenfreude*, really.'

Jamie Broadbent also has his doubts about Chris's drinking habits: 'Dominic Mohan from the *Sun's* Bizarre column was on the telly recently saying Chris drinks like a fish, but he doesn't. He drinks nothing like as much as anyone says. Chris is very clever, because he gives the public that character, but if you were to go out and drink a bottle of wine with him you'd end up drinking three quarters and he'd drink a quarter. That was how he did it. You get everyone pissed around you to make them think what a great party it is. Then people say, "How the hell does he go to bed at midnight when he's drinking so much, and then get up at four?" Well, that's easy. It's because he didn't really drink that much.'

So maybe Chris Evans didn't drink as much as he let on. But what about drugs? The sheer pace at which Evans lived life, the body clock that would go off at five in the morning and be ready to go, go, go, the violent mood swings. Were they really all naturally induced? Or was there a more sinister reason why Evans notoriously couldn't sit still for five minutes?

'There were all sorts of rumours about Chris taking loads of cocaine at Radio 1,' says Jamie Broadbent. 'But if I were a betting man, I'd say he didn't do it. He's too much of a control freak to enjoy being out of control. He would probably have fuelled those rumours, though, because they would have made him look more rock'n'roll.' Evans's friend, TV director Chris Howe, is even more adamant that the star did not dabble in hard drugs: 'That's one thing he *never* does. He's really quite anti-hard drugs, though I think his policy was, "If one of my pals is into it, then I'll get them help rather than sack them." That was what I heard over and over again. I'm sure Chris wouldn't frown if you had a joint, but if it was cocaine he wouldn't like it at all. People just assume, "Oh, he's on the old gear" because he's so hyper and energetic. Me, I reckon it's all that alcohol sugar level!'

In truth, it's unlikely that class A drugs would fit in with Evans's need to be in control, and maintaining control of his burgeoning media empire was clearly of paramount importance to him at this point. Yet according to some who were closely involved at the time, Chris still regarded the TV arm of Ginger as the sickly cousin of the radio division. Even after *TFI* had launched, the feeling – at least, according to Evans's PA at the time, Maria Costello – was that he still considered the tight-knit radio crew which included John Revell, Holly Samos and Dan McGrath to be the A-team.

On the TV side, only Will Macdonald, co-producer Dave Grainger, production manager Clare Barton and girlfriend Suzi Aplin appeared to command much respect from the boss, as evidenced by the fact that many of the people working at Ginger TV weren't invited to Chris's thirtieth birthday celebrations at posh London brasserie Langhams. Costello claimed that the on-screen bonhomie that was so necessary to the spirit of *TFI Friday* was definitely not replicated in the office away from the TV cameras. 'We were always watching nervously to see who was "in",' she explained. 'When I first started, Chris always said hello when he passed, then suddenly he would completely blank me.'

When the Ginger team finally moved out of the BBC buildings at Egton House to their own offices in Great Titchfield Street in 1996, Costello claims that despite overseeing every element of the move, she never received a word of thanks from Evans. Of course, it might be argued that PAs who were experienced at handling highly-strung celebrities would – and should – expect no gratitude for their efforts besides a handsome pay packet. Simon Morris admits that Chris and Maria didn't get along, and that one of his first tasks on arriving at Ginger as MD was to sack her. Why wouldn't Chris do it himself? Because despite what people might think about Chris Evans's incendiary temper, Simon is one of many who believes that underneath it all he really dislikes confrontation and will do anything to avoid it one-on-one.

'I don't want anyone to labour under the misapprehension Chris is a confrontational, antagonistic, fiery, red-haired lunatic,' he says. 'Because that isn't true. Underneath it all, and when it really matters, Chris does *not* like real confrontation. Yes, he's outspoken and yes, he's principled, but he would always duck a fight because he hated it, just *hated* it. On that first day at Ginger I had to sack the PA because Chris couldn't face it. It was awful in a way, because *I* sort of became the hatchet man of the operation.' Awful it may have been, but Simon still defends Evans's behaviour within Ginger at this time.

'He could come down on someone like a ton of bricks, and like anyone he could be in a bad mood in the morning. But a lot of it was that he wanted to normalise things and stop people treating him with kid gloves. He would say, "You don't have to wait two days to ask me if this thing should be pink. For God's sake use your brain. Come on. You'll never be fired for showing a bit of nous, even if it backfires on you. You're not allowed to make the same mistake twice, but use your brain and you'll get on." He would expect people to work to his standards of professionalism, he was short-tempered, and he didn't suffer fools easily. But he was also incredibly generous. Sure, some things could have been handled better, like anything in life. But he's not Boutros Boutros-Ghali and I'm not Kofi Annan, so there you go.'

It's fair to reflect on the insanely busy schedule that Evans was pursuing through 1996. By 9am, when most people in the London media might just be dragging themselves out of the house for a 10.30 start, Evans had already done half a day's intense work. Then there would be *TFI* post-mortems on Mondays; creative meetings for the coming Friday's show on Wednesdays; pre-recording of segments on Thursdays; and then the show itself on the last day of the week. Only on a Tuesday would Chris have any free time in his diary, for those footy games in Regents Park or his new passion, golf. And then there were the ambitious plans for the expansion of Ginger.

'It was always in Chris's mind to be a mogul,' says Simon Morris. 'His first idea was to buy a newspaper. I don't know how the idea came up, but we certainly weren't drunk. We were just blue-skying, talking about maybe buying the *Daily Star*. There was definitely an idea to leverage his success that way. We looked at a *TFI Friday* magazine. We even discussed starting a modelling agency called "Reds". Chris. Red hair, you see. Now, why would you do that? Well, because we *could*. It was just the next thing. You got really charged on doing something new. We didn't want another TV programme. We didn't want to be yet another TV production company. It had to be mould-breaking.'

This constant quest for big ideas was heaping pressure on Evans, but it seemed that the more pressure he put on himself by piling on the work, the more he needed to release the pressure valve by partying hard. Or, at least, being *seen* to be partying hard. Evans could hardly have had a higher profile as leader of the hottest shows on both radio and TV, and with his PR company Freud's deftly manipulating his image, he was the number one celebrity item in all the tabloids.

Such was the interest in Chris that to celebrate his thirtieth birthday on April 1, 1996, Freud's came up with the most amazing April Fool's pranks (to be played, cunningly, on April 2 to lessen suspicions) in order to maximise column inches. Chris would make an on-air marriage proposal 'to someone very special to me' to get the papers frothing over who the lucky girl was. Or he would announce that a screenplay that he'd written had been bought by Hollywood and there would be a photo call outside Broadcasting House with him sat in a director's chair and holding a loudhailer. Or he would 'decide' that, since he'd achieved everything else in life, now was the time for him to run for Parliament.

Freud's also suggested that a select gathering of Evans's showbiz chums – the Gallaghers, Cher, Shaun Ryder, etc – could show up to sing 'Happy Birthday' while Des Lynam presented a cake. If Chris Evans's ego really was out of control, then these elaborate suggestions would have done precisely nothing to keep his feet on the gr████erestingly, though, Evans knocked back the ideas on th██████ds that they were too self-indulgent. Even so, his friends could see that there *were* times when his ego did get out of hand.

'His mates were fiercely defensive of him,' explains Simon Morris. 'Because most of the time he wasn't being an idiot. But there were a couple of times when I was out with him and I thought he was being an arsehole, so I told him. He could be a bit offhand with people, or a bit arrogant. I remember going on

Dan McGrath's stag do after Dan's big on-air proposal thing. I hired this great rock'n'roll bus that we could sleep on, and we headed out on the town. We took over a Chinese restaurant near the Haverstock Arms in Belsize Park, and I have to hold my hands up and say I'm embarrassed about my behaviour there. We were in there thinking we were God's gift, taking over the karaoke machine and spoiling people's evenings. Some of the customers thought it was brilliant and were joining in. Girls were getting up and leaving their boyfriends to get on the bus with us to carry on the tour and they thought it was great. But there must have been other people thinking "You wankers" ... and they were right.'

With his life getting more outrageous by the minute, it's no wonder that Chris Evans didn't often feel like having anyone tell him what to do. He later admitted that his behaviour was frequently unnecessarily aggressive and rude. 'At the time, I don't think I would have done anything about it,' he's admitted. 'Because I wouldn't have cared.'

12 Goin' Crazy

If Chris Evans didn't appear to care what anybody thought of him, Radio 1 controller Matthew Bannister most certainly did.

Despite the fact that he was delighted with the attention Evans brought to Radio 1, Bannister was savvy enough to realise there were dangers in his being seen as the panacea to the station. He also wanted to keep a lid on the ever-more-commonplace notion in the press that Chris Evans was a law unto himself, and that the BBC simply couldn't control him. Of course, the truth was that Evans *did* hold the whip hand and the BBC *couldn't* really control him. This was how he had gained his rabid following, by playing the role of the maverick, the man who couldn't be tamed. All of his shows had been about edge, about attitude, about not toeing the party line. It was exactly what had made people believe in Radio 1 as a vibrant life force again, rather than a fusty, semi-retirement home for satin-jacketed Smashies and Niceys. Evans always appealed to the large minority rather than the all-encompassing majority. So when Trevor Dann got shirty about the fact that Evans didn't fancy playing the game *vis à vis* playlists, well, what on earth did he expect?

'Chris and Revell and his team were all basically 25 to 35-year-old white people and they all liked indie and guitar pop, which is why you never heard any black music on the Chris Evans show,' moaned Dann. 'They just didn't like Shola Ama or R&B, and I found that a real problem. Radio 1's proposition is that it is about generality, it's not about niche.'

This notion of Dann's was palpably nonsense. Evans had never tried to be anything other than what he was. There was never any attempt to be all things to all men. A similar criticism was made of *TFI Friday*'s seemingly endless stream of indie guitar bands. And while music booker Phil Mount's contention that 'that was what was big at the time and those bands were good live performers' is certainly a credible argument, much of what appeared was simply a direct reflection of Chris Evans's personality and tastes. Radio 1 knew all about the cult of personality with Evans. After all, it had been one of the main reasons they were so desperate to get him to come to the station in the first place.

While Trevor Dann may now have been unimpressed by Evans's broadcasting abilities, there were plenty of others who clearly disagreed. In May, the prestigious Sony Music Awards handed Chris a gong for Best Broadcaster, but he turned it down. His show hadn't won in the Best Breakfast Show category, and with at least some semblance of logic, Chris argued, 'So you're saying I'm the best broadcaster, but my breakfast show isn't the best.' To his way of thinking, that made the award 'pointless and meaningless.' Still, turning it down certainly got him some PR.

Dann's carping about the playlist was missing the point. There was a far trickier problem that had to be faced – the fact that Evans's power at Radio 1 was now so great that *any* form of editorial control was nigh on impossible to exert. Chris Evans had been devil-may-care when he was trying to find his way at Piccadilly Radio in Manchester because he had nothing, so he had nothing to lose. Now that he'd made money beyond his wildest dreams (he'd just bought himself and Suzi a five-storey town house in Notting Hill for £600,000 to prove the point), he was equally free in a different way ... and so unburdened by any need to compromise.

At this stage in his career, Evans had been investigated 31 times by the broadcasting standards watchdogs and didn't appear to care too much about how much trouble he was in with the ITC. Most of the time he shot from the lip, and hit exactly the right target. He would use the sparks of ideas that just came

flooding into his brain and create addictive radio almost instan-
taneously ... such as the threat to expose the cowboy plumber
who'd done some shoddy work on his new house by broadcasting
his name and address to anyone listening.

Naturally, of course, there were occasions when Chris went
too far in his efforts to amuse the nation. Telling the joke 'What
do Brussels sprouts and pubic hair have in common? You push
them both aside and carry on eating' at five to eight in the
morning on a national radio station was certainly one of those
times which had Matthew Bannister 'lying in bed with the covers
over my head, thinking, "What's he going to say now?"' And
while the press were up in arms about that particular piece of
poor taste, that was a silly lapse of judgement along the lines of
cat-grilling, rather than the petty vitriol which his diatribes occasionally descended into. A classic case in point was Evans's highly
publicised spat in Scotland with a local radio DJ.

It had all started innocently enough. In August, Chris was
ranting live on air about how horrendous London was becoming
for smog and fumes in the summer, how he'd got terrible catarrh,
and how he really had to get out of the place. According to
Matthew Bannister, it was he who suggested that Chris should
actually do it; get hold of the most remote BBC radio station in
Scotland, and broadcast from there. Evans loved the idea, and
the following week the entire team had pitched up at Radio
Inverness ready to go to work. However, during the week a verbal
slanging-match developed with local DJ Tich McCooey.
Bannister claimed that the falling-out occurred because
McCooey shamelessly attempted to hijack Evans's appearance in
Scotland to get himself some publicity. Not so, according to
McCooey himself.

'Chris had seen a picture of me and said he wouldn't mind
meeting me. He seemed like a decent guy so I thought, "Why
not?" He'd also been joking on air about going round to my
mum's to make her laugh. So we arranged a meeting through his
people at a hotel in Nairn, and I pitched up there with my assistant. Chris was sitting at a table with some of his sidekicks
working stuff out. It looked like they had some maps laid out on

the table. So I went up to Chris, stuck my hand out and for a joke said "Now, what have you been saying about my mum?" He turned to me and said, "I'm a bit busy at the moment", to which I replied "Oh OK, sorry", and went off to the bar on the other side of the room to wait for him to finish. Then at the end of his meeting he got up and walked right past me looking the other way. I thought to myself, "Blimey, he's not chuffed that I've turned up here", so I wrote a wee note and put it through to him saying sorry, and that I really hadn't turned up to hassle him.

'Anyway the next morning he just launched into this attack on me on his show, which to be honest I wouldn't have been that bothered about if it had just been the usual radio shenanigans, a bit of controversy, or something to get the listeners going. The problem was that it was a very personal attack.' Evans, in fact, publicly mocked McCooey and the money he earned in a very aggressive way. According to McCooey, Evans's tactic backfired on him when Radio 1 listeners 'got up in arms about what he'd done.'

Chris Evans had always tried to give the impression that he was just one of the boys, a regular guy who'd made it big, but who wasn't about to lord his good fortune over the rest of us. This incident sent out a completely different message, and one that Matthew Bannister wasn't happy about. 'I thought this was wrong, really patronising, offensive and nasty,' he said later. Predictably, Evans didn't agree, telling Bannister that 'Tich McCooey was completely in the wrong. He tried to harass me, he's a public figure so he deserves what he gets, playing in the public arena with me.'

'Chris always said that he didn't like the fact that I was trying to get publicity for myself off his back, but I'm really not a publicity-seeking kind of guy,' says McCooey. The most interesting thing of all though, is the postscript to the affair. 'I did bump into him a few months after all this nonsense,' says Tich. 'I think it was at some kind of showcase. I thought I'd go up and have a laugh, so I sauntered up to Chris and said "Chris Evans, what have you been saying about my mum?" Well, he was really on the back foot, all nervous and saying, "... I didn't say anything about your mum. I *wouldn't* say anything about her!" I was surprised, but he really was very conciliatory.' If he'd known Evans's past attempts to avoid direct confrontation, maybe McCooey wouldn't have been quite so amazed.

Unfortunately for Chris Evans, avoiding the nasty things in his private life wasn't always to prove so easy. At precisely the same time as the DJ was mocking Tich McCooey's supposedly paltry income, Evans's former partner Alison Ward was making an attempt to relieve him of a further part of his own fortune. Despite now getting £600 per month from Chris for the upkeep of their daughter Jade, Alison had decided that she was entitled to more of a contribution from her extremely wealthy ex-lover.

'He's a millionaire, but Jade has never even had a holiday,' said Alison. Had she known that Evans was already paying Carol McGiffen £150 a month to look after the couple's greyhound Angelina, she might have been even more determined to fight for extra maintenance when she filed Case 94 CP 521, Alison Ward versus Christopher Evans, at Warrington County Court. Evans was required to provide an affidavit detailing his earnings, and duly lodged it on August 2 with a solicitor, Frank Tindal, who had premises on the High Street at Nairn, where Evans was staying during the Scottish sojourn.

In retrospect, the entire Scottish venture was an ill-starred one. Mimicking the local accent and moaning about the antiquarian nature of the studio wasn't going to endear Evans to the locals – or anybody else, for that matter. Of even greater concern, arguably, was the fact that this rather high-handed, world-weary attitude wasn't making for great radio, either. Even one of Evans's staunchest allies, his publicist Matthew Freud, found it hard to defend him. 'Scotland was a mistake,' he admitted. 'Chris had become very negative, very cynical, he was attacking people and it had become quite a nasty programme.' Freud's assessment was that Chris was 'the most reviled man in the country for six or seven months'.

Jamie Broadbent reckons that some of the blame for the press's reaction to Chris Evans at this juncture has to be shouldered by the DJ himself. 'Chris understands how the press works. When he was at Radio 1, they all wanted a piece of him, but the longer I was with him the more he seemed to want a piece of *them*. He didn't need to orchestrate things at Radio 1, because it was such a high profile show that it would do the job by itself and get Chris in the papers. But Chris ended up living his life for the papers – and he's still doing it now. Let's face it, I'm sure he doesn't dress the way he does because he wants to. He looks a twat. But he does it because he wants to be seen as a non-conformist, and that's what keeps his face in the press.'

Simon Morris also felt that Evans was going off the rails at this time. 'My view is that Chris suddenly started to let things get to him,' he explains. 'Everyone who becomes a face goes through a time where they think they're special, and most of them come out of it. Being completely honest, there was a time when he *did* change and become slightly up himself, because he was surrounded by that weird world of people telling him how good he was all the time. I didn't like that and so we'd be out in the West End at 2am and I'd be threatening to knock him out. We did actually come to blows once, I think it was in the Groucho Club ...

'He started having a go at journalists on his radio show. He was a big mate with Gazza around this time, and I remember him having a go at a football journalist, Brian Woolnough, on behalf of Gazza. Chris believed he had the platform on which to fight back and in the end it wore him down, because of course you're not going to win a battle against the media. You're not going to win, and it just makes them more vitriolic. In fact it encourages them, because they think they've got a rise out of you. I saw Chris hurting when people started having a real go at him. He didn't enjoy it, he wasn't happy with himself at that time and also he'd got to the top. I think he was at a point where he was saying, "Right, is this it? This is really hurting me. Why are people doing this?"'

Of course, none of this internal anguish mattered a great deal to the newspapers. And if the tenor of their reaction had shifted from 'Chris Evans, Saviour of the Nation' to a 'love him or hate him?' debate, well, so what? It was all grist to the media mill. The Chris Evans juggernaut was still rolling on. *TFI* was the 'must see' show of the week, the breakfast show on Radio 1 was still successful, and Chris Evans was the celebrity name that the papers craved above all others. Yet Evans was vexed, and when things get a little bit tricky, there is nobody as adept as him at putting a spanner in the works.

'Chris is really hard to pin down,' develops Morris. 'He likes it fast and loose, he doesn't like commitment, and he doesn't like formal meetings. When we had what we called the Ginger board meeting – which was me, Chris and John Revell in some bar in town – I'd have the agenda and say, "*This* is what I'm doing" to make sure I'd pinned him down. If I had a criticism, it would be that he wouldn't commit, and I think he'd hold his hands up to that. It's quite a good business trick, actually. Sure, it was frustrating for the rest of us, but by not formally committing to things he's like the burglar who keeps the back door open. He keeps himself in a position where he can walk away, or say "I didn't have anything to do with that."'

Simon Garfield, who penned *The Nation's Favourite,* an acclaimed history of the Bannister era of change at Radio 1, found himself in a unique position to explain the Chris Evans phenomenon, and has a very clear view on why things were about to get seriously nasty between Evans and Radio 1.

'Chris has a pattern of doing creative things and then getting out at the right time,' he says. 'He clearly gets bored awfully easily. He wants constant praise, and to feel like he's breaking new ground all the time. After a year or so of Radio 1, he was bored. It's classic Evans, a cyclical thing where he reaches a point where he just feels he's done it. He's got in somewhere, and done the hard bit, and once it's fairly smooth sailing he gets bored and starts looking for new stuff to do. He tends to get himself into trouble and upset people, and in a way create his own passage out of wherever he is.

'Chris Evans is very good at creating that sort of friction, and if you want to leave somewhere, then it's a very useful ploy ...'

13 Breaking Up Is Hard To Do

If Evans was looking for a way to stir up a hornet's nest to speed his route out of Radio 1, then he certainly found one on the morning of November 7, 1996. The previous evening edition of the *Evening Standard* had run an article by journalist Lisa O'Carroll, announcing that Trevor Dann had been rewarded for bringing Chris Evans to Radio 1 'with responsibility for the BBC's entire pop music output, from Radio 1's chart show to BBC1's *Top Of The Pops*.' Dann admitted he had indeed applied for the job of Head Of Music Entertainment, a role that he himself had helped to create, but nothing had been announced, and Dann maintains that he still doesn't know where the leak came from. Yet a leak it certainly was, and the idea that Trevor Dann was a) being credited with getting Evans on board at Radio 1, and b) getting a plum job out of it appeared to make the DJ incandescent with rage.

Irrespective of whether this was of any interest to Radio 1 breakfast show listeners, Evans decided to vent his spleen. Reading out the offending article live on air, Evans, John Revell and Dan McGrath voiced their astonishment that Dann was being credited for their success. Then things started to get *really* nasty.

'Here we are,' said Evans, reading from the article verbatim. "His appointment as head of BBC1's music production highlights the extraordinary relationship between the Radio 1 controller Bannister, Evans and Dann." Extraordinary because we unreservedly loathe the man.' 'Pretty much so,' concurred Revell. 'Well, you especially, John,' continued Evans. 'You hate his guts.' On and on the slating went. Revell claimed the loathing was mutual, Evans said he hadn't spoken to Dann in 17 months … and even then it hadn't been about the show. 'He's tried to put this show down more than anybody else I've ever come across,' raged Evans. 'And now, apparently, he's the invisible hand of success behind this show. I'm sick of this, John. I am. I'm boiling over.'

Evans wasn't the only person with steam coming out of his ears. Trevor Dann hadn't heard the on-air slating ('I'd stopped listening by then,' he explained. 'I just couldn't stand his arrogance'), but when he made it into work that morning, his colleagues soon let him know what had happened. Dann got a tape of the show and promptly marched off to see his mate Matthew Bannister to say that Evans had to be stopped. Was Trevor Dann *ever* in for a surprise.

Instead of backing his colleague and wholeheartedly agreeing that Evans had gone too far this time, Matthew Bannister took the opposite tack. 'I've had Evans on the phone and he's absolutely livid about the story you've given to Lisa O'Carroll,' he said. He then proceeded to carpet Dann for constantly trying to undermine the breakfast show. 'They hate you, and I hate you,' Bannister yelled. Dann was utterly dumbfounded. He'd gone into Bannister's office confident that his friend would agree Evans had overstepped the mark, and plot out a course of action to bring him under control. Instead here *he* was on the end of a severe dressing down. Simon Garfield, author of *The Nation's Favourite*, has a lot of sympathy for Trevor Dann's predicament.

'There wasn't really any justification for what Chris did,' he says. 'It's hard to say with any certainty who was in the right or in the wrong as far as the issue of the story is concerned, but there's no justification for insulting someone on air who isn't even known to the public. Chris did a lot of that, though, bringing his own personal and professional dilemmas into the public arena. If he didn't like someone he'd slag them off on air, which is fine if they have a chance to come back or if he did it humorously. But most often it wasn't a balanced debate at all; it was a diatribe. I don't think the attack on Trevor Dann was justi-fied, and if Chris looked back on the incident now I suspect he'd regard it as a rather immature outburst. At least, I *hope* he would. There is, of course, the other argument that it was rather good radio and very compelling listening. And if you're of the opinion that creating great radio is the be-all and end-all, then I suppose you'd say it worked.'

Jamie Broadbent believes that creating memorable radio was *exactly* the reason behind Chris's outburst. 'There was never a problem with Trevor Dann,' he says. 'Chris never *saw* Trevor Dann. It wasn't personal. I don't know if people at Radio 1 didn't like Chris, or didn't like the fact that the breakfast show was an independent production. I never spoke to Trevor Dann in all the time I was at the station, but if I passed him in the corridor he'd look away, I guess because I was a part of Ginger.

'Were they justified in taking against us? Well, we lived by our own rules, and got spoiled to bits by record companies. And yes, we larged it. I did push my luck while still trying to be a nice person, although maybe we weren't *that* nice sometimes. But there was never anything done that was offensive to anyone at Radio 1, and still from their side there was a lot of "What's your game?" and "Who do you think you are?" The on-air thing was a wind-up that came out of that attitude. Chris knew what Trevor Dann was like, and knew that if he said something about Trevor on air, he'd take it personally because he had far too big an ego. I mean, like anyone gives a toss about Trevor Dann! It was all bollocks, but there was a big thing made of it to create a bit of a furore.'

So, according to Jamie, Chris had only been winding Trevor Dann up. It certainly worked a treat. Dann had reacted furiously and his boss, Matthew Bannister, had unreservedly supported Evans in what was far from a black-and-white dispute. But if Bannister thought Evans would have doffed his cap, kept his head down and got on with entertaining the nation, then he was going to be seriously disappointed.

In December, while Evans was on holiday, Bannister received

a call from the DJ's agent Michael Foster, who claimed that his client wasn't well enough to come back to work at Radio 1, though he probably was just about fit enough to present *TFI Friday*. Stress, exhaustion and over-tiredness were cited. A concerned Bannister went down to the *TFI Friday* studios in Hammersmith to see how his star DJ was doing, and didn't like what he saw. Chris was 'white and sweating' and Bannister immediately ordered him to take the following week off and go and see his own doctor. He also visited Evans at home two days later to check on him, but saw little to encourage him that his DJ was making a speedy recovery. Bannister suspected the star wasn't eating properly.

The situation escalated when Evans began to complain that Fridays were becoming a real problem for him. He felt the energy needed for him to hit two peaks, one for his breakfast show and another for *TFI*, was simply too demanding. Again, Bannister showed remarkable consideration for his charge and renegotiated his contract, allowing him twice as much holiday and even giving him what he termed a 'not insubstantial' pay rise.

Matthew Bannister believed that a potential crisis had been averted, especially when Chris went on the following Friday's *TFI* and made light of his problems, showing off all the pills that his doctor had prescribed him. It seemed that everything was back on track, and the end of the year came and went with nothing more worrying to Radio 1's controller than the usual on-air outbursts which Freud's made sure hit the tabloids. Chris took some holiday from his breakfast show over Christmas and New Year, then filmed a *TFI* on the Friday before he was due to return to work at Radio 1.

Evans clearly loved being able to spend all of that Friday focussing on the TV show, because on the following Monday, January 13, Bannister took a call from Michael Foster, who floated the idea of Chris taking Fridays off from the morning show. Bannister's first response was that this was an impossible demand from the man at the helm of the station's flagship show. Not only was it unthinkable to have Evans only presenting from Monday to Thursday, but Bannister was already having real difficulty managing a situation where it seemed as if the tail was wagging the dog. How many more times could Evans be granted concessions before Bannister would be seen as weak, and his role as the ruler of Radio 1 undermined?

Bannister suggested that he and Chris needed to go out together to discuss the issue, but Foster was adamant it was a business issue and as such he, Foster, should negotiate with Bannister, not Evans. There was no way Chris was going to embroil himself in this potentially explosive situation. However, before Bannister could work out how best to deal with the issues, Foster made an audacious move. He sent a letter to Matthew Bannister three days later, citing Evans's contract and saying that under its terms he was hereby giving 90 days' notice to quit unless Chris was given all Fridays off – including the following day – for the remainder of his contract. The terms were very clearly non-negotiable. There had been, according to Bannister, absolutely no mention of a reduction in salary at the time of the increase in holidays from the last round of negotiations. Nor was there this time.

Chris Evans's recollection of events differs wildly from Matthew Bannister's. 'I asked for Fridays off for six fucking months,' he complained. 'One whiff of what they thought was dissent, and that was it. It was a sincere request.' Evans argued that with the extra day off, he would be able to make the other four days' shows a lot better. He also claimed that he got paid five times more for doing his one day of TV work than he did for five days of radio. That may have been so, but many observers felt he had signed a contract with Radio 1 and was obliged to honour it, especially as Bannister had already agreed considerable concessions.

Could Evans not see that by insisting on Fridays off, he was putting his boss in an impossible position? Apparently not. Evans said that Bannister told him that if he acquiesced yet again: 'I'd be seen by the governors as not being in control.' Evans's considered response to the argument was a one-word retort: 'Bollocks.'

As part of Chris Evans's on-air team, Jamie Broadbent knows exactly what he thought of the demand. 'I'd say it *was* unreasonable to ask for Fridays off, when Chris was getting one million pounds plus for the show, which was a massive amount of money at the time. No matter how hard people say presenting on the radio is, it's not brain surgery. And by this time Chris had lost it. However interesting someone is, they're not interesting 15 minutes after they've started talking – and that was what Chris was doing by then. People don't tune in to listen to that.

'In the last year or so at Radio 1, Chris was riding on the back of Britpop and he was big and famous himself. It was all ten-minute links and I was thinking "Shut the fuck up!" I wouldn't have told him that, of course, because I was a junior. The only person who probably could have done was John Revell, and John was more worried about himself. The figures Chris had put on when he first got to the station were on the slide and Chris knew that. He was always one step ahead, so he knew the right time to bail out in order to maintain his profile. And that was the time when he decided he had to leave.'

So maybe Chris Evans had decided that he wanted out of Radio 1 at all costs, and was simply looking for a good fight to pick to enable him to go out with a bang. Simon Garfield doesn't believe this was the case. Or, at least, not right away.

'If Matthew had turned around and said, "Four days? OK, fine", then I think Chris would have been happy to carry on,' he says. 'But I suspect that, after maybe six months, something else would have come up. I don't think that Chris was actively looking for a way out, but the nature of the man meant there would have been some other flashpoint. I think his concern about the work-load he had taken on was genuine. He felt that getting up at 5.30am five days per week was too much when he had a TV show to deal with as well. I think we would all have felt the same way if we were trying to do that. Yes, he had a contract worth more than £1m per year, and was paid well for dealing with the stress. But I can quite understand his problem from a creative point of view.' Bannister, too, understood Evans's dilemma, but thought *TFI* could cut the presenter some slack. 'That was never an option that Chris was prepared to entertain,' he said.

'Chris said that what he was asking for wasn't unprecedented,' says Stuart Maconie. 'He claimed that the traditional American format was that the breakfast DJ would do four days, so that the weekday listeners could be introduced to the weekend guy and would hopefully be carried through by him. He was kind of right about that, but I think the bottom line for Chris was that he was just knackered. It was obvious that he loved being right at the centre of popular culture, and his breakfast show was maybe the last time that show really was in that position. But he was a well-off bloke who liked his leisure. No matter how much he liked the show, it must have been difficult to get up for it every morning.'

However, Jamie Broadbent has a more sensational version of how this drama was really unfolding behind the scenes. 'Matthew was a cool guy,' he says. 'It wouldn't surprise me if he and Chris were in cahoots when Chris left. They probably sat down and Chris would have said "I want to do four days" or even "I don't want to do this any more. Surely it's better for you to get rid of me. That way, you look strong and I look like I'm a maverick. I've got to look like I've stormed out." '

Jamie's conspiracy theory initially sounds unlikely. However, he gives an example of how Evans and Bannister generated publicity: 'Chris was splashed all over the papers once when he was supposedly fined £7,000 for not turning up for work one day. It got Radio 1 on the front page of every single paper. I'm pretty sure that Chris never paid that fine. We sat there after our Christmas party and he wasn't going to tell anybody, but then he told people the way it was going to happen. So we all did it. We knew that Chris was going to miss a day, so none of us turned up for work. All seven people who worked on the show failed to turn up, so what would you make of that? Bannister "fined" him, and loads of press was delivered. It's a big press machine.'

So was Bannister really playing a role? Or was he genuinely bemused and angry when he received the contract termination notice from Foster on January 16? Whatever the truth, Bannister phoned the agent to ask if he really was serious about the demand. Foster merely reiterated the terms. Bannister said that it was impossible to give Evans *the very next day* off, but Foster was unmoved and said if that was the case then he and Evans would have to stand by the decision to resign.

Despite Bannister's pleas to at least have a conversation with Evans, Foster claimed he couldn't track his client down, and the next thing Bannister knew the phones were ringing off the hook in the Radio 1 press office with people asking for confirmation that Chris Evans had left the station. Bannister says he can only assume that Ginger released the information, since only he and his deputy Andy Parfitt knew anything of the crisis. Realising that there was no solution to the problem, Bannister drafted a statement and graciously sent it over to Foster to check. Only a couple of words were changed, and the announcement was made that Chris Evans had given ninety days' notice because Radio 1 wouldn't give him Fridays off.

Bannister still hadn't spoken to Evans directly, with Foster claiming he couldn't get hold of him because he'd gone to a pub with John Revell and neither of them had their mobiles switched on. It transpired, however, that in fact Evans was very close to Radio 1 indeed. He was round the corner, in Needles Wine Bar, with the *Sun's* pop writer Andy Coulson, giving his side of the story for the following day's paper. Bannister said that the interview had 'a certain amount of dignity', because Evans didn't use his platform to slag Radio 1 off. The DJ did, however, claim that he'd been forced out, then forced himself down to the Groucho club with the rest of his team to drink, heavily or otherwise.

14 Please Release Me

It was vintage Evans. With his inimitable feel for the big showbiz gesture, Chris started his show the day the news of his resignation from Radio 1 was splashed across the papers with an ironic spin of 'Please Release Me (Let Me Go)'. He then told his listeners he'd been forced out of the station, and that it was absolutely outrageous. It was a shameless ploy to win people over to his side.

'The perception was that I was taking the pee because I'm a hard-nosed bastard out for everything he can get,' said Evans in self-defence. 'It's not true. I didn't want to leave. Matthew Bannister just thought I was trying to put one over on him.' Maybe so, but the fact that a man who was purportedly really keen to stay on at the station was simply not prepared to discuss the problem with a boss who appeared very willing to talk doesn't quite tally with Evans's view.

In an attempt to look as if Radio 1 wasn't mortified by Evans's resignation and would survive perfectly happily without him, Bannister took out a tongue-in-cheek lightboard ad in London's Piccadilly Circus. It read, 'Radio 1 breakfast DJ wanted. Ginger hair an asset.' Despite Michael Foster's assurances, Matthew Bannister couldn't be certain that Evans would honour his ninety-day notice period, so he sensibly put Kevin Greening on standby to fill in as DJ should Evans not show on the following Monday morning. He even phoned Chris at home on the Sunday to try and straighten things out a bit, but Evans merely put the phone down on him, which made the controller even more sceptical about Evans working his notice like a good boy.

So it didn't really come as any surprise – though the timing could have been more considerate – when John Revell phoned on-air DJ Clive Warren at ten past five in the morning to say that the breakfast team wouldn't be in. Bannister's deputy Andy Parfitt came in to help Kevin Greening out, and chose the first record. It was Oasis's 'Don't Look Back In Anger'.

'There was a feeling of great loss around the station, definitely,' says Simon Garfield. 'I think there was some relief among the other DJs, a kind of feeling that at last they could get on with doing what they did again, because the guy who had stolen their thunder was gone. But Radio 1 was a much quieter place, and some people felt a part of the station had, if not died, then certainly gone into intensive care.' Asked whether he feels it was always going to end in tears given the manner in which Evans came to the station, pretty much knowing that they needed him more than he needed them, Garfield seems to think so.

'Chris has been compared to a child more than once, and I think in many ways his relationship with Matthew really was like that. Before you have a baby people tell you how hard it's going to be, but you're never fully prepared for just how tough exactly. Then you forget quite how awful it can be and go for another one and you know you're going to lose some sleep, but you've forgotten how difficult it is to keep getting up at three in the morning. It's absolutely like that with Chris. He is a handful, and Matthew must have known that he would cause him headaches in the end. But obviously he didn't have any idea of exactly how it would end. Whenever there was a problem with Chris before – like the off-colour joke, or the spat with the Scottish DJ – then Matthew ticked him off, and Chris either said whoever it was had it coming, or that he was in the wrong and wouldn't do it again. That sort of worked. But the four-day issue was undermining Matthew's authority, and that couldn't happen.

'At the end I think Chris believed he was bigger than the radio station. The attitude he had about Radio 1 was that he'd saved its arse, which I don't think is true. There's no doubt that he had a big influence, because the breakfast programme is key to setting the tone of a radio station and establishing a strong listener base for the rest of the day. But, having said that, no one person's impact could be as large as Chris thought his was. It was a smart move to sign him up at the time they did because he was a hot talent and that made Radio 1 a cool place to be.'

So was it worth all the pain and the grief and the personal fallout? Well Chris Evans *had* helped to change the image of the station from a fusty home for fading 1970s hipsters to a place that was, if not hip again, then definitely newsworthy. Nobody but Evans could have delivered the sheer volume of tabloid news coverage. And it shouldn't be forgotten that he had improved the station's ratings performance. In his first nine months with the station Evans increased the breakfast show listening figures from 6.1m to 7.19m, a remarkable feat.

As Evans himself told Brian Appleyard of the *Sun*, with dubious maths; 'We didn't get half-a-million more listeners. We got 7.5m new, younger, hipper listeners.' And while the overall listening figures for Radio 1 were increasing, they didn't grow as fast as his own ratings, which meant he was arguably a better performer than even Matthew Bannister had hoped. Initially, at least, but had his later indulgent broadcasts reversed this effect? The last set of figures covering Evans's tenure showed that the station had lost half-a-million listeners. With the breakfast show supposedly setting the agenda this could be interpreted as failure.

'He clearly had a very significant effect,' says Simon Garfield. 'He came in at the right time and the money that was spent on him was probably justified. There's no doubt that it was a smart move to sign him up. But would the radio station still have been around and doing OK if he hadn't come? I would say yes. Radio 1 may have lost half-a-million listeners or more before Chris came, but who's to say that he wouldn't have lost them again over time once people had had enough of his antics? It's very hard to say what would have happened had he not been there, but what you have to remember is that there were a lot of other people at

Radio 1 who were extremely accomplished and good at what they did. And it has survived very well without him.'

As for Chris Evans, he was back in the bosom of Ginger, plotting his next move and keeping options open. 'Chris put all of the breakfast show team "into development",' explains Jamie Broadbent, 'Which is a media term for doing fuck-all. I didn't mind. It was great getting paid for going to the pub. And we always believed we'd eventually pick things up again on another show somewhere with the same team. Chris was in the office now and again, and I remember that we went away to Ireland with him, just for a break.' But it wasn't only Radio 1 that was in a state of upheaval. Ginger was changing too, with MD Simon Morris heading out of the door.

'I finished because I had got frustrated,' explains Simon. 'I'd done a deal for branded Ginger Beer and Chris's agent Michael Foster basically hijacked it, which just got me thinking. I believed the management structure at Ginger would work, but it was flawed. Foster was Chris's personal manager, with Chris's interests and his own business interests at heart, so he was wary of Ginger and how it would impact on his role – particularly when I arrived, and was already one of Chris's mates. It's understandable, and Michael and I have had some spectacular rows over the years, but I'd like to think we're still on good terms. He's an incredible operator and he's played a large part in Chris's success.

'The problem was that at Ginger we were very aware that the company was a bit of a one-trick pony, reliant on Chris for all the revenue streams. So we had to bring through new talent, and I think Chris never really fully signed up for it – you know, bringing through Johnny Vaughan, or bringing talent through, and pushing them. Performers have that thing in them where they want to be reassured all the time and they're conscious of a threat. Chris had beaten off a lot of competition in his rise, so he wasn't going for the idea of pushing new people through via his own company. Neither was Michael. Plus the fact that we weren't disciplined. Chris, John Revell and I would meet at Stringfellow's, which was very rock'n'roll, and that was good in a way. But it was probably *too* rock'n'roll, and I could see that it wasn't going to work. And Chris and I weren't mates suddenly, and that had gone too far for me.'

Morris left to become a director of an internet start-up, which successful floated on the London Stock Exchange two-and-a-half years later. Back at Ginger, Evans remained overall boss, but John Revell was in charge of radio and Chris's girlfriend Suzi Aplin was heading up the TV arm. 'I know that Ginger was trying to buy Talk Radio and John Revell was putting a lot of work into the deal,' says Jamie Broadbent. 'But that fell through and I think John was quite bitter about it not happening, because he stood to make a lot of money. There were a few things that were in the pipeline. They were trying to do something with Ray Cokes (the man who Chris had so avidly watched when Will Macdonald was working on his show at MTV), and I think there were some attempts to get Danny Baker the breakfast show on Talk. But none of that happened.'

However, it wasn't *all* bad news, as Ginger pulled in a commission to allow Evans to indulge his burgeoning love of golf. Chris Howe, one of the directors of *Tee Time*, explains how it came about.

'Chris was always brainstorming ideas,' he says. 'One day he would be wondering, "What would be the best job in the world? I know, flying here, there and everywhere playing golf? And what would be the second best job in the world? Going round the world drinking in pubs and eating really nice food. Right, let's try and get Channel 4 interested." And that was what became *Tee Time*, right there.'

Yet even if this latest venture was designed as a con and a way to get other people to pay for his holiday between radio jobs, Evans's hyper personality just wouldn't let him chill in places like Dubai, India and the US. 'You'd never catch him kicking back,' says Howe. 'I don't think I ever saw him relax. You'd fly in somewhere, he'd go and have a kip or a sauna to get over the jetlag, but then he would just keep going. He wouldn't fuck about. He hated the time it would take to set up lighting. He'd say he knew what would look best and would want you to do it straight away, get it done and have a beer. Nine times out of ten his instincts about things were right, but I couldn't take that chance. I said, "We have to try other things, otherwise we'll get back and there'll be no rushes and you'll sack me." '

Tee Time was fun and filled a gap, but Chris Evans knew full well that the show, which aired early in 1998, wasn't his next big thing. After eight months out of the limelight he decided that what he really wanted was to return to radio. 'We were all waiting to see exactly where we would end up,' says Jamie Broadbent. But the team wouldn't have to wait much longer …

15 Like A Virgin

On the morning of September 18, 1997, Mark Radcliffe announced on the Radio 1 breakfast show that 'Zoë Ball has got some top new gig, with loads of cash and a brand new alarm clock thrown in for good measure.' Radcliffe and his sidekick Lard had taken over the breakfast slot when Chris Evans walked out, and – in line with their own predictions – had proven an unmitigated ratings disaster. Matthew Bannister had decided that Ball and Kevin Greening would be the pair to get the show back on the rails. Even more remarkably, a day before this news broke, Chris Evans's agent Michael Foster had phoned Matthew Bannister to ask whether he would consider his client for the Radio 1 breakfast show again.

Bannister was very taken aback, and told Foster his timing was appalling, given that he'd only just told the papers that Ball and Greening would be in the chair. Foster's suggestion was that Bannister should tell the tabloids it was all a pack of lies and told the controller to call him back when he'd thought about it. Bannister did call back – within minutes, in fact – to say he wouldn't even consider it. He added that Evans would be more than welcome to do a bank holiday or weekend show. Foster replied that there was only one show that Evans would even contemplate returning for.

A few days later Chris Evans informed the *Sun* that 'Matthew asked me to come back, but I said fuck off.' And Evans did indeed fuck off, to rival station Virgin Radio, who promptly announced that he would be presenting *their* breakfast show, which was due to launch on Monday October 13 – the very same day as Zoë Ball and Kevin Greening.

The scene was set for a very messy battle, and the media saw the potential in a head-to-head of hate. It hardly seemed to matter that the people involved were actually friends. A story appeared in the *Mirror* claiming that Zoë hated Chris; the article was, in her words, 'a complete fabrication'. But it all did the trick, and on the day of the launch of the two shows there was huge interest in who would win the battle for the breakfast-time airwaves. Opinion was divided, but the most perceptive view came from the *Sunday Times'* s Paul Donovan, who identified some major hurdles Evans would have to overcome on a commercial station, regardless of his own on-air performances. 'There are nine minutes of commercials per hour, interrupting him constantly,' he pointed out. 'He also has to stop for three traffic packages and two news bulletins per hour and, as a result, will seem to be stopping and starting all the time.' There was one more, far more serious, drawback: 'Outside of London, he goes out only on unfashionable and booming medium wave.'

Radio 1 were taking a gamble on Zoë Ball, but with her more showbiz-centric approach and the fact that she was an attractive woman who could command column inches, she was never anywhere near as radical a step as had been Mark and Lard. The first set of listener figures reflected that immediately, with Ball and Greening putting 400,000 on the last figures of their hapless predecessors. Simon Garfield believes Ball was crucial to the ongoing development of Radio 1.

'Once they got her on board Radio 1 actually did very well, and while Chris wasn't exactly forgotten, you could argue that she had even more of an impact, just in a different way. To a certain degree her presence was more significant than Chris's as far as Radio 1's long-term success was concerned, because she put the station back on an even keel. To use a terrible cliché, she stopped the boat rocking as much. Whether she would have had that same impact had Chris not been her rival at Virgin is very hard to tell. But I do think that Radio 1 listeners had had enough of Chris. He's an easy person to tire of.'

Down the road at Virgin Radio's studios in Golden Square, however, you could certainly sense Evans's excitement to be free of Radio 1 on his first morning on air. After all, with just a ten-week contract in his pocket, he clearly felt he had scope for a bit of fun. Within the first two hours of his show, he had demanded that William Hague inform the world of his sexual bent, and had even convinced a listener to unveil her new, surgically-enhanced boobs live on the show later in the week.

Evans also managed to pull off a major PR coup by apparently donating the £200,000 he was to receive for his ten-week Virgin stint to the Princess Diana Memorial Fund, which had been set up in the wake of her death on August 31. 'We can confirm that Chris has given the money to the fund,' said his spokesman. 'Other than that we can't comment, because it's a very private matter as far as Chris is concerned.' Well, not now he'd announced it, it wasn't. Chris Evans was back in hog heaven. He was back on the air with his regular crew, except for Justin Bradley who had departed, according to Jamie Broadbent, 'because of financial restrictions.' Their excitement levels were high.

Matthew Bannister finally spoke to Chris Evans again in November 1997. Chris and Suzi had just begun one of the 'off' stages in their on-off relationship, though this time it looked a little more serious. Evans had moved out of their Notting Hill house in Kensington Park Road and bought a six-bedroom house not too far away in Arundel Gardens. Still, he wasn't feeling too depressed to attend a music business awards ceremony hosted by the magazine *Q*, and had in fact agreed to present an award. Bannister was also present and when his former DJ clambered onto the stage, Evans came out with 'I haven't got anything to say except that if Matthew Bannister's here, life's too short, let's go for a beer.' It was just the invitation that Bannister, still a great admirer of Evans and a man who'd been clearly troubled by all the animosity, had hoped to receive. After the ceremony had finished the two men went to a nearby pub, accompanied by

Danny Baker, to kiss and make-up. Bannister later revealed that he also had a conversation about how long Evans intended to stay at Virgin. Evans said that he wouldn't hang around if the other big London commercial station, Capital, bought it, which was a rumour that was doing the rounds. Then, almost as an afterthought, Evans said, 'Maybe I'll try and buy the company.'

'Don't be silly,' thought Bannister. Circumstances were to prove that Evans was being anything but. Virgin Radio were in fact being courted by their London rivals, Capital. Virgin owner Richard Branson was keen to find someone prepared to inject cash into the station to fund an investment in digital technology, thereby putting his station in a stronger position to apply for a nationwide FM licence (Virgin currently had FM only in London) and compete with BBC network radio. Capital had offered £87m for the company, but the deal had been stalled by a Monopolies and Mergers Commission enquiry. The MMC was concerned that Capital was already Britain's largest radio group.

Virgin had signed Evans after Capital's offer but before the MMC's report was due in early 1998, and this had clearly got Evans thinking. What if he actually owned a radio station? There would be no Matthew Bannister or Trevor Dann telling him what to do. Nobody else telling him what records he could and couldn't play. It could be the biggest radio story in years. However, while a very wealthy man, Evans had nothing like the resources needed to fund the purchase of an entire radio station. Nor did he have any real experience of operating at a business level that was infinitely higher than anything he had done before. However, he did have a very shrewd agent in Michael Foster.

He also had the perfect platform from which to talk up any bid he might want to make, and also to appeal for financial backers for his scheme: his own show. It didn't take long for Evans to take advantage. In November, within weeks of taking over the Virgin breakfast show, he was appealing for backers on air. It didn't fall on deaf ears. City venture capital firm Apax Partners were already well aware of the potential that Virgin offered. Having invested £3 when the station was awarded its AM licence, they had watched revenues grow by almost 50% between 1994 and 1997, clearly aided by the award of the FM licence for London in 1995. They further realised that, with Evans as a figurehead to front the bid, they'd have a strong suit with the station's owner Richard Branson, a man who would appreciate Chris's maverick talents. And with the big prize of a nationwide FM licence still to be fought for, there was a huge incentive to acquire the station.

Knowing that Capital's bid had already been referred to the MMC, with a decision expected in January, the new group had to move fast to try to steal the station from under Capital's noses. By November they had bid £80m for Virgin, and Branson realised that Chris Evans really was serious.

This was clearly a calculated risk for Evans. By this stage, *TFI Friday* was Ginger's cash cow, making a clear profit of £100,000 per week – a phenomenal figure. They filmed 40 shows per year: £4m for Ginger. In order for Chris to be able to supply his part of the cash for the bid for Virgin, the banks understandably needed assurance that the *TFI* money would be there for the foreseeable future, so Chris signed up with Channel 4 for another three years to provide 42 episodes per year for £30 million. Given Evans's previous reputation for moving on and making a clean break from shows when he felt that they were past their sell-by date, this was a significant development. It meant that Chris had signed up for a long-term creative venture to ensure that his ambitious business plans could be supported.

On Tuesday 9 December, Chris Evans announced live on the breakfast show that he had bought a controlling stake in Virgin Radio. 'It's great to be boss,' he crowed. 'It's brilliant. It's a very good day. God is Sir Dickie,' he continued, referring to Sir Richard Branson, who had sanctioned the deal. 'And I am his son.'

Evans's group had agreed to pay £87.5m for Virgin Radio, and a holding company had been created for Virgin and Ginger Productions in a deal which valued Ginger at £30m. Evans took a 55% holding in Ginger Media Group, while Branson's Virgin retained 20%, Apax took 20% and the station's management were awarded 5%. Chris had invested £2m of his own money in the venture, as well as his Ginger stake, and signed a five-year contract with Ginger Media, with an option for a further three to prove his commitment to the future. Thanking his lawyers and the money men for bringing the deal to a successful conclusion, Evans admitted that he'd known the bid had been successful since the previous Saturday, but had needed to keep the news a secret until now. 'It's been hard to keep quiet,' he admitted. 'But I can tell you this isn't the end, it's just the beginning.'

This was undoubtedly the most spectacular triumph yet in Chris Evans's extraordinary career. It was one thing to be acknowledged as the country's most influential broadcaster, but upping the ante and becoming the majority shareholder in one of Britain's most valuable radio businesses was something else entirely. Anybody who had assumed that Evans's departure from Radio 1 was the beginning of the end for the Ginger Whinger had received a major surprise. In typically idiosyncratic style, the newly crowned media mogul celebrated his status by cooking Christmas dinner for seven of his best mates' mums!

To rub salt into Capital Radio's considerable wounds, in January 1998 the Monopolies and Mergers Commission ruled that the proposed merger of Virgin and Capital *would* have been allowed to go ahead, with the proviso that Capital divested itself of some of its other stations. By now it was irrelevant – and too late. Chris Evans was back on top of the world, and the Ginger Media Group – complete with radio station – was now his personal fiefdom.

16 Mr Success

It was early 1998, and Jamie Broadbent could not have been happier. He had moved out of development hell (even the breakfast crew had tired of going to the pub without any work to break up the drinking!) and he was back on a radio show with his mate, who now also happened to be his boss. 'Virgin was great when we arrived,' he says. 'The place had a rock'n'roll vibe, and the staff really wanted us to be there. We were seen as the people who had stopped Capital taking over, who had saved the station from corporate clutches. Chris had gone in shouting out the idea that he was fighting for the little guy and everybody loved it.'

Everybody at Ginger felt safe, happy and secure in their new position, because all the key players – the breakfast team, Will Macdonald, Suzi Aplin – had signed three-year contracts. One proviso stipulated by the banks that had lent Evans the finance to buy Virgin was that key personnel had to be locked in. Nobody saw this as a problem. The situation was everything that Chris and his team had ever dreamed of.

The lunatics had taken over the asylum at Virgin … and how it showed. For starters, Chris Evans's penis began to play an even more prominent in proceedings than previously. In meetings held at Ginger – and despite being 'not particularly well-endowed, and with ginger pubes' – the new boss was in the habit of interrupting proceedings by standing up and pulling down the tracksuit bottoms he often wore to reveal his erection, swiftly followed by the words 'What's all that about, then?' He'd happily pull this trick whoever was present – men, or women.

Evans was also prone to wandering out of the meeting room into the general office space stark naked, and nonchalantly asking somebody to fetch him a glass of water as if this were an entirely natural state of affairs. And this was the man who was in charge of the whole shebang!

'This could be interpreted as Chris advertising his sexual prowess, saying, "Look, I'm a stud,"' reflects Professor Cary Cooper. 'But my suspicion is that it isn't really that, because Chris has nothing at all to prove when it comes to demonstrating that he is attractive to women. What he definitely *does* like is attention. In Britain in particular, doing something sexual gains real attention, especially in the media. Chris is not at all conventional, and so exposing himself acts as a real poke in the eye for convention and the Establishment, while making sure that everyone is also talking about him. He's idiosyncratic, he represents the counter-culture, and he's demonstrated all through his life that he's absolutely prepared to get his penis out.'

Indeed, before long Chris was incorporating his apparently insatiable desire to take his clothes off into *TFI Friday*, ending the show each week with The Naked Parade, featuring himself and any other members of the team he could persuade to join in divesting themselves of their clothes. However, as much as Chris loved to present his own (nude) rock'n'roll attitude, some distinctly un-rock'n'roll things were starting to happen behind the scenes at Virgin Radio.

'Chris didn't seem to like the offbeat attitude that was part of the Virgin culture as much as you might have expected,' says Jamie. 'Chris highlighted some of the old guard, including presenter Jono Coleman, and got rid of them. Now, I don't know if Chris's intention was always to sell Virgin to a major media player with a very traditional company culture, but he definitely started to change things to be more regimented at Virgin.' And if this sudden move towards a more respectable face for his radio station was seen as somewhat eccentric for a man who liked to get his penis out in meetings, well, there were other incidents that were just as perplexing.

'At one point, Danny Baker filled in for Chris on the breakfast show when he went away,' says Jamie. 'Now, Danny has never got a bad word to say about anybody. He's the most amiable man in the world and we all loved working with him. He was ace on air and we were dead happy. It was joyous. But then Chris came back after three days – because that's what he does, goes away for three days, gets bored and then comes back – and everyone was phoning in to the show and saying how great Danny had been. Then when we were in the pub after work, someone from Virgin walked in and said it. Chris just looked at him and stormed out of the pub. And Danny never did the Breakfast Show again.

'Jonathan Ross was similar. Chris used to say "Isn't Jonathan fantastic?" and Jonathan would fill in on air sometimes. Then I remember Chris going on air and saying, "Does anyone *get* Jonathan Ross? Does anyone understand what he's doing? Because I don't get it." There was a major falling-out over it, and they had to make up on air.' In truth, Chris Evans had helped to resurrect Ross's media career by inviting him on to Virgin – but this hardly explains the presenter's extraordinary jealousy. It's a behavioural trait that still puzzles Jamie: 'I just don't understand why Chris is so insecure.' Naturally, Chris's control freak tendencies explain a lot about why Evans had the need to play God with his own radio station.

However, even Chris Evans couldn't control certain situations. On June 17, 1998, Warrington solicitor Mike Peake appeared on behalf of Alison Ward before District Judge Hilary Dawson in an attempt to settle a child maintenance dispute between Alison and Evans over their daughter, Jade. Chris was by now paying £600 per month for Jade's upkeep but, given his wealth and status, Alison was launching a bid for more money. Chris was not in court. Clearly it would be difficult to argue a case against providing more financial assistance for 11-year-old Jade, and by July 3 a deal had been struck. In an out-of-court settlement Evans agreed to pay £1,500 per month maintenance, together with a one-off payment of £50,000, and the provision of a home worth £135,000. The regular payments would continue for as long as Jade continued her studies and the house would revert to Chris's ownership once Jade had grown up and moved out.

However, while Evans was battling on the domestic front, as well as behind the scenes at Virgin, he still presented a typically chirpy attitude on air in the mornings. The usual stunts proliferated, including one involving Chris being photographed with prissy fellow presenter Anthea Turner, the latter sporting a saucy nurse's uniform. This PR opportunity turned into a major nine-hour bender that ended with Turner staying at Evans's Arundel Gardens house, although he later denied that anything untoward had gone on between them. In August, he got drunk live on air while broadcasting from Glasgow, and carried on the session in the pubs after he'd stopped broadcasting. It was all typically crafted, PR-friendly stuff from Chris. In the midst of all of the hoopla, did anybody notice that, in July, a 15-year-old from Swindon named Billie Piper had become the youngest girl ever to top the UK charts in July with a single called 'Because We Want To'?

By the end of 1998, it appeared outwardly as if Chris Evans had finally found some contentment in his life. He was the grown-up owner of a radio station, he had resolved the maintenance issues in his private life, and he even seemed to be relishing some domestic bliss of his own. Evans and Suzi Aplin even seemed to be getting along better again. Nobody was sure if they were still an item, least of all them, but for Christmas she bought him a typically offbeat present, their very own greyhound which they named Ickle, a childish adaptation of the word 'little' which had been the basis of a sketch on *TFI Friday*. The last year of the millennium promised to be less unpredictable and more settled than any year of Chris Evans's life, especially when, in February, he bought a two-floor flat, the former home of Lord Mountbatten, in Belgravia's Wilton Crescent for £750,000. With his two cats, Madison and Hobbit, also taking up residence, everything was set up for domestic bliss. But the real question was whether Chris would be able to handle such normality.

Well, 1999 didn't get off to a good start. In January, it was announced that Virgin Radio had lost a whopping ten per cent of their audience in three months, which caused much nervousness at Golden Square. Evans then encouraged his show's listeners to hound a photographer who had been pursuing 'vulnerable' Oasis frontman Liam Gallagher, a stunt that earned his station a £1,000 fine from the regulatory body.

Next came yet another split with Suzi. Evans and Aplin had always enjoyed/endured a seesaw, rollercoaster relationship, but by the middle of the year, the break appeared more serious. Two years earlier, Chris Evans had admitted, 'You couldn't ask for a better girlfriend,' a statement he had then qualified by adding, 'I haven't always been a great boyfriend.' It would seem that nothing much had changed, although to her huge credit, Suzi has always refused to discuss her time with Chris.

Maybe the split was no surprise. In May 1999, Evans claimed that he had slept with his *Big Breakfast* co-presenter Gaby Roslin during their time on the show together. Even so, everyone took this latest 'revelation' with a pinch of salt, as they did the news that Ginger were now lining up a bid to take over the National Lottery. Far more credible was Chris's announcement that he wouldn't host a *TFI Friday* Millennium special, because he had some partying of his own to attend to. But for a man who clearly enjoyed living his life in the tabloids, and whose reputation as a central media figure depended on profile, this lack of newsworthy activity wasn't good enough at all. In November, however, there came a development that delivered blanket media coverage overnight and became the talk of the nation.

In her book *Just For The Record*, former Spice Girl Geri Halliwell describes how, during 1999, 'someone came along and pursued me.' That someone was Chris Evans.

Halliwell claims that the romance began when Evans called her up after hearing her being interviewed on Radio 1. She had described him as 'an inspirational person', before rather cattily adding and sometimes those qualities outweigh more superficial attractions like looks and sophistication.' In her book, Geri paints an idyllic picture of their first few dates together before the media had cottoned on to their relationship, calling Chris 'charming, interesting and funny.' However, she claims that a mere few weeks into the relationship, the tabloids took their first picture of the couple, together in Evans's Ferrari on October 21.

The following day, Halliwell was due to be interviewed on *TFI*

Friday by her 'boyfriend', although the world didn't yet know they were an item. In early November, however, The Artist Formerly Known As Ginger Spice was photographed leaving Chris's flat in Belgravia, at which point the media suggested that the whole 'affair' was a noteworthy PR stunt, to Halliwell's huge indignation.

It's easy to see the tabloids' point. Evans and Halliwell were both represented by Freud's PR company, and their 'liaison' proved an ideal way to boost Chris's profile while simultaneously helping Geri's single, 'Lift Me Up', to reach the number 1 spot in a battle with her former band mate Emma Bunton, who also had a record out at the same time. Or was it just coincidence? In *Just For The Record,* Halliwell claims that her single was originally due to be released on Sunday November 7, a date that had been set for months. It's a bizarre claim; pop singles are traditionally released on Mondays, as sales are calculated after Saturday shopping, and Sunday releases are utterly unheard of. In this context, Geri's word seems very unreliable.

However, November 4 saw photos of the 'romantic couple' splashed across the front pages, with one newspaper even claiming that Halliwell and Evans were about to get engaged. Reporters hot-footed it down to Virgin to catch Chris for his side of the story. On air, he cryptically claimed that stories that Geri never had any luck with men were 'yesterday's news' then made reference to the photographers outside the building, signing off with a weary, 'It's going to be a long day.' Meanwhile, Chris's ex-wife Carol McGiffen was in no doubt that this was all publicity-seeking nonsense. 'When the media has gone completely mad, they'll turn round to the bank of cameras and laugh their heads off at their own hilarious little prank,' Carol wrote in the *Guardian.* Typically, Suzi Aplin, the girl who had spent the most time with Chris but had always said the least, kept her own counsel.

According to Geri Halliwell, she and Chris were together for a month. Then, just as suddenly as romance had blossomed, it apparently withered and died. The fact that Chris was reported by the *Sun* to have disappeared into the loos at trendy restaurant Sugar Reef with his breakfast crew mate and former 'special friend' Holly 'Hotlips' Samos during his time with Geri didn't help. However, Halliwell says she recognised the relationship had run its course with or without the intervention of Holly and her lips. According to Evans's friend John Webster, who was to end up working with him on the breakfast show, Geri's attitude to the relationship was what forced him to dump her.

'Geri kind of stifled Chris,' he said. 'His face was a picture of a man trapped in something he didn't know how to get out of.' Webster claimed that Chris told Geri it was all over after one of his morning shows, though there's no mention of this in Geri's account. Given Chris's track record for avoiding confrontation at all costs, it's hard to know who was telling the truth here. Jamie Broadbent, however, has no doubt about how the relationship began and ended.

'Chris said he was going to marry practically every woman he met. The problem with Geri was that she believed it. He would always be saying things like "I love you. I think you're the greatest thing in the world. Move in with me." So Geri did. And Chris went "Fucking hell, someone's believed me for once." And he couldn't handle it. Most people just thought he was a bit bonkers ...'

Model and TV babe Melanie Sykes may also have fallen for Evans's spiel, because no sooner was Geri off the scene than it was rumoured that Chris was dating the comely Northern lass. Reports surfaced that Chris and Mel had been seen snogging in Soho's Pitcher & Piano bar, although Mel was supposedly dating actor and musician Max Beesley. Then the pair hot-footed it to Tenerife at the end of the year for a four-day jaunt, staying at the Grand Bahia del Duque hotel in Playa De Las Americas and arriving back home just in time for the Millennium celebrations. It didn't seem to bother Chris too much that the hotel cost a cool £500 per night. He had, after all, just written a cheque for £100,000 to a contestant who came close to winning the first £1m prize on UK radio. Chris had devised the competition to steal the thunder from the phenomenally successful TV show *Who Wants To Be A Millionaire?*

By everyday standards, of course, Chris had been rich for virtually his entire career in London. The payoff from TV-AM for *TV Mayhem* had put plenty in his back pocket, then *Big Breakfast*, ... *Toothbrush* and its attendant rights and, of course, *TFI* were all delivering vast sums of money to the Evans bank account. And money had always been of paramount importance to Chris. Maybe it was working-class paranoia about never thinking you've got enough. After all, he had originally claimed that he was going to retire on his *TV Mayhem* money ... and very quickly changed his mind. His attitude now seemed to be, 'Why be just rich when you can be obscenely wealthy?' And by a happy coincidence of timing, as the millennium closed, a major media group were looking to expand into precisely the areas where Ginger was strong. They were also willing to pay handsomely for the privilege.

'SMG started out as Scottish Television, a very small regional broadcaster with one of the 15 or 16 TV broadcasting licences,' explains business journalist James Ashton. 'It became Scottish Media Group when it bought Caledonian Publishing around 1995, so effectively had a TV arm and the *Herald* newspaper. But SMG had much bigger plans and wanted to turn itself from a regional mini-media conglomerate into a proper UK player. The company's chief executive, Andrew Flanagan, actually stated at the time: "Our ambition is to be a national player." With Virgin very much a London station, SMG's decision to make an offer for Virgin was a clear sign of them making a bold move into a new *sector,* as well as a new geographical area. It was good for the company to get into that market, so presumably they were happy to pay a premium for it.' It was also a happy time to hold media assets. The dotcom bubble had yet to burst, and radio in particular was felt to be a fast-growing business.

'The question is, what did SMG want to buy from Chris Evans?' continues Ashton. 'There were four elements. There was the third biggest radio station in London with an FM licence, which was great. Then they had an AM licence around the country, which wasn't quite as good and will die out as we switch over to digital. Then there was the cult of Chris Evans, which was an important, if potentially volatile, factor. They had an online thing that was worthless even then. And then there was Ginger TV. SMG maintained they bought a national radio station. People were paying silly prices for all sorts, and there was another joint bid for Ginger at the time, from a company called Clearchannel, together with Guardian Media Group. So SMG were not the only interested party, which put Ginger in a strong position.'

The valuation being put on Ginger would have made even Chris Evans's head spin – and he was used to dealing with big figures. There would be a payment of £110m in cash and £40m in equity. SMG would also pick up £75m of Ginger's debt. The equity payable to Ginger executives, primarily Chris and John Revell, would be payable in three annual tranches, and Chris would have to continue to present the breakfast show for a further two years to get his hands on what was being estimated at a personal haul from the deal of £75m. The breakfast show, after all, was responsible for forty per cent of the station's ad revenue. Evans knew his value, claiming at the time, 'A lot of the price tag has to do with me,' before quickly adding, 'as time goes on, we're getting away from the reliance on just me.'

James Ashton could certainly see the appeal of the SMG deal for Chris. 'I think he went for it because it gave him more freedom. SMG gave him quite a nice package and they let him stay on, not as an employee but as a contractor to work on the breakfast show.' Yes, and a contractor on a reported fee of £3m per year. But what about the fact that Evans wouldn't be in charge any more? 'SMG wanted him to do what he did best,' says Ashton. 'You have to tie in the top presenters and get the earn-out clauses in, where part of the money is payable only after staying with the company for agreed periods of time, and that's what they did. Yes, Chris got a great chunk of cash and it would have crossed SMG's mind that it could cause problems. But they thought "He's also a businessman. He's got to work his earn-out like anybody else".'

When the dust settled, it appeared that Chris Evans could effectively have his cake and eat it. He would be relieved of all management responsibility, yet would still be the station's figure-head, and perceived by many as the real lynchpin of the operation. He certainly felt happy enough about selling to SMG to announce the plan on his radio show, in the second week of 2000. There again, he was set to pocket £75m. There were many people within Ginger, however, who were much less enthusiastic about the deal. And some were positively hostile.

'Chris's attitude had always been maverick,' says Jamie Broadbent. 'That was why Richard Branson had sold Virgin to him in the first place. Branson had always fought monopolies, that's what he does. But Virgin Radio was an independent station and Chris sold out to a big company and stood to make himself £75m. The day he sold that station was the day he sold his soul. And Chris was a different person after that.'

Other key Ginger personnel were also unhappy, claiming that a single meeting with the suited-and-booted, stiff management from SMG was all it took to convince them that this was never going to work. Mark Donnelly, who acted as Finance Director at Ginger at the time of the sale, claimed that SMG gave the management team a free hand, 'but private companies have less reporting responsibilities, so many of the processes and controls had to be tightened up.'

Yet sitting in the aptly-named Midas Touch Bar, just 10 yards from Virgin Radio's Golden Square offices, on January 13, the day that the deal was announced, Chris Evans must have felt pretty satisfied. What did it matter that some people weren't happy about going to work for a bunch of people they thought of as dreaded 'suits'? Chris would soon have a fortune in his back pocket, which was handy given that he was in the process of buying Hascombe Court, an eight-bedroom Edwardian mansion in Surrey, for £6m. Set in 172 acres and boasting gorgeous gardens, a swimming pool and tennis court, cottages and stables, it was a delightful place fit for, well, a multi-millionaire. However, Chris had also decided to give a bonus of a year's salary to all Ginger staff members to say thank you to them for all their efforts. Surely that was fair enough. What more could they want from him? The nay-sayers were just party-poopers.

'The idea of going to Virgin in the first place was very much that *we*, Ginger, were buying the company,' says Jamie. 'But when it was sold to SMG, there wasn't much "we" about it. Yes, Chris paid us a bonus, but that was nowhere near the £75m he made, was it? And it wasn't so much the fact that he made so much from the deal, but that a lot of people who had really worked to build up all of Ginger's assets made relatively little, and various people who had only joined the company when he bought Virgin were paid a staggering amount out of the SMG deal.

'When I started at Virgin I was paid £18,000, that's all. The thing was, you didn't want to do anything else, so you didn't really question the money. And if you lived it again, you would probably do the same again. But you wouldn't expect to be badly treated and end up out of the company, which was eventually what happened.'

For now, though, the breakfast crew was still the breakfast crew. When SMG took the reins, they took things very steadily with their new baby, trying hard not to rock the boat. If anything, they were making what probably looked like a bit of a ham-fisted attempt to be 'down' with their hip new workmates. Virgin Radio's Head Of Communications Charlotte Blenkinsop claimed, 'SMG executives are now walking around in jeans and T-shirts. They want some of our culture, the "work hard, play hard" ethic.' This didn't wash with some of Ginger's stalwarts, however. Will Macdonald and Dave Granger were unsure of the new regime, and decided that this was an ideal opportunity to strike out on their own.

Will and Chris had been drifting apart for a long time by now. The duo had been working with Danny Baker on a programme called *Carry On Campus*, which had aired for a week on BBC2 with Will as the presenter. However, the series only lasted for a very short run. Macdonald had also given up producing *TFI* in the spring of 1998, now only appearing in the show in spasmodic cameo roles, and since that time had felt 'spare part-ish.' He was also involved with another hit show presented by Zoë Ball and Jamie Theakston called *The Priory*, but according to another person working on it, 'Chris didn't watch any of the first series at all.' As was often the case with Chris Evans, it was all or nothing. If his focus wasn't on a show, then it simply failed to register with him. Will and Dave left Ginger to form their own Monkey Kingdom production company. It was just *time*.

Chris Evans, however, was still working for SMG on his breakfast show, reasoning, 'I'm the only one who doesn't *have* to be here. I'm here because I want to be here, so you've got to start from that standpoint if you're working on a show with me.' SMG, for their part, were even more delighted with new formats, like *Rock And Roll Football*, a Saturday afternoon show which was launched in August to coincide with the new season.

'I remember sitting in a car with Chris one day,' he explains. 'And I said, "Look, football is the new rock'n'roll, but girlfriends get pissed off with their men listening to Radio Five Live all the time, which is nothing but sport. So why not do a music show with a Premiership update every fifteen minutes and have a goal button that goes off when there's a score?" Well that was the exact format of the show that is still running on Virgin today'. But Jamie never got the credit for it.

Disregarding the question of who really had instigated the idea for *Rock And Roll Football*, at least on the surface things appeared to be relatively calm and stable at Virgin. This wasn't the case in Ginger's TV production department. Macdonald and Granger had left, and Chris himself had begun to voice his own lack of interest in the medium. At the start of October, he revealed that he wouldn't be presenting the final series of *TFI Friday*, which was due to come to the end of its five-year run. 'I've had enough of television, I want to concentrate on radio. *TFI* was exhausting.' However, this was far from the whole story. Once the hippest show on television, *TFI*'s popularity had been eroded by a tired format, a lowering of standards, and the fact that people simply wanted something new.

Everybody knew that *TFI Friday* was over. Chris Evans knew it more than most, and so employed one of his classic credibility-retaining tricks that he'd used so often in the past. He bailed out early, leaving the presenter's chair in the last series to be filled by celebrities each week. When the axe finally fell on December 22, 2000, with Sir Elton John hosting, there were few tears.

Evans, for one, certainly didn't need his hanky. There was something developing in his private life that would amaze absolutely everybody...

17 Love Is In The Air

Many people had entered the new millennium with reasonably optimistic expectations. Maybe they'd get that loan for a new car. Or a pay rise at work. Or some sort of unexpected windfall. Chris Evans, for his part, had kicked off the year 2000 by pocketing a cash-and-shares package from SMG worth £75m, making him one of the richest media moguls in Britain. Him! Chris! Nobby No-Level! Tarzan-a-gram Man! Just how much more weird than *that* could you get? Well, actually, quite a lot more ...

Following his split from Suzi Aplin, Evans had been happy to live the bachelor lifestyle. The affairs, real or imaginary, with Geri Halliwell and Melanie Sykes had been followed by a brief dalliance with soap babe Anna Friel, but Chris seemed perfectly content to spend most of the year footloose and fancy free, enjoying his millions. The fact that the Channel 4 contract for *TFI* was due to end in December also felt like a great weight being lifted from his shoulders, given the fact that he'd had to persevere almost to the death with a show he'd clearly grown tired of.

The people who surrounded Chris Evans, however, noticed a more profound change in him. Now that he had his mega-money, it appeared that Evans had crossed the line from wide-eyed, ambitious young upstart to dilettantish celebrity-without-portfolio. Drinking pink champagne with trendy restaurateur Aldo Zilli appeared entirely indicative of his new mindset. In early

December, the *Mirror* claimed that Chris had just broken off a relationship with knitwear designer Louise Miller after a mere eight days, making the Geri fling look like a lifelong romance. It seemed as if Chris really wasn't ready for anything heavy on the relationship front ... until December 13, when a young girl came bounding through the doors of Virgin Radio, ready to be interviewed by Chris.

Promoting her single 'Walk Of Life', 18-year-old Billie Piper from Swindon was subjected to the usual Evans flirtatiousness. A teenage pop sensation who had become the youngest solo artist ever to make the number 1 slot in 1998 with 'Because We Want To' when she was just 15, Billie had been groomed for stardom after appearing in an ad campaign for the teenage pop magazine *Smash Hits*. She and Chris had already met on *TFI Friday* earlier in the year, when Chris had teased Billie about whether or not she was going to marry her pop star boyfriend Richie Neville from the band Five. The pair seemed to get along well, even swapping shirts midway through the show.

This time around, Chris jokingly proposed to Billie on air, and said that if celebrity magazine *OK!* wanted to pay a million pounds for the wedding photos, then the 'happy couple' would donate the fee to charity. There was nothing remotely unusual in this; it was just the usual banter that Chris would make up on the spot to keep himself and his listeners amused. But later that same day, when he was supposed to be at the Ginger Christmas party, Chris sloped off for dinner with this girl sixteen years his junior.

The following night, Evans and Piper met up again after Billie had appeared on *Top Of The Pops* and partied the night away at West End nightspots Stringfellow's, Denim and Brown's. So far, so very Chris. As Jamie Broadbent has pointed out, he pretty much fell in love with every pretty girl he clapped eyes on, anyway. 'We didn't really think anything of it at the time,' he says. 'John Revell had turned Chris onto Billie because he had two kids who were really into her and Chris sort of went along with it at first. Then, even after he'd gone out with Billie a couple of times, he was still flirting with girls and chatting them up the way he always had done.'

Rise and shine. Chris makes sure he doesn't miss the start time for his first Radio 1 Breakfast Show. Note the specially prepared 'just out of bed' look

Chris's Warrington girlfriend Alison Ward. She is seen here with daughter Jade, who was fathered by Chris in 1987. He soon left both mother and daughter

Chris managed to fit in a dalliance with one-time soap queen Anna Friel in 2000

**Playing tonsil tennis with Boddingtons girl
and Northern beauty Melanie Sykes**

Did she? Didn't she? Geri Halliwell emerges from Chris's place at the height of the rumours of the pair's romance in 1999. She is with a little shitzu. Chris stays inside

Chris and long-term girlfriend Suzi Aplin, who looks like she might catch her death of cold

**A day at the races with
former girlfriend Rachel
Tatton-Brown**

Mr and Mrs Evans enjoy one of their many holidays. But wherever they've been the paparazzi are never far behind

Front page news. The ultimate 2001 tabloid sizzler as the multi-millionnaire mogul marries the teenage pop sensation

Tuesday May 8 2001

The Mirror

www.mirror.co.uk

INSIDE

M

10-PAGE SECTION YOU MUST READ

32

Viva Love Vegas

Chris Evans weds Billie .. and it costs £235

FULL STORY AND PICTURES
PAGES 2 AND 3

JUNE 7

WE'RE OFF!

Blair to call June 7 General Election today

By PAUL GILFEATHER, Whitehall Editor

TONY BLAIR will today name June 7 as the general election date, triggering the countdown to Labour's historic second term in power.

The Prime Minister will meet the Queen at Buckingham Palace at the end of the week.

FULL STORY: PAGE 8

Nice work if you can get it. Chris's love of golf led him to create *Tee Time*, a TV show where he could fly round the world and swing a club on the world's best golf courses – at someone else's expense

It was the morning after Billie's *Top Of The Pops* appearance that things started to turn totally surreal. John Webster had been staying with Chris at his Belgravia home after the previous night's shenanigans. Not for the first time, Chris failed to make his radio show, but this particular Friday was about to take a dramatic twist. At 9.30am, Chris announced he had had an idea and took Webster down to car dealership HR Owen in Fulham, where Evans told a rather bemused salesman that he needed a Ferrari – to go! A couple of hours later, and £105,250 lighter (the car cost £105,000, and the red roses and balloons that were strewn all over the interior added the extra £250) Chris knocked on the door of Billie's flat in north west London, handing her an envelope containing the car keys. Billie had just woken up and was completely bemused, as Evans and Webster walked off laughing.

'It's all a bit weird and I don't really know what's going on,' the singer mused, later the same day. 'The car's lovely and it's in safe hands, but I'm just trying to get my head around it all. On Wednesday I was a guest on Chris's show. On Thursday night a few of us went for a drink with Chris and some friends. Then on Friday he gave me the car. It's like something out of a film. I can't even drive.' This was true: Evans had neglected to investigate this facet of the young girl whom he already admitted he was 'completely besotted' with.

This time around, nobody in the media knew exactly what was going on in Chris's head. Was it simply another publicity stunt for a young pop stunner's new single? Was he genuinely interested in this girl? Had he gone completely potty? Tongues were wagging furiously, especially when Billie failed to turn up as planned for the British Comedy Awards in London on the Saturday night. Presenter Jonathan Ross, a man who knows a thing or two about Chris's eccentricities, was merciless in his lampooning. 'Would you fuck Chris Evans for a Ferrari?' he asked fellow presenter Jamie Theakston. 'I don't know,' Theakston replied. 'But apparently he only got Geri Halliwell a Ford Mondeo!' The audience was in hysterics, but the following day Chris and Billie were together again and cruising the roads around Hascombe Court in Chris's own Ferrari. Making no attempt to be discreet, the pair had a passionate embrace in front of drinkers outside the Harrow pub in Compton before Billie headed off for London in a limo that had been parked nearby.

'I met Billie a few times,' says Jamie Broadbent. 'And she was a lovely girl, far too nice for Chris, I thought. She was very level-headed and seemed to take everything that was happening in her stride. She could have been a real prima donna, given the fact that she'd been to stage school and now all this was going on. Maybe she was used to being told what to do, because she'd been in the entertainment business since she was so young. Maybe that was why she and Chris got on so well.'

Kim Dolphin, the mother of Billie's former on-off boyfriend Richie Neville, was unimpressed by Evans's behaviour, commenting, 'He should know better than to do this to Billie. She's a naïve young girl and he's a 34-year-old man. He's gone overboard and is out of order.' The problem for poor Mrs Dolphin, however, was that Billie herself didn't seem to have read the script that stated she should be outraged by all the attention Chris was lavishing on her. On the contrary, she seemed to be absolutely enthralled by this older man and his nutty behaviour.

There was a school of thought building that Chris Evans was losing his marbles, and on Christmas Eve, 2000, he gave an extraordinary interview to the *News Of The World* that appeared to support this analysis. Evans declared that he had decided to give away almost all of his vast fortune. '£5m is enough for anyone,' he explained. 'I've discussed it with my accountant and, after tax, I'll be able to give away £46m. To have that amount of money is obscene. No one person needs that much. I'll keep a little for myself, but the rest will go.' Evans then went further still, claiming that all his future earnings would go to charity: 'That's a great incentive to go to work.' Had the love vibes turned his brain to mush? Did he *really* mean what he was saying? Were he and Billie seriously thinking about making a go of things? Only Chris Evans could have ended the year by eclipsing the start that had seen him make £75m in one fell swoop …

On New Year's Eve 2000, it seemed at least one confirmed party animal was finally mellowing out. Flying back into Heathrow from

Madeira with Billie on his arm, Chris Evans appeared oblivious to the hootenanny potential of the last night of the year. 'We've had a lovely time,' he cooed to waiting reporters, before hastily adding 'We're going to go out with some pals later.' Dressed in jeans and a jumper, Billie left all the talking to her man, other than confirming that she had, indeed, had a great time. It certainly looked that way the following morning, when the *Sun* ran a story headlined 'Double Bed They Didn't Have Sex In'. The story revealed that the couple had stayed in the Madeira Savoy's top-of-the-range honeymoon suite, Room 317, which – unsurprisingly – was equipped with just the one bed.

Chris freely admitted they had shared the room, but in a rare display of chivalry, he insisted that he and Billie had been doing nothing but 'snogging each other's lips off.' And the ever-prurient *Sun*'s 'evidence' offered that something more carnal had been going on – sheets from the bed thrown on the floor along-side towels and bathrobes following the couple's departure – was flimsy, to say the least. If something more intimate than a snogging marathon had been going on during the five-day break, then neither Chris nor Billie was about to admit it. Maybe, this time, the sinner really *was* turning saint ...

18 That's What Friends Are For

The date: January 3, 2001. Chris Evans is enjoying a lazy holiday season day in a comfy little house he has nicknamed 'Christmas Cottage'. For the first time in ages, he is not particularly thinking about work, and is relaxing in the company of the woman he seems certain he loves and surrounded by people he cares about.

A friend of Evans, Debbie Curran, is trying her level best to beat Chris and Billie at the board game Othello, while Debbie's mum Philomena potters about in the kitchen, fussing over the preparation of Irish stew. Love-struck by her new partner she may be, but occasionally Billie's attention still wanders away from both her boyfriend's gaze and the game she's playing, so that she can sneak a crafty peek at *EastEnders* on the telly. She doesn't care that Chris hasn't got a clue who half the characters are any more. After all, he's 16 years older than her, so what do you expect? That only makes him all the more endearing to her … as does the fact that her multi-millionaire man has chosen to spend a peaceful day with friends in the gatekeeper's cottage of his estate when he could be lording it up in Hascombe Court. He is the mansion's sole owner, after all. Yet the cottage is a suitable location for what is developing into a day of friendship and intimacy.

However, tension lies in the air around this apparently happy scene. It's visible in Philomena's face as she stirs the stew in the kitchen, in Chris's eyes as he teases 16-year-old Debbie about something or other, and in Billie's as she glances at her man every now and again. In fact, the only person present who doesn't seem to have something bothering her is Debbie Curran, as she laughs and jokes with her mum and her superstar friends ... which is surprising, given that Debbie is the only person enjoying herself here today who also happens to be very seriously ill.

Just two days earlier, on New Year's Day, Chris had visited Debbie at London's Royal Brompton Hospital. This wasn't easy for him; he'd developed a phobia of hospitals after the death of his dad all those years ago. In fact, he hadn't dared go into a single one until cystic fibrosis sufferer Debbie had come into his life. Debbie, originally from Claremorris in County Mayo but now of Denham, Buckinghamshire, had met Evans the previous May. The Make A Wish Foundation, a charity dedicated to making sick children's dreams come true, had organised a visit for her to the set of *TFI Friday*. Debbie and Chris Evans had hit it off and become unlikely pals.

As Debbie's mum, Philomena, says: 'I think the Make A Wish people thought it was quite an unusual request from a young girl. Most of them wanted to meet the Spice Girls, or something like that. Yet Chris turned out to be really great with Debbie. He brought her on the show and he was very funny.'

At the time, Debbie was in desperate need of a heart and lung transplant, and as her condition had deteriorated she'd been forced to move into hospital permanently. Evans was hugely supportive during her stay at the Royal Brompton, sending cars for her so that she could come to Virgin to watch him present his radio show and even going on the daytime TV programme *This Morning* with Richard and Judy alongside her to appeal for an organ donor. As it became more difficult for Debbie to leave the hospital, Chris would visit her every morning after his radio show to make her laugh and keep her spirits up. He was even there on New Year's Day to help Debbie see in 2001, and when he finally left her side to head down to Wiltshire to spend time with Billie's mum and dad, Paul and Mandy, he revealed that he was to match the £50,000 donated by *Mirror* newspaper readers to the Association of Children's Hospices and The Rainbow Trust children's charity. 'I've been inspired by my young friend Debbie to campaign for people to carry donor cards,' he explained. He was further inspired to invite Debbie and her mum to Christmas Cottage with him.

In the early hours of January 4, transplant surgeon Dr Magdi Yacoub operated on Debbie Curran. Having been woken by the phone ringing with the news that a 12-year-old girl named Natalie Brown who wanted her organs to be donated had died of meningitis, and that Debbie's operation was finally going ahead, Chris jumped in his car. He dashed to the Royal Brompton, where Debbie had returned at the end of the previous night, held her hand and blew her a kiss as she was wheeled into the operating theatre to begin the surgery. Though only scheduled to last some eight hours, the operation would take the entire day.

Seeing somebody involved in a life-or-death struggle right in front of his eyes clearly had an effect on Evans. 'If she can put up with this for 16 years,' he said, 'the least I can do is visit for a couple of hours.' Perhaps even more tellingly, he explained: 'I don't really have a purpose in life. I just earn ridiculously embarrassing amounts of money and have a wonderful, wonderful life.' It looked like the man who many would have willingly dismissed as an arrogant, loudmouthed idiot really did have hidden depths. Maybe the press – who had constantly played up to Chris's laddish image, lampooned it even – had conveniently ignored the kinder and gentler side of his nature. Or maybe he was just growing up.

Whatever. Nearer to home, there was no lack of interest in both Chris's mental state and his love affair, as people finally began to entertain the notion that his new fling was not just a contrived publicity stunt. There was even an atmosphere bordering on disappointment within certain sections of the media, who were desperate to be proved right in their initial, firmly-held belief that The Billie And Chris Show was just another of Evans's well-documented infatuations. Remember Kim Wilde? Melanie Sykes? *The knitting girl?*

However, somebody who definitely didn't believe that this

was just another dalliance was Evans's mate and former Ginger MD Simon Morris. 'We used to talk about looking for love, how it was something that he really wanted to find,' he explains. 'He always wanted to be in love with someone. He always envied that I loved my wife, Helen, and was definitely looking for something that would last. I actually met Chris by chance in London on the day that he bought Billie the Ferrari. It was up by Baker Street, by my company's head office. I was standing on the corner when I noticed this guy on a moped had pulled up alongside me. The visor came up and I realised that it was Chris. He had been driving around the West End on his own, quite obviously high on life. He took his helmet off and simply said, "Si, I've found my Helen".'

Inevitably, rumours began to circulate that Chris had already asked Billie to marry him. Inevitably, they were premature. A typically secret 'source' was supposed to have confided in the *News Of The World's* Rav Singh that 'Chris has asked her to marry him, but Billie hasn't said "yes" or "no".' Even for the notoriously impetuous Evans, though, this would be going some. The couple had been dating for a mere 25 days. During the media circus, Evans continued to visit Debbie Curran. Debbie's gran, Chrissie Mullan, revealed that Evans had been to the Royal Brompton every single day since her operation, and she was convinced the visits were helping Debbie to recover. 'Chris Evans is a pure angel,' said Mrs Mullan, a rare utterance indeed.

Mrs Mullan's opinion was challenged somewhat a mere two days later, when a BBC documentary *Walking With Disc Jockeys*, aired as part of their *Blood On The Carpet* series, raked over the embers of Chris's turbulent last few days at Radio 1 once again, depicting him as a monstrous ego running wild and out of control. Simon Morris, for one, rejects this opinion.

'Chris could be hard when he was working, but that was because he knew what he was doing and he set high standards,' he says. 'He would have a go at anyone who wasn't cutting it – even me. I remember when I was playing "The Man Who Knows What's Going On" on *TFI* – a non-speaking role, very taxing – and all I had to do was look into one camera and nod, then look into another camera, then shake my head or whatever. I was looking for the little red light on top of different cameras, and I kept ballsing it up and getting it wrong, and he lost it. He said, "Fucking hell, Simon. It's fucking *simple*. It's just nodding into the camera! Can't you just get it fucking right?" But that sort of thing is only natural, the kind of thing that happens a million times a day on every TV studio floor in the country.'

Phil Mount, who was on the shop floor at *TFI* and as such might have expected to be on the end of a tongue-lashing, shares this view. 'Chris was certainly never horrible to me,' he says. 'As far as I could see, everyone had a great time working with him. No doubt some people were bawled out, but you have to be like that sometimes to get the results. I'm sure there were some right ding-dongs behind closed doors, and I did see some pretty animated stuff behind the glass when he was in meetings in his office. But that happens in live TV. Chris was no worse than anybody else.'

The miracle may be that it's a miracle Chris Evans could keep any sense of perspective at all, when respected broadsheet journalists such as Chrissy Iley were spending a thousand words dissecting his new relationship, which is what Ms Iley did in *The Scotsman* on January 20. Iley was broadly sympathetic as she attacked the prurient nature of the media interest in the romance ('He's being treated as if he's some kind of paedophile for dating her ...'), but there were enough negatives in the piece about Evans's 'serial monogamy' problem to make him spit out his coffee in moral indignation when he read it. However, Evans may have realised his own personal life was not that difficult a week later, on January 27, when Debbie Curran died.

She passed away just over three weeks after her 18-hour operation, since when she had remained heavily sedated and asleep until her body finally rejected the organs. Chris and Billie were heartbroken at the loss of their young friend and immediately made plans to fly to Ireland, where Debbie was to be taken home to be buried in Kilmane. Debbie's mum Philomena described the funeral as 'amazing' as mourners came from far and wide to pay their last respects. Many of the staff that had cared for her at the

Royal Brompton were in attendance, and even parents of other children who'd shared a ward with her made the journey.

Debbie had written a book of poems that her mum found in her bedroom after she died. 'Some of these were read at the service and brought tears to our eyes,' said Philomena. Certainly Chris was deeply upset by the occasion, and openly cried at Debbie's graveside before moving on to Murphy's Pub for the wake with the rest of the mourners. Chris kissed and hugged Philomena as he left. 'She was such a lovely and brave girl,' he said. 'This is such a sad day for everyone. I will never forget her.' The Make A Wish Foundation agreed to print the book of poems as a final tribute.

If Chris Evans's personal life was darkened by this tragedy, by January it was also clear that things were not well at Virgin. On the day that he and Billie flew to Ireland for Debbie Curran's funeral, Chris's morning show had a message for the listeners whose significance may have been lost on most of them. After livening up the airwaves with a blast of The Jam's 1979 hit 'Eton Rifles', Evans added: 'You'll be hearing a lot more songs like that.' This was an on-air admission that Virgin had to change its music policy.

The station's Chief Executive, John Pearson, confirmed that the move was designed to differentiate Virgin from its competitors, particularly the London-based stations Heart and Capital. With its share of national listeners falling half-a-percent (down from 2.2% to 1.7%), there was clearly concern that Virgin was slipping, and Pearson's decision to play more of what he called 'heritage acts' while jettisoning pop staples such as All Saints, Ronan Keating and Craig David was either bold or foolhardy.

Yet Pearson was prepared to go further. Even crossover acts such as Robbie Williams, Texas and the Corrs – artists who could be construed as pop, but who still retained some credibility with the more serious music lover – were to be shown the door. It was a radical change, instigated as a response to research the station had conducted with its core audience (mainly men aged from 20 – 40), which had shown that sixty-five percent of them preferred music from the 1970s to the

1990s, rather than contemporary chart music. 'Our audience figures have started to plateau,' said Pearson, clearly a man who was fond of his marketing-speak. He went on to stress that Chris Evans was fully behind the changes. 'The music we play is the music he likes,' he claimed, a tad disingenuously.

This major shift in programming policy was to have an equally large impact on Virgin's – and Chris Evans's – fortunes, but that morning the breakfast show's listenership were more intrigued by a casual comment tossed off by Evans during the show. During a section where he'd asked the listeners to phone in and list his former girlfriends who'd since tied the knot, one caller offered up Zoë Ball, who had since married DJ Norman Cook, better known as Fatboy Slim, and had recently given birth to a baby boy, Woody. 'Oh yes, Zoë. That was in the toilets of Harvey Nicks,' Chris blurted out. 'It was great,' he added cheekily, leaving people in no doubt as to what he reckoned had happened in the posh loos.

Zoë had already admitted to having kissed Evans as long ago as 1997 (at a Downing Street reception, of all places). She had been equally happy to recount that Chris had gallantly dubbed her 'Slapper of '97'. 'Probably because I snogged him,' she added, helpfully. 'It was great fun.' Ball's agent, Vivienne Clure, failed to see the funny side of Evans's implication that he had got well beyond a snog with Zoë. 'God, he doesn't half talk a load of bull,' she responded. 'Chris has obviously got a very big imagination, and a very small something else.' Zoë remained resolutely tight-lipped on the subject of sex with Chris Evans, only breaking her silence in an interview with *Heat* the following month, wherein she made it perfectly clear that there was now little love lost between the former friends. 'I snogged him, but didn't shag him,' she explained, before claiming that the pair had fallen out when Evans failed to show up at her wedding to Norman Cook. 'He said us getting married was a publicity stunt,' she sneered.

What Billie would have made of the light-hearted entertainment being manufactured out of her 'love-smitten' new boyfriend's former conquests – on her 'love-smitten' boyfriend's very own radio show – is hard to imagine. But given the truly frightening ordeal she was about to face, she probably couldn't have cared less about such childish horseplay.

19 Somebody's Watching Me

'Why did you give me such a dirty look from the corner of your eye? You are a stuck-up, snooty bitch, an arrogant spoilt brat.'

On Monday February 5, 2001, the trial of 32-year-old Juliet Peters began at Blackfriars Crown Court in London. Unemployed Peters, from the city's Canning Town area, was accused on five counts of threatening to kill Billie Piper, and four of threatening to kill her parents. She denied all the charges. Billie arrived in court with her mum and dad (no Chris Evans, however) wearing brown hipsters and a black top, but didn't give any evidence on the first day. Instead, she sat and listened as details of the frightening messages she and her family had received from August 14 – 25, 2000, were revealed.

Peters was accused by prosecutor Mark Aldred of having become obsessed with Billie after she'd been in the audience at an edition of Channel 5's *Pepsi Chart Show* that Billie had presented in May of the previous year. A few days later, while watching a video of the show, some of Peters' friends apparently suggested that Billie had given her 'a sly, dirty look.' Peters had allegedly thought about the remark for a week, getting more and more worked up, before finally writing a furious letter to Billie's fan club. The note was signed 'Yours angrily, J Peters'.

The letter's content was so reminiscent of a *Monty Python* 'Mr Angry' sketch that nobody initially believed it had been written in all seriousness. However, Peters' anger deepened when she received no reply to her note, and she left an unlucky 13 messages on the answerphone at Billie's fan club. The first one ranted: 'Billie Piper is a fucking cow and a fucking whore that needs cutting up into little pieces. She can sing and dance, but she's a bitch and she's going to die.'

Unbelievably, as the bile-filled messages piled up, they got even more graphic. 'She needs her head kicked in and she needs cutting up into little pieces, where her head will be in the north of England and her body in the south in a forest somewhere,' promised one. 'Billie Piper is a bloody pig and I'm going to kill her parents,' railed another. 'I see them out shopping all the time. They are going to get their heads cut off very soon. The silly cow is a skinny bitch and she's going to be dead.' Another declared: 'Billie Piper's head needs cutting off. She needs decapitating. She needs killing. She needs her body to be set on fire and burnt to cinders where she's banished from our screens so we don't have to suffer her any more.' The most disturbing message of all simply stated: 'Next time she appears on stage, she's going to be shot dead.'

The jury were told that police had traced the first five phone calls to Peters' flat, while one of the later calls was found to have been made from a nearby phone box. When the police then visited the flat in question on August 30, Peters was arrested and cautioned and her home was searched. A draft of the initial fan club letter was found in a cardboard box in her bedroom.

On the second day of the trial, Billie herself gave evidence. On the stand for twenty minutes, she said of the messages: 'They were just horrific. I couldn't understand why anybody would want to say these things. I have done nothing personally. I had no intentions of upsetting anyone and it just seemed very bizarre and it just made me cry.'

Explaining that she had been away working in Canada at the time the calls were made, Billie further explained: 'They were just awful, the worst I ever, ever had listened to, quite scary. I didn't know whether to go out or stay in.' Tom MacKinnon, defending, asked if Billie had ever received abusive mail in the past and she agreed that she had, mainly from fans of her then-boyfriend Richie Neville. Then MacKinnon turned his attentions to Chris Evans, asking Billie's mum, Mandy: 'When Billie is given a £105,000 car by the television presenter and disc jockey Chris Evans and does not hold a driving licence, do you agree the press will give it attention?' This attempt to suggest that Piper should expect intrusion into her life, however, seemed somewhat clumsy and misguided.

Juliet Peters claimed the calls were simply a joke. 'I didn't intend to harm anyone,' she said. 'I had no intention of someone listening to the answer machine and taking the threats seriously.' However, on the trial's final day, Mark Aldred suggested that Ms Peters *had* intended her threats to be taken seriously, given that she'd written each message out before making the call and had clearly then tried to cover up the fact that she was responsible.

Tom MacKinnon echoed his client by arguing that the calls were merely a 'bad joke of the highest order' and 'wild threats that no-one in their right mind could believe.' Nevertheless, Juliet Peters was found guilty of threatening to kill Billie Piper, with the jury further recommending that she should receive psychiatric help. Judge Brian Pryor, QC, adjourned sentencing until March 2 to await psychiatric reports. Billie herself was not in court to hear the verdict, but Detective Constable Victoria Merron, who had first arrested Peters at her flat, praised the singer for deciding to give evidence, saying she felt it would help to deter similar stalkers in future. Piper gave much of the credit for her fortitude to her partner. Calling Chris her 'rock', she said: 'I don't think I could have gone through the court case without his support.' For Billie, at least, this particular nightmare appeared to be finally over.

However, whether down to an understandable sense of relief or something else entirely, just a week after the jury reached its verdict, Billie was making headlines again ... this time, about her collapse following an all-day drinking session with Chris. Friday February 16 had begun at the couple's friend, Aldo Zilli's, Zilli Fish Too restaurant in London's West End, and had also taken in the trendy Groucho Club, as well as the Midas Touch bar next door to Virgin Radio. A friend reported that Billie had downed about ten halves of lager, and Chris a similar number of pints, when she lost her balance and fell over in the Midas Touch.

Evans took her a glass of water and Billie laughed the incident off, saying she'd done nothing more than trip over her handbag. However, this wasn't the first time that she had collapsed very publicly. Eight months earlier, a similar incident at Covent Garden's Bar 38 had been blamed on a kidney infection. But whatever the reasons behind this latest collapse, it emerged two days later that it was definitely no publicity stunt. Vital Publicity, who had been handling Billie's PR for the previous three years, had already stopped acting on her behalf the previous week. 'We feel we got as far as we could with her,' said her former publicist Dave Pittman. 'I wouldn't want to comment about concerns surrounding Billie.' Well if Dave Pittman didn't want to comment, there were plenty of others more than willing to do so.

'I have difficulty seeing how someone in early middle age can have anything in common with a teenager,' said Kate Mulvey in the *Daily Express*. 'What is wrong with Billie Piper?' questioned Rachel Dobson in the *Daily Star*. 'From girl-next-door cute pop star with a glittering future ahead of her, the 18-year-old appears to have changed into a grunge rock chick with a dangerous taste for life in the fast lane.' Even former boyfriend Richie Neville's mum, Kim Dolphin, got in on the act again, saying: 'She has changed completely since she met Chris Evans. I really am tempted to ring Billie and ask if she is all right.' Dolphin claimed that she had only ever seen Billie drunk once before, at Richie's 21st birthday party, and that she used to be scared of what her mum would say if she even heard that she'd been the worse for wear. And Dolphin was also quick to have a dig at Evans, claiming: 'If she'd gone off with a real hunk, Richie might have understood. But Chris Evans is hardly that.'

Given the latest tabloid furore, Chris and Billie decided to make themselves scarce the following week, with a quick jaunt to the sun to forget about things, first in Greece for a short time and then at the Byblos Hotel ('which specialises in healthy breaks for people who have overdosed on the jet-set lifestyle,') on the Costa del Sol. And if the unwanted attentions and career difficulties were affecting the couple, they certainly weren't showing it, kissing and canoodling in the sun as though they hadn't a care in the world, and taking relaxing health therapies in the hotel spa complex. Yet maybe they *were* taking things easier: Chris was sticking to soft drinks, and only supping the occasional beer.

Every celebrity faces the dilemma that they need the oxygen of publicity for their fame to survive, yet they can't simply turn it off at the tap when it suits them. And with the content of Chris's radio show often deliberately created out of his own wild lifestyle, there was no chance that the media would leave him alone when he himself was gaining such mileage out of what he was getting up to. A perfect case in point was the tale he enthusiastically relayed on the radio on his first day back after his break.

Explaining to Virgin listeners up and down the land that he'd decided to drive his green Jaguar XJ8 convertible over to Paris before starting his winter sun break, Evans then revealed that he'd flown directly back into Britain from the Costa del Sol and so needed someone to pick up his motor at Charles De Gaulle airport. Offering to pay travel, accommodation and £500 to anyone who fancied going over to bring the car back for him, he helpfully explained that the car's keys were hidden on top of the offside rear wheel. A listener, Andy from Reading, gamely took up the challenge.

It transpired that Evans's original idea had been for a friend to chauffeur the car back, but then the notion of putting the job up for grabs on air came to him on the spur of the moment. A bad idea, it transpired. By the time the gallant Andy had schlepped over the channel and made his way to the car park in question, the Jag was nowhere to be found. To add insult to injury, the poor guy was stopped by security and taken in for questioning on suspicion of theft. Andy's consolation prize of an invitation to the studio to meet Evans and his team can hardly have seemed too enthralling, but at least Chris wasn't crying over spilt milk. 'He thinks someone might have moved it to a safer place,' said a spokesman. Well ... not exactly. The car had been stolen. 'Chris knows he won't be able to claim on the insurance,' said the spokesman just moments later. But how many people could laugh off the loss of a £60,000 car so easily?

Even if Evans was chuckling, the laugh wasn't to last long. The next day, Friday March 2, saw Juliet Peters up for sentencing following psychiatric reports. To general astonishment, she was freed. Judge Bryan Prior claimed there would be no real purpose served in jailing Peters, and handed down an 18-month suspended sentence together with a two-year supervision order with probation officers designated to care for her. Billie and Chris took small comfort from Peters' lawyer's claim that his client was ashamed of her behaviour, and immediately started reviewing their security arrangements. Yet far from proving to be the most traumatic event of 2001, Billie's court case eventually proved to be no more than a precursor to something that was even more stressful and acrimonious later in the year.

It seemed as if events beyond their control were conspiring to put pressure on Chris and Billie's relationship. Chris's former wife Carol McGiffen, now presenting *Live Talk* on ITV, did her best to sour the mood by shocking viewers – and, no doubt, her former husband – by announcing on air: 'I've had an abortion. I've had two, in fact. I'm not proud of it, but it happens. The first one I had, the guy went a bit loopy. The second bloke, I didn't even tell him.' McGiffen didn't reveal whether Evans was one of the two men involved.

Then at the end of the month, Billie's manager Nicki Chapman, who had recently found fame as one of the judges on the hugely successful *Popstars* TV show, unceremoniously dumped her former charge. A source claimed that it was down to the relationship with Evans, who had 'started poking his nose in where it's not needed.' Maybe, but a more likely reason for the unsentimental Chapman to have ended the association would have been the fact that Billie's *Walk of Life* album and single had disappointed commercially, and a raft of her own TV commitments made it unappealing to continue putting any effort into an artist she would have seen as a fading star. When asked to discuss the split, Chapman would only comment:

'When I stopped working with Billie I always said I wouldn't discuss her publicly, as when you manage someone there is always an element of trust. We're still friends, and I want it to stay that way. If I do an interview, however glowing, the papers will then expect me to comment on her each time something happens in her life.'

Billie's career may have been faltering but if it was worrying her she was trying not to let it show and joined Chris on yet another boozing session, this time to celebrate his 35th birthday. Evans being Evans, the celebrations couldn't be the usual 'down the pub after work on the big day' kind of thing. No, it had to be a 'down the pub after work four days *before* the big day' kind of thing, as he, Billie and another friend ended up guzzling £300 bottles of champagne in the Met Bar.

The ensuing ferocious hangover meant Evans missed the start of his radio show, arriving at 7.45am for the 6am broadcast. His team had manfully held the fort and Evans praised them, saying: 'You all seem to get on so much better when I'm not here.' The incident may have been reminiscent of the old Radio 1 days, but nobody could have predicted that work no-shows would become such a crucial issue within the next three months.

If Virgin bosses were privately seething, at least Evans's girlfriend wasn't. Chris's friend John Webster asserts that Billie paid for seven lap-dancers to perform for her man at Stringfellow's as a birthday present. Such unusual loving devotion didn't bother the media prophets of doom, who were too preoccupied with the question of whether Billie and Chris could actually stay the course as an item to care about the actual details of the relationship. 'Even if there's a wedding, I wouldn't bet on too many anniversaries,' opined an agony aunt. A 'body language specialist' found fault with the fact that in one picture 'their bodies are not in contact and they aren't snuggling up to each other in a genuinely warm and affectionate way'. Even the stars were apparently ranged against them: a psychic, De'ana Dimonte, predicted, 'I have a strong feeling they'll separate by July.'

For their part, Billie and Chris had a funny way of showing that things were all going wrong and they were about to split up.

Evans began his 36th year by adding another property to the couple's expanding portfolio. Not content with the £3.5 million flat in Belgravia and the Edwardian estate at Hascombe Court, Evans snapped up a 40-room, yellow-brick Victorian corner house in Chelsea's Gilston Road for around £7m. No 10 was a spectacular home, spread over three floors, with a singular tower perched right at the top of the property and a particularly pleasant garden.

Just a quick look at the couple's new neighbours, who included Liz Hurley, Rowan Atkinson and David Bowie, immediately showed that the area known as The Boltons is a haven for super-rich show business stars, which should have made Billie and Chris feel right at home. And in another move which would have upset the harbingers of doom for the duo, Billie announced that she would be taking the summer off from her pop career to spend more time with her boyfriend and that her record company, Virgin, had agreed to postpone the release of her new single, 'The Tide Is High'.

By mid-April, the media chatter had swung from declaring that Evans and Piper would never last to speculating on whether they were poised to tie the knot. 'Yes, she will,' said Ruth Hilton in the *Daily Express*, revealing that Billie had proposed to Chris during a trip to Paris earlier in the month as part of those ongoing 35th birthday celebrations. While there was no official confirmation of an engagement as the couple jetted off for yet another break, this time in the Algarve, it seemed that everyone was prepared to accept there would definitely be a wedding. There was even 'confirmation' in the tabloids that the nuptials would take place the coming August at Hascombe, though this information seemed to be usurped by news that the couple had been making enquiries at Chelsea Registry Office. Even Chris's former wife, Carol McGiffen, who had been highly sceptical of his dalliance with Geri Halliwell, was happy to accept that he was about to wed again, although perhaps not for the most altruistic of reasons.

'I hope they will get married,' she said. 'Only because I'm sick of people phoning me up all the time whenever Chris does anything, and if they get hitched, then everyone will leave me alone.' She also gave an interesting, incidental insight into the distinctly un-George Clooney-like Evans's continued success with women. 'He gets women under his spell,' she opined. 'I certainly fell for it and so have a lot of other people.'

Meanwhile, during their holiday at the Dona Felipa hotel in the Algarve's Vale de Lobo, the couple were not to be drawn on whether or not they really, truly were engaged. Possibly they were attempting to lie low as the media yet again attempted to scratch and sniff around their private life. Yet they could hardly have expected privacy, after the DJ had announced details of their destination live on air. Furthermore, if love really was in the air, Chris Evans's choice of travelling companions was an unusual one.

Firstly, this was no romantic break for two; Chris's breakfast show producer Chris Gillett and his girlfriend Zara were also along for the ride. Then, after flying out to the resort before his girlfriend, Chris kept Billie waiting for over half-an-hour at Faro Airport before finally picking her up in a hired green Vauxhall Omega. The following day he left his girlfriend at the hotel, smoking cigarettes and reading *Hello!* magazine, while he spent hours playing golf. Then, on the last day of their short break, Evans again headed for the links, arriving back at the hotel barely an hour before packing up ready to leave. And as if this wasn't bad enough, it appeared that Chris wore the very same hat and the same pair of shorts for all three days of the break!

Not that Billie seemed terribly offended by her boyfriend's behaviour. According to one onlooker: 'Chris seemed very much in love with her, and they looked like they go very well together. She didn't mind at all that he was off playing golf and boozing it up with his pals.'

It was only after keeping everyone in suspense for over a week that Evans 'came clean' and confessed that he and Billie weren't engaged at all. Talking on air with Holly Samos, Evans chided his sidekick with the comment: 'You know better than anybody else not to believe what you read in the paper. When I came back I was dumbfounded that you all said "Oh, you're getting married."' However, as is usual with Chris Evans, things weren't exactly what they seemed ...

20 Let's Get Married

The first that Chris's close friend and reporter on his Virgin show John Webster heard of it was in a phone call from America on Friday May 4. 'Don't tell anyone, and get to Gatwick for 10.30pm,' was the command. This time, apparently, it was for real. Chris really *was* marrying Billie.

Although nobody was aware of any major problem at the time, it was at this point that the seeds of the breakdown of Chris's relationship with his Virgin bosses appeared to be sown. Chris's agent, Michael Foster, knew about Evans's plans to marry, but didn't tell the station's chief executive John Pearson that he would be leaving the country to do so. Foster later said he believed that his client was 'In shock, in a mess, didn't know how to face the team and couldn't go into the building.' According to Foster this had nothing to do with the pressures of a forthcoming wedding. It was because Chris's relationship with the long-standing breakfast team was starting to disintegrate. 'Chris had felt extremely let down by both John Revell and Dan McGrath, whose corner he had been fighting,' said Foster. But none of this internal friction was public knowledge at the time. Chris had simply been ill when he'd missed his first show on May 1 and after he and Billie flew out to the States that day, Virgin listeners were told the following morning was that Chris was still ill. Though not too ill to make for Palm Springs and start planning his wedding.

The gang that headed out from Gatwick on that Friday night

following Evans's instructions consisted of just four people – Webster, Danny Baker, Chris Gillett and his girlfriend Zara – and they were flying direct to Las Vegas. Not even Chris's mum, Minnie, or Billie's parents, Mandy and Paul, were to attend, though after the event the Pipers said they knew about the plans but hadn't been able to make the wedding anyway because of work commitments and the needs of their three other children. The plan was for Chris and Billie to charter their own private jet from Palm Springs to Vegas, book into the Harrah's Casino hotel, and meet their wedding guests in the town. Webster explained that it was only on the day after his arrival, when he met Chris at the Four Seasons hotel where the party had been booked to stay, that even he was made aware of the exact details and arrangements. 'Chris got out a bottle of champagne and told us they were getting married in one hour,' he said. 'We got changed and went to the chapel.'

The Little Church Of The West looks out of place in the midst of all the tacky glamour, glitz and neon of Vegas. Built out of cedar and redwood, it was designed as a miniature version of a typical Wild West frontier town chapel, an attempt to hark back to the older, simpler days of the pioneering West. Yet for all of its aspirations to connect with a less fussy era, it somehow only manages to come across as chintzy, a bizarre construction which almost seems more fake and disconnected than the extravagant casinos that dominate the skyline.

Maybe that's the point. After all, The Little Church of The West proudly claims its place in history as 'the scene of more celebrity marriages than any other chapel in the world.' Zsa Zsa Gabor, Mickey Rooney and Judy Garland all tied the knot there, and Elvis even used it for his screen wedding with Ann-Margret in *Viva Las Vegas*. The chapel literature fails to address the topic of how many of the couples that got spliced there actually lasted the distance as an item. Chris and Billie probably wouldn't have wanted to know, especially when more recent celebrity marriages there included Bob Geldof and Paula Yates, Richard Gere and Cindy Crawford, Angelina Jolie and Billy Bob Thornton, and also Noel Gallagher and Meg Mathews. Even if you weren't much of a tealeaf gazer you might have found *that* information a little bit too disconcerting.

The wedding package chosen by Chris and Billie cost a measly £250, but nobody could accuse them of scrimping. After all, there were another two standard packages out of the four on offer that were cheaper still, and the one they chose came complete with a teardrop rose bouquet for Billie, a buttonhole for Chris, 10 glossy photos, a video of the service and even a bottle of champagne.

The marriage licence cost £25, the minister's fee was £35 and the organist picked up a tidy £20 for his efforts. And besides, in comparison to his wedding to Carol McGiffen back in 1991, Chris was positively pushing the boat out! When the party turned up for the 6.15pm ceremony, the bride wore a pink sarong and a white cotton shirt together with flip-flops, while the groom looked resplendent in sky blue shirt and beige stripy trousers, topped off with a pair of sunglasses.

Billie Piper and Chris Evans were married by the Reverend James Hamilton in a ceremony lasting just five minutes, in front of a mere six guests, including best man Danny Baker. The music played included Wagner's *Lohengrin* and 'All I Ask Of You' from *The Phantom Of The Opera*. 'I don't think they requested that one, but the organist played it anyway,' said Greg Smith, a helpful church official. 'When Richard Gere married Cindy Crawford they made their own rings out of foil chewing gum wrappers,' he continued. 'But this couple were happy to do it without rings.'

That was because, according to Webster, 'Chris hates jewellery on men *and* women. He's got a real thing about it.' Nevertheless, this distaste didn't dampen proceedings. 'We were all emotional, but there were no tears,' added Webster. 'It was just a really happy occasion.' Certainly Evans seemed ecstatic, swigging from the free bottle of champagne and saying, 'We've done it. Isn't it fantastic?' as he left the chapel and headed for a white stretch limo with Billie.

Evans appeared delighted with his new bride, and almost equally happy that he had successfully managed to avoid news of the wedding being leaked to the UK press, thus preventing a media circus. Chris had even craftily moved the booking for the wedding, originally scheduled for midday, back to the early evening as one final precaution. The party drove up and down the strip toasting the newlyweds with champagne (Dom Perignon, ordered from their hotel at £180 per bottle) and took in some of the city's top casinos, including Treasure Island and The Venetian, before heading out to an airstrip to pick up another private jet bound for Palm Springs, the couple's base in the build-up to their big day.

There was one amusing twist in the tale. As Webster and Danny Baker were shown to their Palm Springs quarters, they were astonished to find that they were being ushered into an absolutely amazing room, complete with four-poster bed, kitchen and outside shower. Of course such luxury would have been more than fine with them, had it not been for the fact that the room appeared to have just the one bed. When Webster enquired about the second bed, it suddenly became apparent that the woman who'd taken them to the room had mistaken them for a celebrating gay couple. After all, Americans had never heard of Evans or Piper, and the names of the happy couple *were* Chris and Billie ...

With Baker safely deposited elsewhere, it was only when Webster peeked into the room's mini-bar and found two bottles of champagne chilling nicely, together with a note which read 'Congratulations on your wedding, Chris and Billie', that he realised he'd inadvertently been left in his mate's bridal suite. And when he let Mr and Mrs Evans know about the mix-up, Webster was surprised to hear that they were quite happy in the room they'd found themselves in, thus leaving Webster as surely the only man ever to have spent the night alone in a bridal suite.

It was only when Virgin Radio made an official announcement of the nuptials live on air at 5.45pm on Monday evening, more than 12 hours after the ceremony had taken place, that anyone in Britain knew the first thing about the quickie wedding. 'We are delighted to formally announce that Chris Evans and Billie Piper have married,' said DJ Nick Abbot. 'The ceremony took place in Las Vegas yesterday at 6.15pm local time with close friends in attendance. Virgin Radio knew of their intention to marry last week, but we were sworn to secrecy. We wish Chris and Billie every happiness and look forward to celebrating with them when Chris returns to the breakfast show next Monday.' Carol McGiffen was less unequivocal. 'I told people I didn't care,' she explained. 'But seeing it all in the papers was a really weird feeling.'

However, while the press focussed on the erstwhile media wildman's new-found domesticity, Evans himself was still thinking about the business of business. In classic non-confrontational style, he also used his time away to deal with his breakfast crew issues and parted company with John Revell, Dan McGrath, Jamie Broadbent and Holly Samos. All of them were removed from the show on the grounds that they weren't pulling their weight. Given the years that they had spent together, it appeared a shabby way to treat them, especially when Evans had once stated 'They've been friends for years, and they're friends first and foremost.'

Jamie Broadbent has a theory as to why Evans suddenly jettisoned his entire breakfast crew. 'John had a house in the country, then Dan moved down there and those two became best mates,' he says. 'They became a close alliance. They drove in together and drove home together and Chris knew they talked about him in the car, and he didn't like that.'

There were other changes afoot, too. While Chris and Billie were still enjoying their honeymoon in Palm Springs, it was announced that Evans's long-time agent Michael Foster would now be handling Billie's career, neatly filling the void left by Nicki Chapman's departure. If the rumours that Chapman had dumped her charge because of her interfering boyfriend were still doing the rounds, then this announcement did nothing to quash them. However, at the same time as he was orchestrating his new wife's career decisions, the idea that Chris was also moving away from constantly putting himself in the spotlight appeared to be gathering pace.

Firstly, there were the indications that Billie could already be pregnant. The couple themselves remained tight-lipped on the subject as they enjoyed a barbecue at home on their return. However, one tabloid claimed: 'News that she's three months gone is all over her old school,' managing to ignore the fact that school gossip is possibly the least reliable source of all. Then came the confirmation that the house in Gilston Road – bought less than two months ago, and never lived in – was up for sale already. Hascombe Court and the Belgravia flat were apparently also to go, to pave the way for a move out to Billie's Wiltshire hometown of Swindon.

However, the most interesting news snippet of all was nestling deep inside the May 21 edition of the *Daily Star*. Indicating that Chris was tiring of his Virgin breakfast show, an insider claimed: 'He just goes through the motions'. The paper suggested that Evans was now more interested in developing new TV shows such as the spin-off of movie box office success *Lock, Stock And Two Smoking Barrels*. This was the first hint of any dissatisfactions with his Virgin Radio gig. He had turned up late after the birthday bender, but this seemed a forgivable crime. There were also rumours that he didn't see eye to eye with chief executive John Pearson, but there was nothing new in Evans having a set-to with the 'suits'. But the *Star* was floating the notion that the station had already lined up Steve Penk, recently poached from rivals Capital, to take over the breakfast slot from Chris.

Chris's public behaviour didn't appear to indicate a yearning for a move out of the limelight or a departure from Virgin. Summoned to appear at Staines Magistrates Court in Surrey after being caught speeding in his R-reg silver Ferrari Maranello as he headed for Hascombe on the A3 bypass at Esher, Evans arrived in court together with Billie on May 29, dressed in a white straw boater, three-quarter length coat, cream trousers and brown sandals. He looked more like he was about to attend a regatta than a court hearing, and his curious wardrobe naturally attracted plenty of attention.

He pitched up at the court with the faithful Webster in tow. The idea was to record Chris's comments before and after proceedings, which would then be aired on his show the following morning. A Virgin spokesman, his tongue presumably firmly planted in his cheek, later claimed: 'Webbo [Webster] is a roving reporter for the show. Chris is not out to mock his court appearance.' (Hence the bizarre clothes, presumably). 'He has shared his experience with his listeners and has made it clear he is very contrite.' Contrite Evans may have been, but that didn't stop the magistrates from quickly realising that this was a time-honoured open-and-shut case. After just ten minutes, they handed down a 56-day driving ban, together with a £600 fine and an order to pay £35 costs.

Chris and Billie handed down a swift 'no comment' of their own when pressed on the pregnancy rumours as they left court, before being driven away in a silver Mercedes with blacked-out windows. On the following day's show, Chris admitted: 'We were quite giggly when we went in. But once I was in the courtroom it was really scary.' On the subject of the hat, he impressively improvised: 'I wore it so I could remove it respectfully.' Unluckily for Chris, a court clerk had ordered him to take the ridiculous thing off his head before entering court. 'She stole my thunder,' he whined.

As June rolled around, Billie and Chris were spotted out guzzling champagne and lager yet again, this time in a Knightsbridge boozer. Consequently, the rumours that Mrs Evans was pregnant began to tail off. After all, if Billie was going to have a baby, surely even her lager-friendly hubby would be stopping his new bride from hitting the booze quite so readily.

Billie's mum certainly didn't appear unduly concerned by her daughter's antics. Claiming that Billie was now one half of a scruffier version of Posh and Becks, Mandy Piper explained that she was happy that Chris was looking after her well and was fine about the couple's hi-octane social life, 'because at least she's surrounded by similar people.' She added the sagacious comment, 'I had hoped Billie might have been able to sit back and get out of the public eye for a while. Of course now she's married to Chris, there's no chance of that.' Certainly there was little chance when Chris was still pulling stunts like asking for permission to land a helicopter on the Town Hall lawn back in Warrington. After all, if you can't drive back home to see your mum because you're banned, what's your average multi-million-aire supposed to do?

Meanwhile, Evans's chequered professional life was about to take yet another spectacular turn. Matthew Bannister has no history of clairvoyance, but a column the former Radio 1 controller wrote for the *Times* of June 9, 2001, betrays a remarkable perspicuity.

In an article slugged with the line, 'Chris Evans must invent a new challenge for himself as a radio broadcaster,' Bannister argued that Evans looked bored and, more worryingly, *sounded* bored on the radio. He speculated that the material comforts that the sale of Ginger had given him, coupled with a seemingly happy marriage, had rubbed the rough edges off the bloke. 'Evans feels he doesn't need to try any more,' claimed Bannister, continuing: 'Evans's best days as a sharp, innovative and controversial broadcaster were when he had something to prove; as an unknown working for £50 per show at London's GLR, re-inventing breakfast TV or reviving the fortunes of Radio 1.' Pointing out that audience ratings for the breakfast show had tumbled at Virgin in the past year, Bannister used the word 'complacent' in reference to his former golden boy, and finally suggested that the DJ needed to 'get out of the broadcasting slow lane.' This was pretty damning stuff from a man who once referred to Evans as having produced, 'the most compelling radio I've ever heard.'

Naturally, Bannister's history with Evans meant that his article could easily be construed as the mutterings of a bad loser. With the benefit of hindsight, this was transparently not the case. Later that same month, the pendulum of Chris Evans's career was to swing one more time.

21 Fight For Your Right (To Party)

It all started – as it so often did, with Chris Evans – with booze. And, on this particular occasion, with girls as well. On Wednesday June 20, Evans presented his breakfast show as usual, and then headed for the pub; this time it was The Grenadier, a boozer near to his Belgravia home. So far, so completely normal.

At this point, events of what happened next differ wildly. One version of events suggests that Chris and Billie had 'a furious row' over his flirting with 'It Girl' Lady Victoria Hervey that ended with Billie leaving the pub in tears. According to Chris's mate John Webster, who turned up ten minutes after the supposed bust-up, nothing of the sort had happened, and Billie was still in the pub, looking perfectly composed and happy to confirm that husband Chris had gone off drinking with his pal, the restaurateur Aldo Zilli.

'Billie and her friend and I all went back to Chris's and chatted, and then went to bed,' Webster reported. 'She was as happy as pie.' However, he seems to have got his wires at least slightly crossed, claiming later that after waiting for Billie to finish a driving lesson that day, he had accompanied both her and Chris to meet up with Aldo at Zilli's restaurant in Soho. After a few drinks, he said, he went back to Chris's flat and fell asleep on the sofa, leaving Evans and Zilli to party the night away.

Whatever the truth, Webster certainly missed the mother of all sessions. This certainly didn't seem like one of Chris's rumoured deceptive affairs, where the alcohol flows freely but rarely down his own neck. The booze list compiled during his marathon stint with Zilli included lager, pink champagne, Guinness, Dom Perignon and white wine – just the kind of cocktail to get the two mates in the mood for a night ogling female flesh in Stringfellow's, in fact. And any inhibitions Chris may have had about being a recognisable face in the lap-dancing club were swept away in a booze-sodden fog.

'He was sitting right at the front of the stage,' a source recounted. 'But he just fell asleep. I don't think the staff knew what to do with him.' After the DJ's impromptu forty winks, Evans and Zilli left Stringfellow's looking the worse for wear and found themselves caught short outside a Moroccan restaurant called Souk. This was arguably not the ideal place for one of London's most recognisable faces to relieve himself, but he chose this option nonetheless. Not to be outdone, Zilli then staggered on for another ten yards before promptly vomiting. The odd couple were so obviously soused that the driver of a cab hailed by Chris refused to take the pair because of the state that Zilli was in. And so the two of them lurched off into the night, now looking for a Chinese restaurant to end the high jinks in.

Anyone who had seen Chris stumbling around London after midnight surely wouldn't have been in the slightest bit surprised when he phoned Virgin Radio at 5.30am the next day to say that he was 'too ill' to go to work. At just half an hour's notice, mid-morning presenter Russ Williams filled in for what turned out to be a mammoth stretch lasting right through until 1pm, the finish time of Williams's own show. 'Chris was poorly,' explained a Virgin spokeswoman. 'If somebody's ill there's nothing you can do about it,' she continued rather, limply.

Webster, who had got up early at Chris's flat and not been able to find his boss, turned up for work himself only to find that Chris wasn't there. 'Apparently, he'd come home from Stringfellow's the worse for wear, went to make himself something to eat and ended up sleeping downstairs,' he said. 'I don't know if Billie even knew he was there.' He certainly knew nothing about any illness, yet this mystery sickness, whatever it was, must have continued all through the day on Thursday, because on Friday Evans's agent Michael Foster called Virgin once again to let the station know that his client wouldn't be turning up for work for the second day running. No doubt this would have made Chris's movements on that last day of the week somewhat difficult for his employers to understand.

With the media camped outside their Belgravia flat, Billie Piper emerged at 8.30am on Friday morning and found herself tackled on the subject of her ailing husband and even rumours that their marriage was already in trouble. 'There's been no major bust-up,' she said. 'Everything's fine. I'm just going to buy Chris breakfast in bed. Thank you for your interest,' she added politely and went off to the nearby Tyler's food hall to stock up on milk, bread, fruit salad, yoghurt, mineral water, tea and coffee.

After breakfast, Chris and Billie re-emerged and walked to a local pub, the Nags Head, where they arrived just before 10.30. One can surmise it wasn't their first visit, as they felt confident enough to climb in through an open window to get a cup of coffee before opening time thirty minutes later. Once the towels were off, an unshaven Evans ordered a pint of lager, quickly followed by cider, Bloody Marys and whiskies with water. Billie opted for three vodka and Red Bulls, then settled down with lemonade. The session lasted for six hours before the pair ran out of money and started a tab.

Now whatever his motivation for this second booze session in three days, Chris Evans is palpably no fool. It is inconceivable that he would have gone to such a public place to drink, knowing that Foster had phoned Virgin to tell them he was sick, and have believed that the media wouldn't see him. Without further explanation, the only conclusion that can be drawn is that Chris wanted people to know he was out drinking – and by definition wanted his Virgin bosses to know it too. But he later denied this in the ensuing court case, saying, 'I didn't know it would embarrass them. I thought it would be more publicity.' He simply must have known, particularly by refusing to answer any journalists' questions about his 'illness', that this would have caused tension between the two parties. The manoeuvre had all the hallmarks of a classic Chris Evans strategy, whereby he manufactures an exit from a job he no longer wants in such a way that allows him to avoid any direct confrontation.

Virgin may have hoped a weekend of recuperation would help their breakfast host get over his mystery illness and report back fit and refreshed on Monday June 25. No – once again, Russ Williams was called upon to fill in. However, if the station bosses Virgin were irritated – possibly furious – with their star turn, then they certainly weren't showing it to the outside world. 'We're concerned about Chris,' said a spokeswoman, on the Monday 'He must have issues he's dealing with and who are we to know what they are?'

Maybe the regulars at the White Horse, near to Hascombe Court, would have been able to shed some light on the matter. After all, Chris and Billie had been in there with a friend that very lunchtime and the absentee DJ had drunk a couple of pints of lager, sitting in full view of everybody, soaking up the sun in the pub's front garden. It's no surprise that, by the end of the day, cracks were starting to show in Virgin's spirited defence of Chris's behaviour. The company's media representative, Charlotte Blenkinsop, who had been so keen to tell the world how loose SMG executives were becoming thanks to Virgin, was now more formal, explaining: 'There are contractual obligations. It's public knowledge that when Chris sold the company there would be certain payments over a period of time. His contract ends in December 2002, so if he were going to renege on the contract, which isn't the case at the moment, then there would be comebacks.' She then added: 'But it is by no means at that stage at the moment.' Evans himself was less willing to talk about the issue. 'This is private property. Clear off,' he told journalists who approached him back home at Hascombe that evening.

This fast-developing real-life soap opera threw up yet another dramatic twist the next day as an astonishing scenario unfolded in the Waitrose supermarket at Godalming. Chris and Billie had apparently decided that now would be the perfect time to do some shopping – for booze. The couple spent twenty minutes filling their trolley before emerging with a handsome haul of alcohol: 24 cans of Fosters, 12 cans of Carlsberg, five bottles of Chardonnay and one bottle of Cabernet Sauvignon. Admittedly, the load had also included Diet Coke, lemonade and even some groceries, all of which was loaded into a white van driven by a friend – Evans, after all, was still banned from being behind the wheel.

Once again Chris and Billie were photographed heading out of the store with the alcohol, and must have been aware that they were being watched. However, this particular brinkmanship was slowly starting to become easier to understand. Evans couldn't really have been unsettled by the arrival at Virgin of Capital golden boy Steve Penk, as he had played a part in recruiting him, but intriguingly, beleaguered Charlotte Blenkinsop refused to reveal what Evans thought of his new work colleague. Her only comment: 'We've got a job to do to build a radio station and Chris was totally aware that Steve was coming.'

This wasn't exactly the greatest seal of approval for the new boy from the star turn. Yet then again, was Chris Evans really the star turn any more? Sara Cox's Radio 1 breakfast show was pulling in 7m listeners, in comparison to Evans's 1.74m. Virgin now had fewer listeners in the London area than Heart FM. Executives admitted that Penk had been earmarked to do a fifth of Chris's shows in the coming year, and word was leaked that the station's new programme director, Paul Jackson, was spitting feathers over Evans's erratic behaviour. Still, Blenkinsop manfully tried to maintain the party line on the illness issue. 'Our position remains the same as it has all week. Chris is off sick. We will be in contact with Chris's agent today – as we are every day – and we will be talking about Chris's state of health and whether he is too sick to work. We are taking things on a day-by-day basis. We still believe he's unwell and aren't expecting him for the next few days.'

Blenkinsop somehow forgot to mention that she had already been spotted trying to talk to Evans in a pub in Knightsbridge while the DJ was drinking whiskies. Nor that the station had been trying to set up a face to face meeting with Evans since the very start of this farcical affair ... without, so far, any success.

However, if it had been a strategic decision by Chris to neither apologise nor explain his absences and actions over the last week, he suddenly changed tack on Wednesday June 27. John Webster later claimed that Virgin were at this point merely *pretending* to be trying to woo Evans back, and that they'd already decided he was going. Webster claims that he was told to get to work early on the Wednesday morning, as Chris would be coming back, although it's unclear why he wouldn't then have phoned his best friend to find out whether or not this rumour was true.

In any case, Webster asserts that he arrived at Virgin's Golden Square HQ early in the morning to be greeted by a large number of press camped outside the building and the sight of security personnel changing the electronic locks on the building's doors. 'I couldn't believe it,' he later reflected. 'GMTV were broadcasting live and there were loads of paparazzi. It was a bloody set-up. All the management had turned up at 5am. If Chris had arrived he wouldn't have been able to get in. They were trying to set Chris up and publicly humiliate him.'

If so, their efforts were in vain. Once again, Chris Evans didn't show up. After visiting the White Horse in Hascombe for a couple of hours before setting out for London, Billie and Chris arrived in Belgravia in a racing green Bentley at 7pm. They were wearing matching floral Hawaiian shirts. Whatever Virgin were up to, it was time for Chris to put his own plan into action. He picked up the phone to talk to the *Mirror* editor Piers Morgan and the *Sun* showbiz editor Dominic Mohan.

Trying to create the biggest possible platform on which to get his message across, Evans's emotional comments were splashed across the first three pages of the following morning's *Mirror* in a piece headlined 'Chris Evans Bombshell: I've Been Offered £3m To Go, But I Just Want The Job I Love. By Talking To *The Mirror* They'll Probably Fire Me'. Written by Morgan himself, the story carried a number of new revelations, foremost among them that Evans had been issued with a formal letter from Virgin owners Scottish Media Group, stating that his recent behaviour had 'humiliated and embarrassed' them. Evans further claimed that he had a doctor willing to confirm that he really was ill, that he wanted to return to do the breakfast show, that he'd been offered a lump sum payment to leave the company (thus forfeiting the third tranche of shares due to him the following January), and that he felt he was being shabbily treated by the executives he had made rich.

'I've been ill and there's a doctor in my kitchen right now who'll confirm that to anyone,' Evans told Morgan. Despite this, no doctor came on the line, nor was there any explanation of the precise nature of Chris's illness. 'I want to come back and do my show today,' he explained. 'But they've said I'm banned and if I try to turn up they will physically stop me broadcasting or even entering the building.' Morgan described Evans's voice as 'shaking with emotion' as he contemptuously dismissed the £3m offer to walk by arguing 'the current share price is £1.60 and it's been as high as £3.75, so with my five million shares they know if I accept this offer they will be saving themselves up to £15m.'

Despite this, the logic behind Chris Evans's arguments appeared to be somewhat muddy. The severance offer would not have been designed to give Evans full parity with the value of his shares, and the argument was irrelevant, given that he himself admitted that, 'By doing this interview with you now I accept that there is a strong chance they'll fire me today. They will say I've breached my contract and I guess I have.' In which case, it could be argued, the DJ really didn't have much of a leg to stand on.

However, the real issue behind the seemingly irrevocable breakdown in relations between the two parties appeared to be revealed when Evans ranted about the culture of the radio station. 'The management have been constantly poking their noses into the day-to-day running,' he claimed. 'They've changed the music policy four times in eighteen months, which anyone in the industry will tell you is a ridiculous thing to do. But, despite that, we were the only show on the station to actually increase our ratings in the last quarter.'

Was this the crux of the issue? Evans's reputation for demanding full creative control is well known and, as he himself admitted,

'Like anyone who runs a fast-moving, populist, creative business, I like to be in charge and do things my way.'

In the *Sun*, the DJ was even more open about the perceived cultural divide between himself and his bosses. 'I was sick to death of the atmosphere at work,' he explained, citing the fact that when he originally bought Virgin, he personally paid for every member of staff to get a bonus of their annual salary as an example of his commitment to the rank and file of the station. 'I wanted it to be a nice place to work and it's not,' he added.

Cynics will naturally observe a recognisable pattern in this behaviour. The entire row is easily viewed as one more example of Chris Evans making an exit in the only way he appears to know how, by causing a stand-up row that left his bosses with no choice but to get rid of him in a manner that still makes him seem like the maverick outsider. Naturally, the City's insatiable need for quoted companies to deliver more and more profit can result in dilution of the creative spirit, while the notion that profits do not simply expand exponentially and that creative products naturally have peaks and troughs doesn't cut much ice with money men. Business journalist James Ashton believes that it was exactly this perhaps inevitabale culture clash that led to the SMG/Evans impasse.

'In buying Virgin, SMG were trying to move into a new market – radio – to build on their TV and publishing arms, which was a good idea at the time,' he says. 'But what they also bought was a very, very volatile personality, and it was difficult to see how SMG's chief executive, Andrew Flanagan – a trained accountant, and a hard-headed businessman who just happens to be in the media – would get along with a maverick personality like Chris Evans. What sort of premium do you pay for Chris Evans and what he as an individual brings to the party? Then how do you tie a highly creative personality like that to a long-term deal? It was always going to be very difficult. Like any media business it's a people business ... and that's where the risk lies.'

In the position in which he found himself after the sale to SMG, with his financial future assured, it was perhaps inevitable that Evans would have little time for the people he'd so often pejoratively referred to as 'suits'. His is not the personality to change easily from being a boss to an employee. However, on this latest occasion, even this master schemer was having trouble finding the moral justification to bolster his actions if he wanted out. 'Now it's all apparently ending because I've had a few days off sick,' he finished, somewhat weakly. 'It's madness.'

Even if he were too stressed to go to work, or did not think that he could present the show in his current state, he knew full well that by publicly flaunting his absences in pubs and bars he was openly, and very publicly, challenging the authority of his bosses. What were SMG supposed to do? Turn a blind eye and risk every other DJ on the station's nose being put out of joint? Allow Evans simply to do what he liked, when he liked? The management would have come across as both spineless and pliable. And, given how the assets sold to them by Evans had performed thus far, they were most likely in no mood for compromise and certainly not for backing down.

'Virgin was always the jewel in the crown,' explains James Ashton. 'Ginger TV was always a little bit extra, and I think there was very little value ascribed to it even at the time of the deal. Today the combined TV business of SMG, its Scottish TV production arm for programmes like *Taggart* and *Rebus*, together with Ginger is only valued at something like £30m to £40m. SMG is still only the sixth largest TV producer in the UK, so that gives you some idea of Ginger's value. But after the SMG purchase of Ginger, *TFI Friday* was cancelled, they did a few things that didn't really take off and they had really high hopes for a programme called *Red Alert With Lulu*, but that didn't come to anything either. So effectively SMG paid for not a lot with the TV business.

'Even on the radio, you could also argue that something needed doing. Virgin was losing listeners even before the deal was done, so you either stuck with the format that Chris had and tried to build the station around him, or you had to try and take it off in a different direction. I think that with such differences of opinion about things like music policy, not to mention him simply getting bored, it was almost inevitable that Chris Evans was going to have to go.'

22 D.I.V.O.R.C.E.

Something would have to give in this Mexican stand-off between Chris Evans and his bosses – and Evans surely knew it. By talking to the *Mirror* and the *Sun,* he was very publicly forcing the issue. It hardly mattered that Billie came on the line while he was on the phone to *The Mirror* to inform Piers Morgan that Chris was 'a kind and generous man who just wants to do his show and entertain people.'

However, even more fuel was added to the fire by a close friend of Steve Penk, who revealed that: 'Steve was told in the early stages of his negotiations with Virgin that he was being lined up to take over from Chris Evans. He was told that he would be presenting the show solo.' Which may well have explained why Evans – had he known this was the plan – opted to force the head-on collision, deciding that it would be far better to burn out than to fade away, just another DJ unceremoniously ousted when his figures started to slide.

After speaking to the two tabloid newspapers, Evans then opted to throw a few titbits to the rest of the media. As a strategy for stating his case it was nigh on faultless. He knew that he had already bagged the front page of a major tabloid and the lead showbiz story in another. Now all that was left to be done was make sure he fed the others something which was worth writing about, but which wouldn't hand over anything too meaty and effectively spike the big two.

After speaking to the *Mirror* and the *Sun*, Evans left the house and headed for the Nag's Head, the pub where he and Billie had climbed in through the window five days earlier. Dressed in a red floral shirt, shorts and a floppy hat, Evans told reporters: 'I've not been sacked, but it's going to happen soon. It looks like it's all over. I can't go into work tomorrow, even though I want to.' He then explained exactly what he meant by that. 'I wrote them a letter saying I wanted to come back, and they wrote back saying "Your letter is like a knock on the door, but we are not opening the door".'

Evans further claimed that he had taken the time off due to 'stress' and had only been given the all clear by his doctor during the day. 'Virgin have offered me £3m not to speak to the press about our row for a year,' he continued. 'You wouldn't offer money like that unless you have something to hide.' This is not necessarily true; many companies adopt this same procedure for any high profile departure, to protect both parties from anything that might be said in the heat of the moment. Evans, however, was not in any sort of mood for holding back when it came to his employers.

'SMG own cinemas, newspapers and radio stations. Virgin Radio is the only one that's making money, and I'm their biggest star. Why treat your biggest asset like that?' he complained. When questioned about what he was planning to do next, he answered: 'I've no immediate plans.' And, as he reached the entrance to the pub just before the bell, Chris merely added: 'Now I'm going in for a pint.' By contrast, Virgin's spokeswoman, Charlotte Blenkinsop, played the press with a straight bat, as she had throughout the entire chaotic saga. 'We are going to make a statement tomorrow,' she confirmed, 'but will be saying nothing until then.'

Understandably, Chris Evans's former boss at Radio 1, Matthew Bannister, was watching these developments with a keen interest and a wry smile on his face. Not to mention, one imagines, a certain sense of déjà vu. In an interesting article in the *Times* that appeared on the same morning that both the *Mirror* and the *Sun* printed Chris's version of events, Bannister put forward three theories as to why Evans was once again in conflict with his bosses.

Bannister's first hypothesis was that things really were as they seemed: 'Chris is cracking up. He's gone AWOL without a satisfactory excuse ... The new owners of Virgin are livid and are just waiting for Chris to turn up at the studio to hand him his P45.' His second theory was that it was all a ruse designed to garner maximum column inches for both Evans and Virgin: 'If your radio show needs to attract more listeners, why not create a national hue and cry about when you might or might not turn up again to present it? Why not fail to explain your absence in the newspapers, thereby creating a reason for people to tune in to hear your explanation on air? And why not make the story even more irresistible by apparently jeopardising a £12.8m payout which you don't really need anyway?' His third explanation was that Evans wanted out, but wasn't going to leave like any other member of the company: 'Why would anyone with £52m, houses in Belgravia and Surrey and a nubile young wife want to get up at the crack of dawn every day to do a radio show?'

Bannister sagely concluded that the most likely reason behind all the kerfuffle was a combination of all three of his theories. Interestingly, he said that the tabloids were genuinely important to Chris: 'He seems to have reached the stage at which, if he doesn't read about himself in the papers, he begins to doubt his existence.' Bannister also claimed that: 'Evans once told me he had more money than he knew what to do with. He said it wistfully ...' Bannister's implication was clear. Now that Evans had a financial safety net, life was simply too boring. He had to almost wilfully destroy it to keep things interesting for himself.

Professor Cary Cooper thinks that there is another, more likely reason, why Chris was heading for a confrontation: 'Empire-builders like Chris can simply get fed up when they've got what they set out to achieve. But there is often conflict when someone bigger takes that empire over. Some people can happily reap the benefits and move on, but others are like painters. They've created a canvas and someone is suddenly starting to go over their painting. So what they decide is that they'd rather rip up the canvas than let someone cover up their work. Chris loves the creative process of building something that's identified with him.

So to then have someone else come and take it over, well, that's going to be hard for him to take.'

If Evans's intention was to force a confrontation that could only be resolved in one way – him leaving Virgin – then the plan worked to perfection. At 3.25pm on Thursday June 28, spokesman Ben Brewerton stepped outside the radio station's offices to issue a statement to the waiting press. 'I can confirm that Chris Evans is no longer a presenter,' he stated. 'He has been in breach of his contract and Virgin Radio was left with no option but to terminate it. It is not just the events of the last week, although his high-profile absence from work obviously brought it to a head. We are sad that it has ended, but Chris clearly has not been focusing on the show.' He then added: 'With all due respect to Chris, the programme wasn't doing very well. No one DJ is bigger than any station. Radio 1 survived and prospered after Chris left it and so will Virgin.'

It was no great surprise to anybody when it was confirmed that Steve Penk would take over the breakfast show from July 9. Nor was anyone flabbergasted when Virgin confirmed that the third tranche of shares due to Evans, estimated to be worth about £9m, would not now be paid. It was also confirmed that the doors where Chris's security pass would have given him access to the building had had their locks changed.

Interestingly, the City appeared not to back Evans's vociferous claims to be SMG's biggest asset. The company's share price began the day at 165.5p: by the end of trading, in the wake of Evans's dismissal, it had closed up at 171.5p. If this was the financial world's reaction to the firing, it was clear that they believed Virgin's decisiveness was in the best interests of the company. SMG had argued that: 'We don't believe there is any Chris Evans premium in our audience rating,' and it seemed the City agreed. Of course, given that Evans still held almost 10m SMG shares, the irony could not have been lost on him that on the day he lost his job, he also managed to net a £600,000 paper profit.

Reaction to the dismissal – and there was an awful lot of it – also appeared to back Virgin's decision. Veteran Capital Radio DJ Chris Tarrant generously observed: 'In a very strange way he's made an awful lot of people aware of radio, so it will be sad not to have him around.' He then rather less benevolently added: 'The fear for Capital is that they might replace him with someone *good*.' Chart countdown DJ Neil Fox said: 'No one DJ's bigger than their entire radio station.' And a media psychologist, Professor Alex Gardner, pulled no punches when he claimed Evans had demonstrated 'vanity, bombast and towering egotism' during the dispute. 'He has an exaggerated sense of his own importance,' he asserted, concluding that Evans had an 'edgy, puerile outlook on life.'

Then there was 'radio trends analyser' Robert Tedder, who claimed that Evans was 'surrounded by yes-men who provide no service to advertiser, listener or investor.' And London 'shock jock' Caesar The Geezer wasted no time in putting the boot in either: 'To tell people he's sick and then go out boozing is disgusting,' he moralised. Even Virgin Radio staff got in on the act, sticking a handmade sign in the window at Golden Square that echoed Radio 1's reaction to Chris's departure: 'Wanted – breakfast show host. Hair colour optional. Apply within.'

Broadcaster Dominik Diamond pinpointed hair colour as the secret behind Evans's success in the radio business: 'He's an ugly ginger bastard. TV bosses are always trying to find gimmicks, and his ugliness was a gimmick.' Even former school secretary at Padgate High, Jan Leicester, wanted to have her say: 'Chris has gone too far this time and needs a good clout round the ear. He would have never behaved like this at school.'

It was to be expected that Matthew Bannister would be unimpressed with his former charge's behaviour. 'I think Chris survives on an adrenalin rush,' he said. 'Recently that has been taken up with buying and selling the radio station, and with his off-air antics, and not with his broadcasting. I would think that any media business would be deeply sceptical about Chris Evans's reliability after this.' However, the most vitriolic comments of all came from Steve Penk, the man who was to replace Evans. 'Chris became lazy and tired,' he said. 'He lost his touch, and that's quite sad. Chris always seemed to be drunk, and his show was past its sell-by date. Can I get the ratings up from what Chris was getting? Of course – easy.'

Unusually, as the media feeding frenzy reached fever pitch, the only person who didn't have anything to say about the outcome was Evans himself. There was no sign of either him or Billie at Hascombe, where the staff seemed to have no idea as to his whereabouts. Nor were they at the Belgravia property, where a women turned up to pick up a bag of golf clubs during the day. The only indication of how Evans had reacted to the news of his sacking came from an unnamed source, who said: 'Chris is going to fight this to the end. He's furious with the shoddy way that he's been treated. He doesn't care how much it costs him, he will try to prove that Virgin have treated him unfairly.' This didn't appear to come as any great shock to his former employers. 'There may be legal action at some point in the future,' conceded SMG spokesman Callum Spreng. Asked if this was because Evans might take the company to court, he replied: 'Not specifically ... perhaps.'

Despite the huge numbers of people prepared to go on the record, the weekend papers were still absolutely full of 'Virgin sources' and 'former colleagues' who were now also ready to make their opinions, if not their names, known. One cited an instance when Virgin boss Paul Jackson told off the DJ after listeners complained about his drinking on the show: 'Jackson put him in his place and Chris didn't know quite what to do. So he went out and got pissed.' A 'senior Virgin exec' took a more personal view of his former work colleague. 'He's screwed himself,' he said. 'He would walk around the station, refusing to talk to people. He treated everyone like dirt on his shoe. He would only speak to people through memos. Even if they were sitting five feet away, he had to write a letter to them. His bad behaviour was tolerated when he was doing the business. But he's lost it, and nobody will put up with him.'

Reflection on the cause of Evans's downfall was one thing. Speculation on his uncertain future was another. One friend said: 'I wouldn't be surprised if he just upped sticks and went out to Portugal for a while. He started saying this two months ago, so he may have felt for some time that he was going to leave Virgin.' The DJ's pal Aldo Zilli confidently asserted: 'Chris will definitely be back as a broadcaster, but on radio not TV, because he finds that too much work. He wants to say what he thinks, without being censored, so he's likely to come back with an evening show.' The bookies shared this verdict, as William Hill declared odds on what Evans would do next. They gave an ungenerous 1-20 on him turning up on another radio station, also offering 25-1 against Chris investing in a pub chain, 80-1 against him buying the Betty Ford Clinic and a mere 100-1 on him becoming the first ginger James Bond. You could only get a cagey 2-1 against him aping David Beckham and appearing in public with a Mohawk haircut.

Evans may have been remaining tight-lipped, but his wife's granny, Margaret Piper, didn't follow his example when she gave an interview about Billie's new husband. 'She's hanging around with a crowd of his that always seems to be going to pubs and night clubs. Her husband isn't setting a good example,' she said. Meanwhile, public opinion seemed to have turned against him. 'In the early days Chris was talented and funny,' said John Yeomans of Putney, south London, in the *Sun*. 'Now he is no more than a greedy show-off.' 'Goodbye and good riddance to Chris Evans,' said Lesley Mills of Wolverhampton. 'His sacking is only the same treatment that anyone would receive if they were boozing day and night when they were supposed to be working.' William Cooke of Margate indulged in sarcasm: 'Chris doesn't appear to understand the meaning of being fired,' he commented. 'When he received notification of his dismissal from Virgin Radio he vowed he would never work there again. Wasn't that the general idea?' Cheekily, a rival radio station took out full-page newspaper ads suggesting that, as Evans no longer broadcast for Virgin, his listeners might want to give their breakfast show a try.

Evans's publicist, Matthew Freud, received over 300 requests for interviews with his unemployed client. None of them were granted, and the *Mirror* had to make do with John Webster, himself sacked from his £50,000 job after Chris's departure. Webster claimed that interference from the Virgin top brass had infuriated Evans, and had been a calculated move to force a confrontation that would lead to his mate leaving the station and allow Steve Penk to slide into the breakfast slot. Webster pointed to a 'furious' memo from boss Paul Jackson after Chris played Sheena Easton's oldie 'Nine To Five' after 'Billie Piper, from Belgravia, London' had phoned in to request the song. The memo had insisted that Evans should always stick to songs on the Virgin playlist – and 'Nine To Five' most definitely wasn't on it. Webster also claimed that, because the breakfast crew had sung along to the song on air, another memo arrived banning singing or talking over records. 'Bloody absurd,' he said. 'It was like they were telling us: "Make sure your show isn't too much fun. Keep it nice and boring."'

It was clear that relations between Evans and the station management had completely broken down, and the presenter had had enough. Webster concluded: 'Chris told me, "I don't need all this grief and I don't need the money. So I'm just saying bollocks to it. I just want to get on with my marriage and not have to worry about these suits trying to wind me up."' At the end of the whole sorry affair it really did look as if that was the main reason behind Evans's divorce from Virgin. And in choosing to pick a very public fight, at least it meant that when he left it was as front-page news rather than as a snippet in a gossip column somewhere.

Virgin's owners SMG might have been feeling just a tiny bit smug and self-satisfied about their refusal to buckle under the provocation dished out by Evans. However, even a cursory look at their accounts would have quickly wiped the smiles from their faces. The company's debts in 1999, shortly before they bought Ginger for £225m, stood at £104m. In May 2001, just before the row with Evans broke out, this deficit stood at £363m. Considering that the Ginger purchase was intended to buy them a slice of lucrative revenue from the teen and twenty-something advertising market, that made for sobering reading. SMG had so far failed to prove the value of their purchase.

Indeed, the ratings for the breakfast show, where the majority of a radio station's ad revenue is generated, had dropped by a million in less than two years. In the previous week, the group had been forced to make 20 job cuts at two of their three news-papers. It could be argued that it was too soon to expect a new acquisition to be performing and yes, the city had appreciated chief executive Andrew Flanagan's no-nonsense approach to the Evans problem. However, it was also nervous about the ability of a traditionally cautious company to establish itself as a major media player when it appeared to find it difficult to work with volatile creative talents.

'You'd be inclined to believe that they don't give their people much freedom, which someone like Evans needs,' said one insider. 'After all, he did build up a company which last year they felt was worth more than £200m.' SMG may have felt they'd won the battle, but had they won the war? They didn't even seem to have resolved the basic issue of handling uncontrollable DJs. Chris Evans's replacement, Steve Penk, hit the ground running on the breakfast show. 'There's some tosser here who has e-mailed me to say he hates me and that Chris was much better,' he ranted on air. 'If you don't like it, tosser, turn it off. Show me what a tit you are by starting a campaign to get rid of me.'

With comments like these, it was almost as if Evans had never left ... but he *had* gone, and gone to ground too. While local radio stations desperate for a bit of publicity came up with the tired routine of offering him work ('I'm willing to give Chris some cover work over the summer to help him out,' said programme manager Gary Burgess at Warrington's Wire FM. 'His mum lives round the corner, so he'll have somewhere to stay,') there was nothing concrete from Evans himself outlining future plans. A rumour circulated that Ginger were hoping to win the contract to produce Channel 4's replacement for the *Big Breakfast*, and Evans would have a weekly on-camera slot. However, if this were true it would be surreal, given that he would then be working for SMG again.

Broadcast magazine declared that Chris Evans had slipped from eighth to twelfth place in their list of broadcasting tycoons, and a magazine poll named him the least sexy star in showbiz (Billie, incidentally, was voted third in the least stylish woman category). However, there was nothing of substance reported, because for the first time in years there really *was* nothing to report. Chris headed for Orlando on holiday, together with Billie and Danny Baker's family. All he would say on the unbelievable events that he'd just been through was: 'This is desperately unfair. I feel really hurt and need to take time off to relax.' Exactly how long he was going to take off was anyone's guess ...

23 Sunshine Of Your Love

As Chris Evans disappeared into the sunset to lick his wounds and prepare his next move, there were plenty of commentators who simply didn't believe that Mr Publicity would go to ground for long. Yes, since he'd been with Billie, Chris had been happy to pop off to Madeira, the Algarve, Paris, wherever to snatch a bit of R&R, but his focus had always been work, work, work.

Yet as the summer unwound it seemed as if, this time, Evans really did mean it. 'I'm on a hundred-day holiday. Come back to me at the end of it,' he claimed, and did his level best to avoid any contact with anything or anyone work-related. There was a short break on the Isle of Wight, the supervising of £500,000 worth of renovations at Hascombe, a longish stay in Hollywood at the Sunset Marquis, and sightings at a number of cricket matches in England. However, the closest Chris came to anything remotely approaching 'business' was getting involved in a few good local causes.

'He's had a lot to do with financing the rebuilding of the village hall,' said one local. 'And he's kitted the local football team out in a new strip.' Evans also mused over the idea of starting his own cricket team at the White Horse and spent £12,000 on a caravan. There was, however, a twisted logic behind this purpose. As renovations on the mansion continued, Chris and Billie had spent most of the year staying in the gatekeeper's cottage where they had entertained Debbie Curran and her mum at the start of the year. And as Billie turned 19 on September 22, despite the fact that both she and Chris were enjoying marital bliss, the quarters seemed a little cramped. The solution, then, was to buy a caravan, park it outside the cottage and turn it into an office, thereby freeing up more of the house. Simple.

A quick trip to Hollywood in October fuelled the notion that Chris might be taking his talents to America, but as December came around that didn't look too likely, as Chris told a friend: 'I liked the hundred days' holiday so much that I've just awarded myself another hundred.' However, this time he was lying. Out of the blue, there Chris Evans suddenly was, back and working … in his local pub.

Or, to be more precise, just outside it. Wearing a Santa hat and with Billie as his able assistant, Chris spent the first weekend in December flogging Christmas trees outside his Hascombe local the White Horse. The trees were taken from his own hundred-acre estate and Mr and Mrs Evans were selling them for £20 each, with a quarter of the profits going to the local church, a quarter to a Cystic Fibrosis charity, and half to the Chase Hospice in Guildford. 'I chopped down 150 myself and hope to sell a thousand by Christmas Eve,' Evans explained. 'I'm going to be selling the trees every Saturday and Sunday until Christmas. It's all good fun and the money goes to local charities. It keeps me out of the pub, at least.'

Well, not entirely, though. There were various sightings recorded in Godalming pubs as Christmas approached, and Lee Sharp of the Jack Phillips boozer claimed that Chris was drunk. 'He was only in here for a couple of minutes, but he was wrecked as usual,' he said. There again, a generous soul might argue that it's not so unusual to find somebody wrecked in a pub before Christmas, enjoying the festive spirit and the simple things in life. 'I'm not missing TV and radio at all,' Chris reported. 'I'm looking forward to a nice family Christmas with Billie.' However, it wasn't just Christmas trees that Mr & Mrs Evans were selling, as news emerged that the house in Gilston Road, Chelsea, bought just seven months earlier, had been sold to pop star George Michael, netting the couple a tidy £400,000 profit in the process. No wonder Chris Evans was looking forward to a nice Christmas.

While Evans was happily spreading festive cheer around Surrey, none of the top brass at his former employers SMG would have been expecting a Christmas card. In fact, what they actually received by way of an early Christmas present was an action brought by Evans through his lawyers, Harbottle & Lewis, and issued in London's High Court. It claimed that SMG still owed him the third tranche of shares allotted to him under the terms of the original sale of Ginger, and due to be released in March 2002. Evans was also seeking damages for unfair dismissal, as well as interest on anything that the High Court might award him if his action proved successful.

'I can confirm that Chris Evans is taking legal action against us, for shares he would have received if he had not broken his contract,' said an SMG spokesman on December 14. 'We plan to launch counter claims, and to defend the case rigorously. He breached his contract in a high-profile manner, and we have strong evidence to support this. If he insists on us proving this in court then, while it will give us no pleasure, we will.' The shares that Evans claimed he was still owed – 1,245,355 ordinary shares in SMG Television, and 4,981,420 shares in the parent company – were estimated to be worth just shy of £9m to the man whose 3.18% stake meant he was still SMG's fourth-largest shareholder. Chris Evans was effectively suing a company that he owned a large chunk of. SMG's case, predictably, would be based around the fact that his boozing sessions had left staff uncertain whether he would turn up for work or not.

Regardless of their belief in the strength of their case, and no matter how rigorously they were prepared to defend it, SMG did not relish the court battle. This was a company whose share price at the end of the year was running at less than half of its year high of 275p, with pre-tax profits in the first half of the year down a third to £20m. These figures also predated the September 11 US terrorist attacks which had had such a catastrophic impact on the world economy, and particularly on the advertising industry on which SMG relied so heavily. And for the saving of £2m that the company had made through the sacking of Evans (his estimated annual salary), a protracted court case could easily end up costing them considerably more.

'From what I understand, I don't think either side is going to back down,' says business journalist James Ashton. 'Most cases like this tend to be settled out of court, but not this one. It all depends on what doctor's notes can be produced to explain Evans's absences. He clearly thinks he's got a strong case, because it's not that he needs the money. There was a bit of gloating when Evans was ousted because of the drinking, but he retaliated with "Stop kidding everybody. You're SMG, a Glasgow company that's bitten off more than it can chew. You can't retain volatile celebrities and they're what you need to make your station successful." Now that's a bit harsh, in my opinion. Since the fallout with Evans Virgin have lost a load of listeners, but SMG bought Ginger at the height of the boom and nobody could have known that advertising revenues were going to crash so spectacularly.

'In any case, listeners were being lost even before the fall-out with Chris. Paul Jackson was brought in as controller and his appointment was always seen as one made with the specific intention of shaking things up. And if Evans was determined to take on Paul Jackson, then he should have known he was in for a fight. Jackson is Richard Park's son and Richard Park is behind *Fame Academy*, he discovered Craig David and is the man who brought Chris Tarrant to Capital. So Jackson is well connected, still has the backing of the management to turn Virgin round and has got time on his side.

'Jackson has admitted that it's going to take a long time to shake off the Chris Evans effect, and an asset – namely, Chris – that was seen as a great halo became a bit of an albatross. When Richard Branson sold the majority of Virgin to Chris Evans it was almost the plucky underdog being carried forward by one big personality. I think what SMG needed to do was broaden that appeal out, and you probably couldn't do that without treading on a few toes. I would have liked to see how other companies could have hung on to Chris. Could they have made him a director of the company? He probably wouldn't have wanted it. But this issue hasn't been resolved and there's no doubt that both sides are determined to fight their corner.'

Yet Evans remained hot property. Even with a court case pending, having been sacked for breach of contract and having made it clear that he wasn't in the mood for working, the rumours of fresh employers were never far away. As Christmas approached, he was said to have agreed a deal with Radio 2. 'Although there is no official word, Chris is going to Radio 2 next year,' said one supposedly informed insider.

The only company that appeared to be making no claims at all about any involvement with Chris Evans was his former operation, Ginger. The far-fetched idea that Evans would be involved in their putative replacement for the *Big Breakfast* was revealed as nonsense when Sky won the contract to produce *RI:SE*. Tellingly, it was also announced that the 'thick glasses' logo that Ginger always aired at the end of their shows was to be dropped after eight years, effectively signalling the final severing of ties between the company and its founder.

Then, just as everybody seemed to have had his or her say on the Chris Evans enigma, a highly unlikely contributor to the great debate hove into view – Sir Cliff Richard. The 61-year-old singer made the arguably rather fanciful claim that the broadcaster's run of bad luck was all down to his refusal to play Cliff's 'Millennium Prayer' single, a musical rendition of the Lord's Prayer, on Virgin back in 1999. 'He terrorised my record,' Cliff said. 'People got really upset on my behalf. He lost that battle hands down, and things have never been the same for him since.'

However, as 2002 approached, maybe a perspective was called for on Chris Evans's fortunes. Technically he was unemployed, and had yet to bounce back with a high-profile media gig, and pending the court case he was still being denied the third tranche of shares promised to him in the original SMG takeover of Ginger. However, he was still worth around £52m, had a beautiful 19-year-old wife, and had just awarded himself another bumper hundred-day holiday.

'I was talking about this very thing the other day,' says broadcaster Stuart Maconie. 'That people were looking at Chris at this point and seeing him as some kind of underachiever. But Jonathan Ross pointed out that he was an underachiever who was sitting on a beach on holiday somewhere with his lovely 19-year-old wife by his side and with £50m in the bank. Well, that's some kind of underachievement.'

Indeed, Evans the loser was putting some of his money to good use by buying two luxury villas in Portugal's Algarve. The purchases were completed in January, the idea being to take the two adjoining villas in upmarket Quinto do Lago and knock them through to form one giant luxury pad. Chris and Billie decamped to the sun to oversee the conversion work on their new project, which was being handled by Billie's builder dad Paul, since the Pipers had left Swindon and moved to Mijas, near Fuengirola, in 2001.

Evans certainly didn't appear to find supervising his Portuguese workmen too stressful, though. Staying at a white-washed Moorish villa just five minutes away from his new apartments, Chris took to driving around in a gold Range Rover, swinging his clubs at the world famous San Lorenzo golf club nearby, and enjoying a pint or two at English bars like the Pig & Whistle. 'I've never seen him remotely tipsy, and he's always friendly and polite,' said one ex-pat. 'He likes to watch the soccer and he's a sociable bloke, so I think he doesn't want to watch it alone.' Chris was also spotted getting lessons to improve his golf at the local Pinheiros club, where his cousin Brian was a director. And when Billie wasn't driving an olive green Jaguar convertible, she was sunning herself by the pool.

The couple's idea was to use the larger of the two villas, with its seven bedrooms, as living quarters, while the smaller one would be converted into a recording studio and offices. The two villas combined would share a large swimming pool and two acres of beautiful landscaped gardens. The neighbours were also high class. Footballer Alan Shearer owned a property in Quinto and his England successor Michael Owen had bought a place for his parents nearby, which had once been owned by the racing driver Ayrton Senna whom Chris and Simon Morris had hung out with back in the early 1990s. With little nightlife and a host of low-key, wealthy individuals in the area, maybe the choice of Quinto do Lago was Chris and Billie's way of sending out a signal that their attitude to wild partying had changed, and their one-time seemingly all-consuming thirst for publicity had pretty much fizzled out.

According to John Revell, that wasn't the only change. Not only had Chris Evans cut himself off from the media: he'd also severed all links with his former right-hand man and business partner, who was dumped from the Virgin breakfast show when Evans canned the original 'zoo' format. 'I've not heard from him in at least six months,' said a hurt-sounding Revell. 'My last conversation with Chris was that we'd no longer be working together.' Explaining that former breakfast crew members Holly Samos and Dan McGrath hadn't heard anything from their former boss either, Revell continued, 'It's very sad. I really didn't think it would end the way it has.'

However, not everybody felt deserted by Chris's move to Portugal. 'You know the phrase, "As happy as Larry"?' asked John Webster, now back in gainful employment in a somewhat more low-key position as a presenter at Kent's Mercury FM. 'Well, Chris makes Larry look like a miserable git.' Webster also claimed that Chris was hardly drinking now and had told him he wanted to start a family with Billie, just to add to the increasingly convincing picture of domestic bliss. Danny Baker also confided that he felt Evans was delighted with his new life. 'I still speak to Chris all the time,' he said. 'He's very, very happy. He's just living life for pleasure, and there's nothing wrong with that.' 'I think he's lost interest,' concluded John Revell. The question remained – had the industry lost interest in him?

Virgin's programme director Paul Jackson thought not. In fact, Jackson blamed a combination of the loss of Evans and a listener switch to more news-based radio items post-September 11 as the prime reasons for his station's tawdry set of figures. 'The abruptness of Chris Evans's departure last summer forced us to change the schedule without the station or the listeners being prepared for it,' he confessed. Virgin revealed that they'd lost 300,000 listeners over the past year … not to mention the DJ heralded as the perfect replacement for Evans, Steve Penk. Penk's show just wasn't working and he was moved to the drive time slot. So much for Penk's 'Easy!' prediction when he'd been asked about increasing Evans's listener figures on taking the job.

To make matters worse for Jackson and Virgin, not every music station had suffered. Chrysalis-owned Heart FM cheerily reported that hours spent listening to their station had leapt by 43% in one year. Sitting in the sunshine of Quinto do Lago, checking out his beautiful new villas, nobody could have begrudged Evans having a laugh at Jackson's expense, even if he was a major SMG shareholder himself. It was small wonder that he'd decided to double his 100-day holiday.

Jackson himself, however, remained defiant. 'Chris was being outperformed by the rest of the station,' he told the *Stage* in February. 'That's a situation that you don't want for your break-fast show.' Yet Evans may have found some vindication in Jackson's even-more scathing verdict on Penk's performance: 'The bottom line was, it just wasn't working,' he confessed.

Chris Evans was also very happily not working, as he proved emphatically when he finally left Portugal and breezed back into London on Monday February 18 for a day of booze-fuelled shenanigans with old pals. After a day spent in various pubs, Evans ended up back at his favourite old haunt Stringfellow's, 'completely surrounded by naked women' as one clubber put it, while his wife went for dinner at trendy nearby restaurant The Ivy. Peter Stringfellow was pleased to hear his old carousing mate was back in business. In fact he was phoned on his yacht in the Mediterranean to have a chat with his old pal, but Chris managed to drop the mobile into a champagne glass. No matter, Peter was delighted, saying: 'Chris hadn't been in for about a year. It's brilliant to have him back.' And if Peter's memory was failing him – it was actually June when Chris had last been in the club – then his generous spirit certainly wasn't. Evans accidentally left Stringfellow's without paying, only to realise halfway back to his place in Wilton Crescent and send one of his pals back to settle up. 'We'd hold a cheque for him anytime,' said Peter.

Chapter 23

The following morning, Evans headed out for breakfast with his mates, then swiftly moved on to Knightsbridge wine bar Motcombs, where he bumped into former England football manager Terry Venables and enjoyed a few more drinks. It was just like old times – without the hassle of having to get up for work in the morning. And was it really such a bind not to have a radio show to present, when you had millions in the bank and even more palatial potential homes to take a look at … this time over in Hollywood?

24 Back For Good

Los Angeles beckoned, and at the start of March Chris and Billie flew out, heading straight for the Sunset Marquis, Hollywood hotel of choice for media stars (and also the venue where Chris and Will Macdonald's shorts had caused such a tabloid furore years ago). The couple began to view houses in upmarket areas, including Coldwater Canyon and Laurel Canyon. 'We're looking up in the hills, and may buy a house,' Chris explained. 'But we've got a few to look at.' He didn't even mention the vintage Mercedes and Porsches that he was also spotted having a peek at.

Two days after the couple's arrival there was a distinctly sticky moment when Geri Halliwell checked into the same hotel and Chris ended up chatting to his 'Was she? Wasn't she?' former lover. Billie appeared less than amused and stormed off in tears, seemingly overcome with jealousy at the encounter. Evans resolved the tiff in time-honoured fashion by handing over a wad of cash for Mrs Evans to blow on a shopping extravaganza while he took root at the hotel bar.

By mid-March a decision had been taken, and the couple snapped up a 6,000 sq ft place up in the Hollywood Hills. Smoochy singer Lionel Richie had once owned it. Complete with swimming pool and tennis court and with neighbours including Brad Pitt and Leonardo DiCaprio, it was no wonder the new owner was happy with his purchase. 'We wanted somewhere with a great view,' he explained. 'This is the best place to find a good home in the city. We looked at several houses, but went back to this one a few times and decided it was what we wanted.' Evans also seemed excited by Hollywood itself, claiming: 'This town's great. The weather's good and the people are nice. There isn't any other place like it. Who wouldn't want to live here?' It certainly compared very favourably to Orford.

Hollywood had one further, crucial attraction for Chris and Billie. Neither of them had ever become known in America, and given their new-found taste for keeping a lower profile, a £6m bolthole in a town where, if they so chose, they could look to develop new projects away from the intense media glare back in London made perfect sense. And with Hascombe Court and the Portuguese villas both undergoing extensive work, the actual timing was excellent.

Besides, what was £6m to Chris Evans? Especially when, according to the *News Of The World*, he had reneged on the promise made to them fifteen months earlier, when Ginger was sold to SMG, that he was going to give away £46m of his fortune to charity. His words were reprinted in full: 'Really, £5m is enough for anyone … Money doesn't mean anything to me any more, so I'll try to make all I can so I can give away all I earn from now on.' In the fervour of his zeal back then, he'd even challenged other top earners to give similar chunks of their fortunes away. Suddenly, this looked like a case of Evans both shooting his mouth off … and shooting himself in the foot. He did set up a charitable trust for needy causes into which he donated £1m at the outset. But clearly, he'd not given a lot of the money away. Clearly, he was spending some of it on himself. The *News Of The World* even printed a hotline number for Chris to ring in and tell them what had happened to all the cash that was earmarked for charity in an open invitation to come clean.

Yet if the latest piece of media gossip doing the rounds was to be believed, Evans could well be needing every bit of spare cash that he could find. There were increasing rumours that he was seriously looking to buy Virgin Radio back from SMG, whose debts were by now recorded at £390m. 'The sale of Virgin Radio will certainly interest him,' said a friend.

As Evans looked to the future, one significant element from his cluttered past bit the dust. On March 29, 2002, Channel 4 finally pulled the plug on *Big Breakfast*. The consensus was that it wasn't before time. In marginally less than ten years, the show's viewing figures had slumped from 1.5m at their Evans-led peak to less than 300,000. It clearly was time for Evans's *alma mater* to go.

The last ever *Big Breakfast* ran for an extended three hours and featured recorded messages from many of its former presenters, including Gaby Roslin, Denise Van Outen and Johnny Vaughan. Talking from his new LA home, Evans reminisced about how he'd actually managed to get himself locked in the toilet just seconds before the very first show back on September 28, 1992. He also, perhaps surprisingly, criticised the decision to axe the show, saying that it would take years to build up as good a production team again. The final show – number 2,482 in the series – attracted almost one million viewers, a tribute to the esteem in which its alumni were held.

In the inevitable media inquest that followed the show's demise, most commentators acknowledged Evans's pivotal role in the establishment of a new form of early morning TV entertainment in the early 1990s – less stuffy, more attitudinal and, above all, fun. James Jennings, from advertising agency BJK&E, hit the nail on the head when he said: 'People started to realise that the show's success was less to do with the format than the fact that they were exceptionally lucky in finding two presenters as good as Evans and Johnny Vaughan.' Clive Crouch, sales & marketing director of rivals GMTV, said: 'It will be difficult for anyone to create the level of excitement that Chris and Gaby Roslin did initially.'

Yet any residual fondness for the *Big Breakfast* would have felt like ancient news as Billie and Chris began to settle into their new life in Hollywood. They were obviously enjoying themselves. Starting their day in a leisurely fashion around noon, the couple would most often take a stroll to pick up the papers from a news stand, then enjoy a laid-back brunch in town. Billie started going to the gym and took up yoga, and the couple were seen at car auctions (Chris actually bought Billie a new Range Rover), bowling alleys and record shops. And while Chris was spotted giving $50 to a beggar (Gareth Johnson from *TFI* similarly recalled Evans giving £200 to a beggar in London once), the couple were hardly ever seen out after dark; they were too busy watching old videos together.

The one time that the pair *were* noticed out and about, at a Celine Dion concert, Billie and Chris couldn't keep their hands off each other. The earlier prophets of doom for the marriage appeared to have been vanquished. 'I never had any doubt they would make their first anniversary,' said Billie's mum, Mandy. 'They're very happy and I'm very happy for Billie.' Meanwhile, a sudden invasion of rats into their LA dream house led to a visit from pest controllers as the couple spend their first anniversary in a local Indian restaurant, Flavors Of India, rather than in their own home.

'In many ways being free of the pressure of money makes you think about different things,' philosophises Simon Morris. 'I think when Chris had time away with all that money in the bank, that was when he really started to focus on family and love. His pot of money allows him to do whatever he wants, and there was a time when he went off the rails. But stepping out of things for a while made him grow up and realise what was important. There's always that saying about people with loads of money: "Ah, but is he *happy*?" There's a lot of truth in that. If you're a person who's driven, someone who's an achiever, then there *is* a price to pay, be it relationships, friendships, your personal health, whatever ... And maybe it was a price that Chris decided was too high.'

Los Angeles location aside, Chris Evans clearly wasn't chasing the dream career-wise anymore ... but there were the first signs that he was beginning to at least start *thinking* about a return to work. Firstly, there were secretive meetings with American TV executives while he was in Hollywood. Then out of the blue he spoke to the *Mirror* again, putting forward a proposal for calling off the legal action against SMG. 'I will drop my legal action if they give me what is rightfully mine, which would mean they can sell Virgin Radio to at least two parties that I know of,' he offered, then added: 'I will also run the station for free for the new owners and present the breakfast show.'

Explaining that he had always been fully committed to Virgin, even to the extent of offering to sign a ten-year contract with the station, Evans reiterated his belief that he had not broken his contract (despite what he had first said in the *Mirror*) and was still owed the outstanding shares. 'The only person who has not been paid in full for one of the most famous deals in British media history is the one person who bought and sold the station,' he claimed. 'Take into account that I was sacked by a man who I made a millionaire and whose job I not once, but twice, saved, and I hope you understand why I have now taken legal action to attain what, in my opinion, is rightfully mine.' SMG appeared to be unconcerned with this new offer, stating simply: 'We are not prepared to comment on the court case. Virgin Radio is not for sale.' More interestingly, the company's annual report divulged that it had made no provision whatsoever for a payout in the Evans case, and had merely set aside funds to cover legal costs.

SMG may have wanted nothing more to do with Chris Evans, then, but by mid-2002 it became clear that there were plenty of top media figures who were more than happy to discuss possible future projects. First there was a meeting in London with BBC1 controller Lorraine Heggessey, then a lunch with the same channel's controller of entertainment commissioning, Jane Lush. A spokesman for the Beeb admitted that Heggessey 'met with Chris Evans recently at his request,' before rather sniffily adding: 'She often has meetings with talent.' There was talk of a game show and a chat show, and with the BBC without a major Saturday evening entertainment show *à la Noel's House Party*, it didn't take a genius to see where his talents could possibly end up.

Evans's good mate Danny Baker claimed to know nothing of these clandestine talks, but did say that where Evans was concerned, the BBC was, 'still in his blood. He still answers the phone: "Hi, Chris Evans, ex-BBC".' This information would not play well with Channel 5 boss Dawn Airey, who was allegedly in the final throes of talks with Evans about a new breakfast show, to be co-hosted with Anthea Turner, to rival Channel 4's *RI:SE*. Evans and Airey had met on a flight from LA and had apparently hit it off. Finally, on July 7, it was announced that Evans would indeed be involved in a new show for Channel 5, but his return to TV would not be in front of the cameras but *behind* them, as executive producer of a new live evening entertainment show.

This show was yet to be blessed with a name, but Channel 5 confirmed that it would run for 13 weeks each weekday evening and would be hosted by Radio 1 DJ Chris Moyles. Moyles, whose schtick of confrontational radio with a liberal dose of sarcasm and humour was hardly a million miles away from Evans's own style, already had a reputation for sometimes being difficult and controversial on air. The plan was that he would head straight for his TV slot after finishing broadcasting on the radio in the afternoon.

Evans said: 'Chris Moyles is the man of the moment and I couldn't be more excited to be working with him. The early evening slot offers a golden opportunity to provide programming for disenfranchised viewers who aren't currently being served. At the moment there's nothing available for people who don't want game shows, soaps or news. We want to provide something different and bring new viewers to the table.' Moyles himself added a more prosaic: 'It's going to be great.'

While refusing to confirm rumours that Chris Evans was being paid £4m for his role in the new venture, Channel 5 director of programmes Kevin Lygo decided: 'Chris Moyles is a unique talent. He's straight-talking, irreverent and unpredictable. I'm delighted we've been able to attract him to 5.' How these virtues made Moyles a unique talent among all the other straight-talking, irreverent and unpredictable DJs and talk show hosts wasn't fully explained. However, moving on to Evans, Lygo expressed equally effusive admiration: 'Chris Evans is one of the most original on and off-screen talents British broadcasting has produced, and the fact that he's chosen 5 for his comeback project demonstrates the strides the channel is taking.'

Nevertheless, this latest development flummoxed many

people, who believed that Evans would want to make as much of a splash as possible on his return to television. Working behind the scenes on a half-hour show on the baby of terrestrials seemed so low-key as to be almost off the radar. 'It just seemed bizarre,' said one insider. 'It didn't seem very Chris at all to be coming back in this softly-softly manner.' Charlie Catchpole, one of the *Express* newspaper's pundits, was also of the opinion that the new job was too low-key for Evans. 'I suspect he won't be able to resist sticking his face in front of the camera for long,' he claimed. However, he was still glad to see Evans back. 'With *Big Brother*, we've been reduced to watching people sleep,' he said. 'One thing you can be sure of – when Chris Evans is around, *no-one* sleeps.'

If anybody was left in any doubt that Chris Evans was poised to return to the media arena, it was Channel 4's turn a week later to announce a new project. Evans was to produce two shows for the channel through his new production company, UMTV, which he had set up with agent Michael Foster and friend Chris Gillett. While one of the programmes, both of which were commissioned by 4's head of entertainment Danielle Lux (iron-ically, the girl who had co-presented the pilots of the *Big Breakfast* with Chris back in 1992), was being kept under wraps and being referred to simply as an entertainment show, there were more details about the other project, a weekly prime time feature called *Boys And Girls*.

Based much more in traditional Evans territory – live-in-the-studio and an hour-long format à la … *Toothbrush* and *TFI* – *Boys And Girls* was to be aimed at the 16-34 age group, with an initial run of 12 shows beginning in early 2003. No presenters were yet confirmed, which meant, of course, that Chris hadn't actively ruled out taking the job on himself. Channel 4 made no comment on this subject, merely insisting that the show was, 'bound to be something completely different yet again, because that's the way Chris works. What we're all aiming for is some-thing that has the same degree of reinvention that *TFI Friday* and *Don't Forget Your Toothbrush* had.' Lux was also quick to let the world know how marvellous she thought Chris was, claiming

Channel 4 was, 'the natural home for his unique brand of bold, totally original broadcasting. The ambition, energy and scale of his ideas are qualities we want to see more of in Channel 4 entertainment.' Evans, for his part, was also full of praise for the station, saying: 'I'm thrilled that Channel 4 has shown the level of commitment required to support these two unique show propositions. We will try to create two stand-out television programmes, unlike anything currently on UK screens.'

What the Channel 4's positivist statement *didn't* mention was that the company was in desperate need of a creative catalyst to rejuvenate its fortunes. The station has posted its largest ever loss of £28m in 2002, as well as warning of up to a hundred possible job losses. If they were prepared to take a gamble on Evans in such a difficult market place, it was obvious that being away from the media spotlight and having an almighty fall-out with his former employers had done little to damage his market value.

Further media speculation hinted that Evans was close to signing another deal with Channel 5 to produce a daytime chat show hosted by the unlikely pairing of Gaby Roslin and Terry Wogan. Neither presenter spoke of the plans, though Roslin did admit that she would be thrilled to work with her former *Big Breakfast* sparring partner, adding that she wouldn't have a bad word said about him.

Wanting an effective media platform to discuss his return, but loath to face a string of interviews with separate journalists, Evans agreed to be the subject of the Richard Dunn Memorial Interview at the Guardian Edinburgh International Television Festival on August 25. The interview was to be conducted by Channel 5's Kevin Lygo, who had been so effusive in his praise of Evans when he announced their recent deals. It was clearly a home banker: the chance of Lygo upsetting 'The Talent' with a hard-hitting line of questioning was nil.

Nevertheless, the festival's advisory chair, Charles Brand, was more than happy to have bagged the media mogul, no matter who was interviewing him. 'Everyone is always interested in what Chris Evans has to say,' he gushed. 'Because among other things, he has an amazing ability to know what people want and how to deliver it. He is a key voice of innovation, invention and importance in television today. Delegates will undoubtedly benefit from his unique and potentially controversial views on the present state of the broadcasting industry and his views on its future.'

Possibly, some rather more realistic analysts might have argued that an individual who had not been involved in television since ducking out of *TFI Friday* over two years back was hardly in a strong position to comment on the state of the industry. Nevertheless, such was the reverence for what Evans had achieved in the past, and such was the need for someone – anyone – to find more winning formats, that nobody was prepared to air that opinion.

Like a prize-fighter readying himself for a big comeback, Chris gathered his wife and headed off to the four-star Grayshott Hall health farm near Hindhead, Surrey. A mere ten miles from Hascombe, the establishment, which charged up to £1,000 for a five-night stay, was known to cater for celebrities in need of a spot of rest and relaxation. Such diverse people as Monica Lewinsky, Dale Winton, the Duchess of York and Emma Thompson had all graced its premises. Grayshott didn't allow its guests to drink alcohol, but offered a variety of health-oriented entertainment, including gym and swimming pool, sauna, steam room, tennis and badminton. And, importantly for Chris, there was also a nine-hole golf course.

However, if the couple felt that a short break would allow Chris to rejuvenate quietly and ready himself for his grand return to television, the events of Wednesday August 7 soon put paid to that idea.

25 Death Of A Friend

It had been a great day. James Ward, the 50-year-old landlord of Evans's favourite Hascombe local, the White Horse Inn, was also Chris's good mate. So when the experienced sailor had the idea of celebrating his business partner Susan Barnett's 54th birthday with a trip across the Solent to the Isle of Wight during Cowes week, it was only natural he should invite his famous pal.

There were seven people on board Ward's 31ft Nausicaa yacht, including Evans's buddy John Webster, and everyone had a fine time on the island, finishing off with a calypso party at Salty's in Yarmouth before boarding the boat to make the journey home early in the evening. Then, at approximately 9.15pm and with twilight having descended, the boat was nearing Brambles Bank in the Solent just one-and-a-half miles from Cowes when the yacht's boom unexpectedly swung around and caught Ward a glancing blow on the head. He was thrown into the water and disappeared from view.

As James was the only experienced sailor in the party the alarm was raised straight away via a 999 call from a mobile phone, as someone also tried to put out a mayday call on the yacht's radio. The coastguard scrambled a rescue boat, a police launch and a helicopter as John Webster bravely dived into the water to try to rescue Ward. 'It was absolutely freezing,' he said later. 'I dived in near to James but once I was in I lost sight of him because it was very dark. And the waves were high. I kept shouting from where I was. I couldn't see him, but still felt I was near him.'

Thirty-year-old Jason Ludlow was in a rigid inflatable boat leaving the Cowes regatta when he heard the coastguard's call for assistance. 'I had five friends with me,' he said, 'and told the coastguard we could help. We got to the area very quickly and another yacht was shining a powerful beam into the water.' This was because nobody on board the Nausicaa knew how to switch on the boat's own lights. Another man on board Ludlow's boat, Justin Bloomfield, dived into the water and swam towards a body they had spotted. 'He was wearing just a T-shirt and shorts,' said Bloomfield. 'I turned him over, but there was no sign of life. He must have been knocked unconscious from the boom, because his body was floating very close to the lifebelt and he should have been able to swim to it easily.'

Bloomfield then put James Ward's body across his own to support him and was trying to get back to a boat and get him out of the water when the rescue craft from Hamble, near Southampton on the mainland, arrived. Both men were pulled on board. At around 9.45, James was rushed to shore in the fast rescue craft. A doctor and an ambulance were on standby and the medic worked on the body for twenty minutes, but James Ward was pronounced dead shortly afterwards.

PC Stuart Revell, of Southampton Police Marine Unit, was one of those involved in the attempted rescue. 'It's something that happens, occasionally, even to the most experienced of sailors,' he said. 'I went on board the vessel and everyone was dazed. One man was saying, "What did I do wrong?" I didn't see any evidence that there had been a great deal of drinking. In my opinion, that wasn't a factor. They were totally coherent. Chris Evans didn't say a word. He was traumatised, and very upset.'

However, there were harsh words over the fact that nobody on board besides James Ward had even rudimentary knowledge of the boat's workings. 'Unfortunately, the only man who knew how to sail and operate the vessel properly was the one who was knocked overboard,' said coastguard spokesman Mark Clark. 'It's probably fair to say the rescue attempt was hampered by their inability to operate the yacht and its radio.' But the police were quick to confirm that no blame was being attached to any of the party for James Ward's death.

The following day, as Chris and Billie comforted Susan Barnett at The White Horse, John Webster said, 'Chris is really carved up and shaken, but he's playing a blinder and being a rock for them all down there.'

'It is a very difficult time for all of us,' reflected Evans. 'We want to get together to remember James in the village. I have been helping to organise the funeral, which will be held here for his friends and family on Monday 19.' Later that weekend, he spoke in more detail of how the tragedy had affected him: 'It was a terrible day, I mean a terrible day. It was the worst. James was one of the most beautiful, warm people you could ever come across. He was a great community man and loved by everyone. His death has left a huge gap in village life and in all our lives. We're all trying to mend right now. The spirit round here has been fantastic and of course Billie has been supportive. Everyone is trying to look after each other.'

The funeral of James Ward took place at St Peter's Church in Hascombe on Monday August 19. Dressed in a black suit, blue shirt and purple-tinted sunglasses, Chris Evans, together with Billie, was among the 300 mourners who packed into the church. A further hundred listened to the service, which included a poem written by one of the crew members the day after the accident, on loudspeakers in the graveyard. The coffin was then taken from the church for a private burial, which Chris did not attend, and a wake followed in the White Horse.

James Ward's death had unexpectedly thrust Chris Evans back into the media eye in a highly unwanted fashion. His more stage-managed return to the spotlight was followed at the Edinburgh International Television Festival on August 25. Every seat in the 1,200-capacity hall in the Edinburgh International Conference Hall was filled, which showed that, if nothing else, his year away hadn't made Evans any less of a draw – or any less interesting.

With a few flecks of grey peeping through his trademark ginger mop, Evans was lively and energetic in a wide-ranging discussion that saw him comment on everything from his time out of the spotlight to the state of British television, and on to why he didn't want to present shows in the foreseeable future. 'I planted some vegetables,' he answered, somewhat wryly, when asked what he'd been up to during his year away. 'Went back to nature. Just looking at how beautiful everything is, and listening to the birds more closely. I know it sounds like bullshit, but that's what I did, and what Bill did.'

Of his time spent in America, Evans was no less enthusiastic while discussing the place than when he'd actually been out there. He declared: 'The place that entertains the world is Los Angeles. They don't see problems: they see opportunities. It struck me how positive they were. I started watching television again in America, and I fell back in love with it. It was like being free again. I didn't know who made the shows, I didn't know the hosts. It was fantastic.' He went on to discuss his new production deals, and was adamant on one point: 'I'm not going to present again because I want to do all this stuff. Presenting is entirely different and trying to do both wouldn't work. It's far more important for me to encourage everybody, get some talent in and say "Why don't we do this?"'

Evans also brandished forthright opinions about the state of contemporary British TV too. 'Standards have slipped,' he regretted. '*TFI* was a show that was really of its time. I think … *Toothbrush* was, the *Big Breakfast* was, *Big Brother* is and *RI:SE* definitely isn't.' However, even a programme that obviously appealed to him, like *Big Brother*, wasn't exempt from criticism. 'What about the four weeks afterwards?' Evans asked. 'It's such a lost opportunity. What about the guy who went over the roof? Did he regret doing that, and what do his mates think?' Referring to the huge commercial potential that temporarily accrues to contestants after the show finishes, Evans asserted: 'What Channel 4 do is let everyone else benefit but them. I'd have liked to see Brian Dowling return home. Don't tell me that you wouldn't want to watch that.'

His love of reality TV was obvious. '*Pop Idol* was life-affirming, aspirational TV which featured the public entertaining the public,' he explained. 'And the public are good at it, much better than TV professionals realise. The public look better than we do. They are really cool. So why aren't we seeing people like that presenting programmes?' He went on to itemise one particular Saturday night's viewing: 'It was *You've Been Framed,* then on the other side it was *Star For A Night* with Jane McDonald, then *Stars In Their Eyes,* and then Jane McDonald with a voting update. I thought, "For two hours and fifteen minutes, the public have been entertaining the public. That's because they're better at it than we are."'

Yet it was the subjects that Evans declined to discuss during the interview that were arguably more interesting than the topics he did. His dismissal from Virgin Radio was predictably glossed over due to litigation pending. There was confirmation that there would be a new morning show on Channel 5 with Gaby Roslin, and possibly Terry Wogan, which he would begin work on in February 2003, but no more details were forthcoming. There was also the tantalising titbit that Evans had spoken to financial backers about taking a stake in a TV company, possibly Channel 5, but he gave no more details there either. Evans clearly had not forgotten the golden show business rule dictum of always leaving the public wanting more.

Yet regardless of how much – or, rather, how little – Evans wanted the public to know about his return to the fray, Simon Morris is certain why Evans stopped twiddling his thumbs and finally got down to some real work: 'He doesn't have to work, clearly. He doesn't have to prove he's a talent, because he's done that many times over, and he could go off and do whatever he wants. But my sense at that time was that he was back in a driven mode. He had something to prove about *something*. He was back on a mission, and that was good, because to my mind that's when Chris Evans is at his most creative. To have a Chris Evans who's fired up and bouncing off the walls could only be a good thing for television.'

26 Trying To Get The Feeling Again

So it was official. Chris Evans's behind-the-scenes return to television would be the uninspiringly titled *Live With Chris Moyles*. The show would air daily at 7pm, going up against *Emmerdale* and *Channel 4 News*, beginning on September 23 and running for 13 weeks. Broadcast from the Babushka bar in Islington's Caledonian Road and with a budget of £3m, the half-hour show would be filmed in front of an audience of just 16 members of the public, making it effectively a mini-*TFI Friday*. Moyles claimed that the show's 'unique take on the day's news, regular games, challenges, outside broadcasts and audience participation' would be – guess what? – 'straight-talking, irreverent and unpredictable.'

To many ears, however, the format simply sounded predictable, and put the onus very firmly on Moyles' personality to make the show must-see TV. Chris Evans had made *TFI Friday* – a unique broadcasting concept at the time – culturally important through the sheer strength of his own personality as a presenter, and his enviable ability to think on his feet and provide a high 'laughs per minute' quotient. Now it would be down to Moyles to do the same on a station that was significantly less powerful than Channel 4 had been, and with a format that had now become recognisable, jaded even. It would be a tall order.

As summer slipped into autumn, Evans announced another

new project. Publishers Harper Collins had handed him a seven figure sum to write 'a full and frank account' of his life in an autobiography entitled *Little Big Shot,* due to be published at the end of 2003. Harper Collins' publishing director Susan Watt announced that she had been 'thrilled to find on reading the material that Chris Evans's creative energies encompass writing. His author voice is strong, lively and original and I know this is going to be a brilliant read.' Evans, for his part, simply said, 'It's good to have the chance to write at greater length and make sense of what's been happening around me.'

More pressingly, Evans began to turn his mind to the *Live With Chris Moyles* show. Going back to the future, he hired two former Ginger employees, Clare Barton and Chris Gillett, to act as joint managing directors at his production company, UMTV. Their role appeared to be operational, relieving Chris of the more mundane day-to-day elements of the business and leaving him free to devote all his energies to the executive producer's role. Barton had been head of production at Ginger while Gillett operated as special projects manager, producing Virgin's *Rock And Roll Football* and *Terry Venables* shows. It was also revealed that Evans had given up almost twelve per cent of the company's equity, which would be shared between Barton and Gillett, Evans's longstanding accountant Kirit Doshi and his agent Michael Foster. All four were listed alongside Evans as directors of the company.

Just before the final rehearsal, Evans explained that he didn't consider his new show a comeback. 'Of course, I feel anxious,' he confessed. 'I thought about it last thing last night, first thing this morning. But I had eight hours sleep in between. It's good old genuine nerves, like the first day at school. You just want to get on with it.'

However, there was no getting away from the fact that if people were looking for something revolutionary from *Live With Chris Moyles,* they were going to be seriously disappointed. Moyles had bandied around the word 'unique' when referring to the show, as all media folk are obliged to when trying to hype something new. But with a 'live in a bar' format, an audience of 'real people', a mouthy DJ fronting things and gags such as grabbing people at a nearby bus stop and asking them to sing a song for the princely sum of £100, the parallels with *TFI Friday* were simply too strong to ignore. 'It's zoo telly,' admitted a more realistic Kevin Lygo. 'I don't think people should turn on and expect to see a revolutionary show.'

After the initial fanfare and perceived PR coup of signing up both Moyles and Evans, it seemed that at the eleventh hour Channel 5 were suddenly extremely keen to play the realism card. They put out the word that they would be satisfied to increase their average 7pm viewing figures of 300-400,000 to, say, half a million. Evans confessed that the show was aimed at 'three million disenfranchised young males' – and young working males were also the admitted target market for the advertising people, who are obliged to justify any programme's existence on a commercial station by bringing ad revenue in.

In this respect, at least, Channel 5 had already had a big win, with brewers Carling having stumped up £500,000 in sponsorship money without even seeing the show. 'We're going to give ITV a serious kicking,' said the bullish Nick Milligan, 5's deputy chief executive with a responsibility for ad sales. Lygo, however, was once again keen to temper such a gung-ho attitude. 'One of the advantages of Channel 5 is if it doesn't work, you haven't got very far to fall, have you?' he reasoned.

This, though, was all conjecture. The reality was that the first *Live With Chris Moyles* was unloved by critics and punters alike. Leaving aside the fact that for many people the simple fact that it was on Channel 5 meant that it was already off their personal viewing radar, those who did tune in seemed utterly underwhelmed by the antics they saw. These included: the lardy Moyles running in a 10k race the day before broadcast with a flash on the screen screaming 'knackered': a game involving sliding pints down a bar with pinpoint accuracy to prevent the 16 members of the audience (student nurses, for this lift-off edition) receiving an electric shock: reviewing the morning papers at 7pm: Moyles' mum warning him, 'Don't fucking swear.' It all seemed precedented. Nothing seemed to work.

The public spoke ... and they were not impressed. 'Boring ... yawn,' said viewer Chico Mendez at BBC Online. 'It promised so much but it was a big let-down. I ended up watching *Channel 4 News* instead. If this is the best Chris Evans can come up, with then he'd better stick to pub crawls in Chelsea.' Ray in Scotland concurred: 'Trash. The type of TV that Channel 5 is famous for. When is their licence up for review?' Naturally, it's human nature that people who are prepared to e-mail their opinions are more likely to want to bury than praise, and there were viewers who argued that both Moyles and the show should be given time. But it was *Live With Chris Moyles'* obvious similarity to *TFI Friday* that irked most people.

'The fact that it's produced by Evans explains a lot about the format of the show,' said Graeme West. 'The audience participation, the bar set, the gag segments, etc. It reeks of *TFI*.' 'A talentless, sub-par Chris Evans impression,' commented one viewer. 'This is 5 going upmarket?' However, the most sardonic viewer was one TJ, who sarcastically noted, 'Hasn't Chris Evans put on weight? And dyeing his hair too, that's a bit extreme. Pity he's not funny any more on his new show. Not sure why he calls himself Moyles, though. What? Is it not him? Oh. Why is he doing the same show then?'

If the fans were disapproving, newspaper critics were no kinder, concluding that the show was merely trying to replicate its forerunner on a lower budget and without the celebrity guests. Nor did the ratings provide any comfort. Just 400,000 tuned in to the first show, the same number that had watched an arty programme about cathedrals called *Divine Designs*, which had appeared in exactly the same slot the previous week.

First shows are often heavily – and unfairly – criticised. Everybody needs time to find their sea legs, and with Moyles making the leap from radio to TV, some felt it would be churlish to lambast his early performances too cruelly. The beleaguered team did receive some good news, as Channel 5 recommissioned the show after just three weeks on air. They reported that advertisers loved the show's irreverent format, and even though the viewing figures were reported to be settling around the 400,000 mark, rather than the modest half-million that the station were hoping for, executives seemed pleased with *Live With Chris Moyles*. However, some analysts speculated that a canny TV veteran like Evans may well have insisted on a second run as part of the original deal. That way, he would be able to guarantee the programme would appear to be a success if an announcement of the re-commission was made early on in its first run.

Phil Mount, who worked with Evans at *TFI Friday* and is now series producer of Saturday morning music show *CD:UK*, has his own view of the programme. 'A lot of people didn't like it,' he says. 'But I don't know whether that had more to do with Chris Moyles than the format of the show. You could certainly see where it came from, what with the pub idea and all the rest of it, but I really liked the programme and think it was just a shame that it wasn't one big long show with time to breathe like *TFI Friday* was.'

Fellow radio presenter Jono Coleman was far more damning of Moyles. 'It's a Chris Evans show with another Chris fronting it,' he said. 'It's just *TFI* on another channel and I think Evans would do it a lot better than the dated, laddish way in which Moyles presented it.' Meanwhile, behind the scenes it appeared that changes were being made in an attempt to sharpen things up. Evans was reported to be taking a far more 'hands on' approach to the programme, with one colleague graphically reporting, 'If anyone tells you it's fun working for Chris Evans, they're a fucking liar!'

It soon transpired that the show had one fundamental flaw: it had failed to tap into the cultural consciousness of British youth in the way that Evans had always been adept at doing. People simply didn't talk about *Live With Chris Moyles* in the way they had discussed the *Big Breakfast*, *TFI Friday* and Evans's Radio 1 breakfast show. All three of those shows had provided what market researchers habitually refer to as 'water cooler moments', the conversation-generators that office workers discuss when they gather for a five minute break from work under the pretext of getting themselves a drink. *Live With Chris Moyles* simply wasn't there, in the air, important almost by a process of osmosis.

Arguably, this was not entirely the fault of the content and format. The fact that it was airing on a less popular channel, together with advances made by digital TV in splitting potential audiences, could both be argued as mitigating factors. Somehow, though, this didn't seem to be the real story. The harsh truth was that the ideas seemed old hat and Chris Moyles wasn't very good as a presenter. He was criticised by one journalist for being unable to engage with the camera and for 'having a habit of switching off his facial muscles between questions to audience members – par for the course on radio, but a glaring distraction onscreen.'

Given that young people had eventually turned their backs on *TFI Friday,* dismissing it as hackneyed and irrelevant, it was hard to see how this new show could ever be cutting edge or significant. *Live With Chris Moyles* was shaping up to become a niche show for young men who responded to tried-and-tested lowbrow conventions. It might fill a hole in the schedule ... but it would do no more.

Before the first series had even ended, the rumours began that 'Man Of The Moment' Moyles had fallen out with Evans, and his contract was not renewed. XFM DJ Christian O'Connell took the slot, while an insider explained, 'The failure of the first series will not be Chris Evans's fault, in his eyes. It will be down to the fact that nobody liked Chris Moyles. And if the second series doesn't work out, then it will be because nobody knows who Christian O'Connell is. Chris won't take any of the blame.'

Some people might even go so far as to argue that this was exactly why Chris Evans had taken the job on in the first place. If *Live With* ... was a success, it would be down to him. If it was a failure, well, it was only a low-key production for a low-key station, wasn't it? There would be no such excuses for Chris's next major comeback project, however. No such excuses at all ...

27 Boys And Girls

The word was out in student unions and on local news websites. Chris Evans was looking for contestants for his new programme, *Boys And Girls*. And while these first steps on the road to producing 'Britain's biggest game show' may not have caused seismic tremors in the offices of the country's media moguls in November 2002, *Boys And Girls* was underway nonetheless.

Live With Chris Moyles' unadventurous format and lack of ambition may have been a disappointment to viewers, if not to advertisers ... but early indications were that *Boys And Girls* would be a production far more in the Chris Evans tradition; bold, large scale, adventurous and, yes, unique. The central idea was that 100 men would battle it out against 100 women in a series of challenges described as 'the ultimate battle of the sexes' with a £100,000 jackpot up for grabs in each episode. Naturally, in the new spirit of the public entertaining the public that Evans had praised in his Edinburgh speech, the public would decide the fate of contestants via phone-in polls. Indeed, each show's winner (and a partner chosen from the opposite sex) would be required to return the following week to be judged by the public on whether they should keep their booty or not. Such devices open up another lucrative revenue stream besides advertising – and *Boys And Girls* was going to need it. At a cost of a whopping £500,000 per episode for 12 weeks –

including outside broadcasts – nobody could accuse *this* new production of lacking ambition.

Denise Van Outen was heavily touted for the role of female presenter. The former *Big Breakfast* presenter had a chequered track record in TV, having excelled alongside Johnny Vaughan in the early morning slot with her sexy image and saucy banter. However, some people remembered with a shudder her disastrous time hosting an appalling late night Channel 4 show, *Something For The Weekend*, which plumbed new depths of boorishness with a feature entitled 'Privates On Parade' wherein women had to identify their male partners from an ID parade of willies.

Denise soon ruled herself out of the *Boys And Girls* role, and Chris began casting around. Then he had a brainwave. He was going to be putting his arse firmly on the line with this show. The £500,000-plus costs, the Saturday night prime time slot on Channel 4, the lavish marketing campaign that saw huge billboard ads being put up around the country in signature blue (for boys) and pink (for girls) asking provocative questions such as whether girls prefer length or girth ... a lot was riding on this. If he was going to make the splash needed to make *Boys And Girls* a massive success, he would need to bring in a name that would get tongues wagging and tabloid papers excited. And he so nearly did.

Chris Evan's time in America, it appeared, had not entirely been spent sitting in coffee shops with Billie. The *Boys And Girls* format had been sold to the ABC network, in a deal brokered by Celador (responsible for *Who Wants To Be A Millionaire?*), and Evans's agent Michael Foster. Chris had also landed himself a consultancy deal on top. Through contacts he'd picked up out there, Evans now launched an audacious move that, had it come off, would surely have been the TV coup of the year. He wanted Pamela Anderson, *Baywatch* babe and star of her own home porno movie, to present *Boys And Girls*.

'That would make more sense than you can imagine,' says an insider. 'The show is very "birds and blokes". The blokes are in control and the girls are there to look good and show their boobs off. Any show that Chris has been involved with has had a large element of that to it. *Boys And Girls* isn't about reconstructing sexual relationships, and that's very Chris – he's not reconstructed either.' With Anderson fronting the show, *Boys And Girls* would surely have been a guaranteed ratings winner. As it was, however, Pammy declined to sign on the dotted line and Chris was forced to look elsewhere for his figurehead.

Channel 4 youth presenter Vernon Kay came into the frame, and it certainly seemed like something was in the air when he was spotted with Evans on a pre-Christmas bender at the end of 2002. Evans, Kay and four mates ordered six bottles of pink champagne in the Groucho Club before the two of them headed off together for a pub in Dean Street. And sure enough, Kay was announced as the sole presenter of the show, which would air for the first time on Saturday March 1, 2003.

Chris Evans had started the year on a break in Barbados with Billie, while sporting a rather unfetching beard (drinking with Michael Winner, and getting told off by the missus for doing so, was the most newsworthy episode of the holiday), but by the time he headed home, he was clean-shaven and ready to get down to serious business. The pressure to succeed with *Boys And Girls* was immense. Predictably, Evans was his usual bullish self. 'I believe this show has all the ingredients for a hit,' he frothed. 'The atmosphere we create by splitting 100 boys and 100 girls, and making them play for such a large sum of money, is the most volatile I have ever witnessed in a TV studio.'

Yet tellingly, according to insiders on the show, Chris was saving the shrieking for the media. Behind the scenes, Evans was no longer the ranting, raving lunatic of ... *Toothbrush* and *TFI Friday* days. 'He's stopped shouting,' claimed someone who was involved with the show, and who knew the worst of Evans's excesses. 'It's very Californian, actually. He's still vehement and decisive, but he now speaks very calmly and in a measured way when he says "Look, I don't think this is right."' Nevertheless, such a new age, laid-back attitude didn't stop Chris pulling rank as boss when he scrapped a £200,000 pink-and-blue set at the very last minute, driving designers and builders to distraction as they strove to ready a replacement in time.

The first *Boys And Girls* programme contained plenty of easily recognisable Evans trademarks. It was fast, fun and young, yet with elements of the Saturday night variety shows he had so loved when he was a kid. Vernon Kay introduced each section of the programme with a dance routine performed alongside luscious girls. The show was bawdy too, featuring segments specifically designed to embarrass trendy contestants. Their parents featured, snogging and prancing around naked. Many of the stunts were regurgitated from *TFI*, but the big difference in formatting was that *Boys And Girls* followed reality TV's penchant for focusing on members of the public rather than on established celebrities.

Predictably, Evans wasn't entirely true to his promise to stay behind the camera. As the winning contestants whooped and hollered at the end of the show, a golf buggy appeared on stage to transport them away. Dressed in a chauffeur's outfit and baying for the winners to get on board was none other than Chris himself, making sure everyone remembered that at the end of the day, and when all was said and done, this was *his* idea. *Live With* … was dipping a toe in the comeback water but, make no mistake, *Boys And Girls* was The Big One.

Given the early critical response to *Boys And Girls*, Chris may well have been better advised keeping his ginger head down. Not only did the critics savage the show, but the viewing figures for the first programme were disastrous, drawing a measly 1.1m, a mere 5% of the available viewing audience. 'This wasn't trash TV, it was just plain scrappy. All the fun of a hangover,' said BBC Online's Tom Bishop. 'While *Don't Forget Your Toothbrush* was engaging and well-structured fun, this show was just a crass mess.' The *Independent*'s Tom Sutcliffe appropriated one of the show's catch-phrases when he declared, 'To my mind, nothing can conceal the fact that it's a minger,' while *The Guardian* suggested the show was only entertaining, 'if you're very young, very drunk, or harbour an ambition to be a *Big Brother* housemate.'

Channel 4 had trumpeted *Boys And Girls* as a winner even before a show had been aired, claiming: 'We will revive Saturday nights with bold new shows like *Boys And Girls*.' The trouble was that, while the show was certainly bold, there was very little that was charming about it. It was a good job that Chris had filled in his name as 'Christopher Pressure Evans' on his application form to work at GLR all those years ago. With his first two 'behind the scenes' projects off to less than auspicious starts, then pressure would be something he would have to learn to cope with during his comeback.

And things simply got worse. The second *Boys And Girls* show was watched by 1.3 million viewers, a rise of 200,000 on its first week. But once again audience share was incredibly low – just 6% – and most worrying of all for a show that was designed to add some spunk to Channel 4's Saturday night offerings, it was 3% *down* on the station's 2003 average peak-time share. Chris Evans's big comeback show looked in serious danger of turning into a total turkey. Then on 21st March – just three episodes into the run – it was revealed that series producer Rob Clark had quit the show, only for Chris to quickly talk him into returning. Things were hardly going smoothly – and Chris also had to cope with the huge extra burden of taking on Virgin Radio-owners SMG to recover the £8.6 million in share options he claimed he was still owed after his sacking from the station in 2001. The action had begun in the high court just two days earlier, on Wednesday 19th March.

Channel 4 were spooked, but put on a determined and brave public face. 'We have not had a big entertainment show such as this on a Saturday night for some time, so it will take time for the audience to find us and we are already in talks with Chris about a possible second series in the autumn,' Head Of Entertainment John McHugh claimed in the *Daily Mail*. Well, if the audience were having trouble finding *Boys And Girls*, then Channel 4's next move would only make their job more difficult. On Wednesday 26th March a spokeswoman for the station admitted 'We are moving it to 10.30pm because we think a later slot will help it get the audience it deserves.' Such a statement could be interpreted in more than one way, of course. 'We are looking for the 16-34 age group audience and moving it later,' continued the valiant spokeswoman. 'Let's have a look and see if there are more of those at that time. It is not at all a demotion. It's a proactive move to help it get the audience it deserves.' But the move, which would start from 5th April, certainly looked like Channel 4 and Chris had got things disastrously wrong.

The failure of *Boys and Girls* to set Saturday-night audiences alight raised serious questions about whether Chris's once impeccable instinct for providing the right entertainment at the right time had deserted him. For the first time ever he was faced with not one, but two critical flops. *Consecutive* critical flops. And to rub further salt into the wound, on 11th April Channel 4 announced with a grand hurrah that it was launching a peak-time quiz show titled *Grand Slam*. Who would be making this high-profile new show? None other than independent production company Monkey, which had been founded by Will Macdonald and Dave Granger, the two former Ginger men who had decided that they really didn't want to hang around when Chris sold the company to SMG.

28 Courthouse

On Wednesday 19th March, 2003, Chris Evans finally got to do battle with his former employers Scottish Media Group, in his attempt to get what he believed was nothing more than simple justice. The issues being argued over were relatively simple. Chris was claiming around £8.6 million in share options which had been withheld after his contract with Virgin Radio was terminated by SMG in 2001. He maintained that he'd been unfairly dismissed after missing a series of broadcasts and as such was entitled to 4,981,420 shares in the SMG radio group, and 1,245,355 shares in SMG TV. He was also claiming damages for a breach of his breakfast show contract. For their part, SMG were of the view that it was Evans who had breached *his* contract 'in a highly public manner' when he went on a very open three-day drinking binge, and as such wasn't owed a single thing.

Given that on the very first day Chris entered the high court in London his big comeback show *Boys And Girls* was taking a battering in the ratings wars, maybe Channel 4 should have rush-commissioned a drama based around the court battle itself, because there was more than enough excitement, tension, emotional breakdown, greed and alleged double dealing to keep viewers glued to their screens for weeks.

Putting the case for Evans to Mr Justice Lightman was 47-year-old Christopher Pymont QC, a barrister specialising in property, company, commercial and insolvency litigation who qualified in

1979 and became a QC in 1996. He worked out of the Maitland Chambers. Facing him and representing SMG was Geoffrey Vos QC, who heads his own chambers named 3 Stone Buildings, qualified in 1977 and became a QC in 1993. Vos had previously represented the estate of renowned artist Francis Bacon in a 2001 case against the gallery that represented him.

Christopher Pymont opened by claiming that the relationship between Chris Evans and SMG began to break down after his client had an idea during his breakfast show on 6th June 2001 – the day that the England football team met Greece in Athens in a World Cup qualifying match – that he would stay on air all day. Pymont claimed that it would be 'an excellent commercial opportunity' for the station. 'It was exactly the sort of idea that would excite the station's core audience and exactly the sort of idea he thought it was his purpose and job to bring off,' said Mr Pymont. When Virgin's bosses refused to entertain the idea Evans wrote to the station's management to express his frustration at their 'lack of respect for his opinion', as Pymont put it and to say 'Please don't seek my advice about anything else.' It was because of this breakdown in the working relationship, suggested Mr Pymont, that Virgin put Chris under so much stress he became too ill to work. The people who owned the station refused to change an entire day's scheduling at the eleventh hour. Then Chris Evans said that because of this they shouldn't ask his advice about anything else in the future.

When Geoffrey Vos stepped forward for SMG on the same day, he painted Evans as a man of 'overbearing arrogance and conceit.' By refusing to communicate with Virgin's management team Evans had shown that he only wanted to do what *he* thought was right. 'His defence is, in short,' said Vos, 'that he knew best. He says he should have been allowed to do what he thought best; we say this is not the case at all.' Vos also claimed that Evans would not communicate with management or consult with them in any way about the breakfast show, 'except in the most guarded terms through his agent.' Given the way that Chris had dealt with his departure from Radio 1, this would not be the first time he'd adopted such a tactic. And anyway, in Vos's – and therefore

SMG's mind – this was a clear-cut case. Chris hadn't turned up to present his breakfast shows simply because he was too hungover and so Virgin had sacked him. 'It is a breach of contract fair and square,' he argued. 'Virgin had no choice but to sack him.'

Even Christopher Pymont admitted that Chris did 'go out and get very drunk' after his show on 20th June. Evans did not go in to Virgin the next day, but he was used to working with hangovers and Pymont argued that his absence stemmed from the fact that no-one from management had turned up for a scheduled meeting with Chris and because Chris was afraid he was about to be sacked. This wouldn't appear to be the way most people would respond to the fear that they might be losing a job they wanted to hold on to, but when he took the witness stand the following day it was clear that Chris Evans really isn't like most people.

Some of his confessions were incredible. 'I prefer my opinions to other people's,' he acknowledged, while admitting to once unilaterally changing a promotion for Boddington's beer because he didn't think it would work. He said he didn't have 'any real friends', yet changed his mind when Vos read out a list of witnesses due to appear in court for him, including Chris Gillett, Michael Foster and former head of PR at Virgin, Charlotte Blenkinsop. Yes, he agreed, those people were, in fact, his friends. Chris claimed he was happy to attend management meetings and 'made strategic decisions for the station.' When questioned, though, Evans admitted he never read his contracts and that his agent Michael Foster never told him what he was actually expected to do under their terms. 'How can you perform your contractual obligations if you don't know what they are?' asked Vos. 'That's a very good point,' Chris admitted weakly.

Perhaps the most poignant moment of the day, though, was when the subject of The Breakfast Team came up. 'We had been through hell and high water together,' Chris said. 'Births and marriages and deaths, literally. It had been a fairytale.' At this point he broke down and cried, but Vos suggested that he had deliberately tried to 'destabilise' and 'cruelly humiliate' his co-presenters John Revell, Holly Samos, Dan McGrath and Jamie Broadbent because they were holding back his career. Evans blamed new Virgin

Programme Director Paul Jackson, saying that Jackson said something along the lines of 'Every time you fly they bring you down.'

The following day's proceedings led to Evans admitting he'd been 'childish' on the day of the Greece versus England match, when he had signed off at the end of his show with a comment of 'sod 'em' directed at Virgin's management because they'd refused to allow him to broadcast all day. He had then refused to talk to the Virgin head John Pearson by returning a note which he'd received from Pearson unopened.

But the supposed crux of the whole case in SMG's eyes – the three day drinking binge which began on Wednesday 20th June, 2001 and which tried their patience beyond endurance – provided even more astonishing revelations. Chris claimed that it was usual ('my normal working zone') to appear on air hungover, then suggested that the reason he didn't turn up for work for those three days had nothing to do with being too hungover. It was rather because he was still upset with his bosses following the incident back on 6th June. 'I was unable to broadcast, in my opinion,' he explained. 'To do a show like I was doing you have to be in a good mood and I was as miserable as sin. I was upset. I didn't know what to do.' He said he believed there was a conspiracy 'to get me', but refused to entertain the notion, put forward by Mr Vos, that being seen and photographed drinking in pubs when he was off work could potentially embarrass his employers. 'I thought it would be more publicity,' he offered by way of explanation and said it was definitely *not* his intention to embarrass his employers. This, despite the fact that he was seen by a solicitor in The Nag's Head pub at lunchtime on that first Wednesday being talkative and active, even crawling around on all fours to impersonate a female journalist. Geoffrey Vos then put it to Evans that, in fact, he *wanted* to be sacked and got in touch with national newspapers 'to go on the offensive and contact the press and spill the beans in all their gory details.' Mr Vos claimed that Evans was deliberately trying to let his show unravel and also pointed out that Chris had told *Mirror* editor Piers Morgan, 'I like to be in charge and do things my way, but the management have been poking their noses in.' Evans said he'd exaggerated because he was angry.

To counter the claims of SMG's barrister, Evans's team first focused on Virgin programme director Paul Jackson, a man Evans called 'scary'. According to Chris's new business partner in UMTV, Chris Gillett, who was working with Chris at Virgin at the time, Jackson's arrival at the station created 'an atmosphere of fear;' and that Jackson had been trying to provoke Chris. Vos suggested this was nonsense. On Tuesday 26th June 2001, Pearson offered Evans £3 million to quit after the offer of a sabbatical and a weekend radio slot had been rejected by his agent Michael Foster. The offer was good for two days, but if it was not accepted, then SMG would terminate Evans's contract on the grounds of breach. Foster turned this offer down flat without even consulting Chris, who gave evidence that he would not have accepted it. After visiting his client at his home in Hascombe, Foster then agreed to write a letter to Virgin saying the DJ was coming back to work. Vos picked up on this and clarified that if this was the case, then that meant Evans was by this point suddenly no longer ill. Foster agreed.

When John Pearson took the stand the full extent of the breakdown of communications between himself and Chris was outlined. He explained that he'd had lunch with Chris on 30th April, but there had been no mention of the fact that Chris was intending not to present his breakfast show over the next few days and head for America, where he eventually married Billie Piper. Christopher Pymont suggested it was not Chris's fault if Virgin had no contingency plan in place for such a 'crisis'. Pearson also claimed that Virgin Radio's revenues and profits were damaged because of Chris's behaviour. Actual sales for 2001 were down 27.7% on 2000 and profits were almost £7 million less than predicted. Pearson explained that the 'fundamental changes' to Chris's show on 14th May, when his original breakfast crew had been replaced, had produced a show of 'a very poor quality'. He also said that on the last day Chris had broadcast for Virgin – 20th June – the station's management had discussed terminating his contract 'if things did not improve.' The fact that the DJ was then off drinking in the pub meant that 'Chris was making a fool of the station and its management and demonstrating his contempt for us,' said Pearson.

Later in the trial, however, Trevor Morse, a commercial radio expert, suggested that the losses suffered by Virgin since Chris's departure were not entirely the DJ's fault inasmuch as the market trend for commercial stations broadcasting on the AM waveband (as Virgin did outside of London) had been declining since 1998. In fact, he suggested that 'one might wonder whether the cure was worse than the disease.' Christopher Pymont also hit back by suggesting that Virgin were keen to make PR capital out of Chris's wedding when they had no right to do so and that they put too much pressure on him at the time of his marriage by expecting him to cope with the break-up of the breakfast show team as well as putting a new show together.

On Thursday 27th March the trial took a dramatic twist when Virgin bosses were accused of trying to cover up a meeting where programme director Paul Jackson was alleged to have said he didn't want to work with Chris Evans. The meeting supposedly took place on 28th March 2001, while Jackson was still on 'gardening leave' from Capital Radio and before he joined Virgin. Neither Jackson, John Pearson or SMG business development director Bobby Hain had previously mentioned this meeting in their witness statements. But when Ian Grace, a Virgin radio consultant, had brought it up, suggesting that Jackson *had* made the comment about Evans during that meeting, it was admitted by Pearson that the meeting had, in fact, taken place. He said he had no recollection of Paul Jackson saying he didn't want to work with Chris, though. Mr Pymont suggested 'that you and Mr Jackson and Mr Hain put your heads together to make sure all mention of this meeting was expunged from your witness statements.' 'Absolutely not,' said Pearson. In fact, Paul Jackson claimed that working with Chris Evans was one of the reasons why he had wanted to come to Virgin in the first place. Mr Justice Lightman asked Mr Pymont to find out when Ian Grace, who lived in Australia, could either fly in to give evidence or do so by video link.

If these new allegations might have altered the judge's view of the whole affair, then on Monday 31st March more revelatory information came to light when Paul Jackson came to the stand

and admitted he'd already commissioned new breakfast show jingles for the DJ Steve Penk in mid-May of 2001, again while he was still on gardening leave. Jackson joined Virgin on 11th June, less than a fortnight before Chris Evans left the station, and admitted that working on Virgin Radio business before officially joining the station was not allowed according to the terms of his severance deal with his former employers Capital. But he said he had commissioned the jingles simply because Penk had been hired to cover the breakfast show when Chris was away. In addition, Mr Pymont also told the court that John Pearson had written a draft report on the breakfast show on 27th May 2001, which said Chris Evans had made 'significant effort' to address concerns about his breakfast show, thereby seemingly contradicting his earlier statements about Chris's refusal to deal with management and the lack of quality of the new format. Indeed, Pearson supposedly also stated that the changes to the show would ultimately *increase* its audiences.

By Wednesday 2nd April John Pearson had been accused of lying under oath when he was recalled to the witness box. There he admitted he had, in fact, contacted Ian Grace in the last month after previously saying that he hadn't. Pearson claimed it was an honest mistake, saying 'It seemed a lot, lot longer ago.'

Claim and counter-claim. Revelation and counter-revelation. The longer the trial went on, the more the intricacies of the case seemed to become murky, complicated and difficult to fathom. But one thing at least was crystal clear – besides the fact that Chris had drunk a whopping 833% more than the recommended level of alcohol during his notorious three-day binge, that is. No matter what the outcome of the case, neither side will surely ever accept that they were in the wrong. And it's hard to believe that after this affair Chris will dust off his 'life's too short, let's have a beer'"speech that he once made for the benefit of Matthew Bannister. Not for John Pearson and Paul Jackson, anyway...

29 Epilogue

They say the flame that burns twice as bright burns half as long. Yet Chris Evans, the man who has lit up the world of British broadcasting for more than a decade now, is still going strong. On the surface, a lot of things have changed. Gone are the days of wild carousing and endless partying. And the endless streams of women. And those very public bust-ups with his bosses. Gone too are the days when Chris had the ear of the nation, when the Radio 1 breakfast show simply had to be heard, and *TFI Friday* was 'must-see' television.

Nowadays, Evans's preoccupations are rather different. There's marriage, of course, and a determination to help wife Billie develop her own career. Chris's agent Michael Foster now looks after her as she attempts to kick-start a film career with a movie titled *The Cinnamon Kid*. Then there's his own, oft-stated desire to work behind the scenes rather than in front of the cameras with shows like *Live With* ... and *Boys And Girls*. The fight for justice in the high court. He wants to develop his new Ginger, the production company UMTV. And he appears, on the surface, to be happy that he has finally grown up. 'Billie is my inspiration,' he says, with a touch of Zen-like karma. Which is a far cry from screaming that he wanted to marry every good-looking girl he once came into contact with.

'There could be a whole load of reasons which explain the dynamic of Chris and Billie's relationship,' says Professor Cary

Cooper. 'Maybe Chris is looking to recapture a youth that's fading. Billie is young and vibrant, and he responds to that. It could be a sexual thing – being married to someone much younger so he can prove that he still has sexual prowess. But I doubt that's the case, because his other partners have not been significantly younger than him, so there's no pattern there. But it could certainly be a control thing, in that he's so much more worldly and experienced than her, so he will always set the agenda in their married life.'

Many of the people who know the pair, though, believe this is for real. 'One thing I can tell you is that Chris and Billie are truly in love and very happy,' says Nicki Chapman, who should know Mrs Evans well enough after managing her pop career for so long. 'Chris's ego doesn't demand that he's in front of the camera,' says his erstwhile director Chris Howe. 'He's absolutely happy to make television. I don't think he cares.'

Professor Cooper thinks maturity may very well allow Chris to continue in his new role: 'Once vastly successful people get a bit older, they change a bit and begin to let go. They will never do so *completely*, because they will never lose that need for some sort of control. But they tend to understand better that their success can also be based on the skills and talents of others and that they gain kudos from the success of their protégés, because they are still clearly associated with their successes, even if it's not directly.'

Chris Evans himself is adamant that his future lies behind the scenes, despite his golf buggy cameo on *Boys And Girls*. 'When I'm behind the camera I really, really love it,' he says. 'I thrive on it, I feel like I'm capable of it, and that it's within what I'm good at.' But there are plenty of others who feel that Chris's broadcasting talent will be sorely missed if he stays off camera for too long.

'He really has revolutionised both radio and television,' says his old mate from the Nobby No-Level days, Paul Carrington. 'Chris has been such an influential figure that, had he not been there, it's impossible to say what the shape of the media would be today. Chris broke the mould and made the rules up as he went along, and broadcasting in general owes him a huge debt.'

'I assume he'll want to come back at some point,' says broadcaster Stuart Maconie. 'I just don't see him as this behind-the-scenes wheeler-dealer, because he's much more creative than that. He won't do a breakfast show, but something on Channel 4 or Radio 2 or a high profile TV gig would make sense to me. For somebody who's been off the scene for a while, Chris is still really fascinating to people. I saw he was number 23 in a list of the 50 most important people in comedy recently – and he hasn't done anything visible in ages!'

'Chris still has huge value as a media asset,' says James Ashton 'He's quite unpredictable, but is obviously very talented and has been a bit of a rainmaker really, so he's always going to get the commissions. Coming back with *Live With Chris Moyles* wasn't culturally significant, which is what you tend to expect from him. But, really, what on Channel 5 is?'

Professor Cary Cooper feels it unlikely that the negative reaction to *Boys And Girls* will have a significant psychological effect on Chris Evans: 'Successful people tend to be insecure and feel a constant need to prove themselves to others, no matter what. But above all they need to prove something to *themselves*. They have to keep demonstrating that they are as great as other people say they are, because deep down they actually don't think they're that good. Success or failure will in many ways bring out the same deep-seated feeling of inadequacy. So in fact, these people are not particularly disturbed by failure, because in a funny way they *expect* to fail. But that also means they have a remarkable capacity to bounce back.'

'Chris is in an odd position now,' adds Simon Garfield. 'He's already done some very high-profile and original TV stuff and has had the best job on radio, so what does he do to top that? I think he'll want to come back eventually and be a kind of Michael Parkinson or Terry Wogan figure; older, hugely respected, well-paid and a very reliable broadcaster. Chris doesn't need to do any more shows where he's exposed. He doesn't need new formats, and has more sense than to jump into anything risky. He'll have thought very long and hard about his reputation and how he's regarded now, too. He's no doubt aware that he's seen by some as too much of a hothead, but that's a fairly easy reputation to change once you've been in a job for a while and proved that you won't fly off the handle every five minutes. I actually don't think Chris will want to be outrageous any more.'

Tim Grundy, however, isn't so sure that Chris Evans's image can be re-branded quite so easily. 'I think TV bosses might need more proof than an expensive Savile Row suit that Chris has calmed down and grown up,' he says. 'There are probably one or two bridges to be rebuilt, because I've had people who worked with Chris on *TFI Friday* and *Don't Forget Your Toothbrush* come up to me at awards ceremonies and parties and say, "I'd like to shake you by the hand, because you're the only person who's ever told the truth about Chris." There's a lot of confidence to win back – not least his own. Presenters love to be loved, but if you're not being seen you don't get the love. And even people like Jonathan Ross have ended up ridiculing Chris, the very people he adored, and whom he used to get to the top. If you think the world has stopped loving you, then it makes sense to go on holiday for a year to a country where nobody knows who you are, to repair the damage. And it does damage, because that's what we broadcasters are all about. We all need the love that comes back from being admired in our jobs.'

So is Grundy right? Underneath the new, sober exterior is there still the same Chris Evans who's never quite got over the death of his father? Who craves the attention of the media and the adrenalin high that it brings? Is he still the same guy who's been all the way to the top and thinks 'it ain't all there'? Still the same bundle of perpetual motion, always looking for the next peak rather than standing to admire the view for a minute? Simon Morris feels this may be the case: 'I sense he's got something to prove. The gun's gone off in his head again. He's an incredibly talented bloke, and he needs to do something with that talent.'

Jamie Broadbent may come closest to the truth when he argues that, beneath all the surface movement, it's nigh on impossible to know what's going on in Chris Evans's mind.

'You don't know where the playing starts and stops and where his proper life starts and stops,' he explains. 'Even regarding the year away. It could well be that Matthew Freud advised him to bugger off for a year, to go to LA to get loads of ideas from American TV and come back with them as his own. Plus, you're always more interesting when you've been away, aren't you?

'You have to really think about things with Chris. Like the "I'm selling Christmas trees outside my local pub and the locals love it" thing. Do you think he really wants to stand there for a day? And if you really want to give money to charity, aren't there much easier ways of doing it than standing around flogging Christmas trees when you've got £50m in the bank?'

Broadbent is not alone in portraying Evans as habitually cynical and manipulative ... but has the perennially driven star simply realised that, in the upper echelons of entertainment, everybody is simply using everybody else? His childhood friend Trevor Palin tells a story that illustrates the point: 'A few years ago, Chris and I bumped into each other outside a hotel in Knightsbridge. I'd spent a lot of time abroad while Chris was making his fortune, but it felt like we'd just met up after a few days of being apart. He invited me up to *TFI* so I went. After the show we went down to the pub and got sloshed. Chris had the usual cronies hanging around, which was something I could never get a grip on. They seemed to be jealous of our relationship and were constantly hassling me for information. Then I started to go down to the radio station just to hang about and do some jingles for his *Rock And Roll Football* show. After every show we'd all go down to the pub – he was very generous with the people around him, but I couldn't help but feel that many of the hangers-on were just there for the ride. I asked Chris what kept him ticking over. He replied that every Monday morning, he looked at his bank balance.'

'Chris doesn't have friends, he just has colleagues,' concludes Jamie Broadbent. 'For five years, I was one of them. Three times a week after finishing the Radio 1 show I'd leave with him straight afterwards and be in the pub all day with him. Then twice a week I'd go and play golf with him. So, three times a week, I was spending from five in the morning until midnight with him. I thought he was a very close friend and he's charming company, funny, a good laugh and great when you're out. But after I left Virgin, we never spoke again.

'He was like that with other people too: all of a sudden that would be it – and they were gone. Take Paul Gascoigne. Now Gazza is a genuinely nice guy and was big buddies with Chris round the time of France 1998. He was a lonely bloke who thought Chris was his mate, but things changed after he got all the bad press when the picture appeared in the papers of him holding a kebab. That picture cost Gazza his World Cup. Chris showed no loyalty at all. Holly Samos was always of the opinion that Chris was only it for himself and the rest of the breakfast team would say "No, surely he's always going to look out for us". But she was right.'

One former close colleague of Evans, who understandably wishes to remain anonymous, is even more forthright.

'I've looked into his eyes, and they are the coldest eyes I've ever seen. Very dark and very empty eyes. They're almost scary, actually. To me, this reflects the fact that he's a very Chris-centric person. He finds it impossible to see things from any perspective other than his own. Like, he would always see the favours he's done for others, never what they've done for him. At the end of the day he thinks it's *all* about him, but Chris has a seductive personality and people respond to that. A lot of people who work for him now started off by saying he'd changed. Now they're saying, "Well, he *has* changed. But underneath he's still the same person."'

Simon Morris has a different view: 'Chris is flawed, sure. But anyone who is a bit colourful in life has that side to their character. He's been his own worst enemy at times and he's tripped himself up, but he's not an evil or vicious person. He's incredibly generous, and when he's on form he's great, great company. And he's stuck by me over the years.'

'Who knows if he's really changed?' ponders Simon Garfield. 'But the fact that he's been working behind the scenes a lot suggests that he's at least able to work with other people in a satisfactory manner. His reputation for mad antics has always been a little OTT. In the main, Chris is fantastically professional, and his outbursts are fairly well manufactured to produce those "water cooler" moments. I think he probably has matured. He'd have to be a seriously infantile person if he hadn't. Mind you, I don't understand the whole Billie thing. Goodness knows what they talk about!'

Tim Grundy, for his part, doubts that Evans has reached the level of inner serenity that some friends and commentators now ascribe to him.

'I still worry for Chris,' he says. 'I'm still frightened that Chris will self-destruct, because he's that kind of person. And the day it happens I will be heartbroken because there's still a part of me that loves him. He's one of those people who burst onto the scene spectacularly and then disappear in tragic ways. You see it all too often in the media. People who ... *stop living* tragically early. I hope beyond all hope that's not the case, but I have this niggling worry in my head that Chris could be one of those.'

'There are few people whom we meet in our lives that have a profound influence on the way we live,' says Trevor Palin. 'But Chris has that effect – big style.' Indeed, twenty years into a glittering, tragic-comic and turbulent media career, Evans's ferocious impact on all around him shows little sign of diminishing. The gun went off to start the race back in Orford all those years ago. But Chris Evans hasn't stopped running yet ...